Mountain Sheep and Man in the Northern Wilds

Mountain Sheep and Man in the Northern Wilds

Valerius Geist

CORNELL UNIVERSITY PRESS
Ithaca and London

QL
737
453
G45

68730

International Standard Book Number 0-8014-0943-8
Library of Congress Catalog Card Number 75-5481
Printed in the United States of America by Vail-Ballou Press, Inc.

To Renate

Acknowledgments

It is with pleasure that I thank a number of persons who aided me during my course of studies and the writing of this book. In particular I wish to thank Mr. and Mrs. T. A. Walker, Mr. and Mrs. W. B. Smith, and Mr. and Mrs. M. Hess for their helpfulness during our Spatzisi days, and Mr. F. J. Coggins, Mr. J. Rimmer, and Mr. J. C. Holroyd during the time of the bighorn studies in Banff National Park. Dr. I. McTaggart Cowan and Dr. J. B. Cragg have been a never-ending source of stimulation as mentors, and I am grateful for their concern. I wish also to thank Mrs. E. L. Wittig of the former Stenographic Services of the University of Calgary for her work on the manuscript. The sheep studies were financed by grants from the National Research Council of Canada, first to Dr. I. McTaggart Cowan and later to me. These funds provided the opportunity to ask how man had coped with primitive tools in the cold climates, and that question led to studies the conclusions of which are, in part, reported here. Permission has been granted by the University of Chicago Press to reprint three of my photographs from my earlier book, *Mountain Sheep: A Study in Behavior and Evolution,* © 1971 by University of Chicago Press.

VALERIUS GEIST

University of Calgary
Calgary, Alberta, Canada

Contents

Illustrations

12   Illustrations

Mountain Sheep and Man
in the Northern Wilds

1

The Cabin and the Man

Ø Once upon a time a cabin stood in the wilderness. It was
surrounded by tall, rugged mountains, their peaks often hidden in clouds, with dark valleys below. These were young and
craggy mountains, most vulnerable to the water that eroded
them, for when the heavy gray clouds sailed in from the Pacific
across the Coastal Ranges of Alaska, the mountains caught the
clouds and were bathed in rain. The water worked endlessly.
In winter it froze in the rock cracks, and when warm weather
came in spring, it forced pebbles and boulders from their foundations. On a mild evening in May, when the wind was hushed
and the hermit thrush sang from a dark spruce, a steady murmur and rumble could be heard in the valley. Then the rumble
increased to a clatter and roar. It was the sound of rockslides
far and near—the sound of the mountains disintegrating—and
while it told of the water's mischief, it spoke also of the youth
and growth of these reckless ranges.

The water seeped from the high snow blanket down the
slopes, past pebbles and boulders, past moss plants and grasses,
past roots and over ice, down to the little trickles; then on to
the creeks, where it became a silt-laden foaming brew; down
past the boulders of the moraines left long ago by valley glaciers and on to the lake where the little cabin stood. Here it
waited awhile in company of other murky waters, cleansed it-

self of silt, and finally ran off—down to Fish Creek, down to the Spatzisi River, on to the mighty Stikine, past Telegraph Creek, through the towering Coastal Ranges, and on past Wrangell in Alaska, where it mixed with the salty waters of the Pacific and the odorous effluent of fish canneries.

The water had the fool's freedom on those ranges. It stayed in the cirque glaciers forming into blue ice; it stayed in the cornices that gave caribou welcome relief from mosquitoes and black flies in summer; it trickled down the cracks into aqueducts in the mountains and emerged again as a crystal-clear spring on the slopes, surrounded by flowers and herbs that almost all bear girls' names. There are *Valeriana* and *Luzula, Arnica* and *Veronica, Campanula* and *Dantonia, Potentilla* and *Achillia.* In winter, the water formed the hoarfrost on the aspen and willows; it covered the mountains, valleys, lakes, and rivers in fluffy, soft white. It blew in long silky streamers as dusty snow from the mountain tops, carried by roaring chinook winds; it sang as ice when the lake worked in winter, and its tune filled the canyons and rocky walls around with eerie echoes. But above all it ground away at the mountains. It polished rocks and ate through cliffs; in spring it tore new melt-off channels on the slopes; it cut and churned, foamed and gurgled, while carving up the mountains and cracking boulders from their peaks. And the mountains were implacable. Their height shadowed the valley; their slopes shed mist and rain into the valley, where it poured and poured and poured. The chinook wind coming from the Pacific made the mountains sing as it rushed through the cliffs and canyons. The wild chinook tore clouds of snow off the slopes and carried it far before dumping it, piled snow on wet snow in the valley, or made the snow melt under its warm breath, till in midwinter the water ran freely as if it were spring. Then the spruce trees and pines stood dripping while big puddles formed at their feet, and moose sloshed through the soupy snow. The warm wind brought relief for some of the hostages of the mountains. The white goats and black sheep had no need to paw snow from forage; the chinook exposed it. Gone were the cold days of the arctic front. The wind might be blowing and howling, but it was a warm wind and kindled a memory of far-off spring.

The chinook never stayed. Soon it was gone, and the great, gray clouds opened up and showered snowflakes on the land below. The mountains grew silent. The snow descended. Soon the goats had to paw; the sheep stood in snow, belly deep, working hard for every meager bite of food. Then the cold front came back, the skies cleared, and an icy hush fell on the land. In the night, the sky was black and the mountains white. Stars in countless myriads sparkled overhead. The northern lights quivered in green ribbons, and the bright moon made long shadows on the white snow. Then a sound drifted in from afar, pure and delicate, a tune faint and sad. It was a wolf, howling somewhere in a valley distant from the cabin. The goats stopped feeding to listen; the sheep moved closer to the cliffs, and the moose became nervous. The wolf would have to eat, and someone would die on those slopes.

The noisiest spirit in winter was the lake. It rested in a hole dug by an old glacier. Its shores were formed by terminal and lateral moraines, and the creeks that fed it were flowing on glacial till. The lake froze over in October, but before the first heavy snows had come, it stood steaming in the cold weather, filling the air with tiny crystals that glimmered and created sun dogs if the sun chose to shine. And then it froze. The ice thickened and began to work. Overflows burst on its surface and spread water below the snow blanket on the ice. For days it banged and hummed, sang and split, while cracks ran hither and yon on its surface, and water gushed out through the slits. Only the inlet and outlet never froze.

During the long winter the wind sculptured the snow on the ice. The caribou and wolves used the ice as a runway—the wolves to run down caribou, the caribou to escape wolves. Some willow ptarmigan buried themselves in the lake's snow blanket and slept there through the night. When the days lengthened, the trout and grayling began to swirl at the open inlet, and whitefish made a few ascents up the creeks under the ice. That was the beginning of the end for the ice. The sun

Large mature bighorn sheep ram, at the peak of his life

shone down on it. On a few warm days the creeks guided melt-water to the lake; its level began to rise. The ice developed dark spots and grew rotten. The wind pushed the ice pan up against the rocky beaches and ground the ice at its edges. Ever higher rose the lake. Ever hotter grew the sun. Evermore the ice creaked against the shore where it was crushed and finally melted. The clear winter water ran from the lake, and the murky melt-off took its place. Spring had arrived.

No one knew who was first to herald spring: it may have been the pair of mallards that stopped on the open waters of the lake, the junco that had arrived in a snowstorm to pipe and peck around the roots of the white spruce in the hope of better weather to come, or the varied thrush that came on a mild, lovely evening and sang so all were aware of his presence. Whoever came first mattered little to the Canada jays or the whisky jacks. They had been courting for weeks and had built nests ready to raise their young in the short summer. With the warm days came the mud on the trails and the odor of rotting leaves which is the smell of life and fertility. The snowshoe hares wasted no time insuring offspring. They chased each other through the willows on the creeks, shedding their winter secrecy. The goats and sheep grazed on the slopes, looking like little figurines, delicate and dainty in the clear mountain air. On the willow flat a calf moose that had survived the cold and the wolves began frolicking about its thin but gravid mother. On it came, raising its hackles, shaking its head, splashing with its front legs in a water puddle on the trail and kicking at it with its hind legs. The water flew in sheets. The old cow shook her head and moved on, followed by her offspring.

On the mountain slopes, the first green began to show. Grasses pushed their tips through the soil, first where it was warmest on the south slopes, around the well-fertilized beds used by mountain sheep at night. From there the green spread, just as the melt-off had spread from the cliffs and rocks onto the slope. More green followed. More warm days followed. The coats of the sheep began to look moth-eaten, faded, and ragged. Soon the old coat would be sloughed off, and bits of matted wool and guard hair would cling to the shrubbery, some to fall down and decay, some to be picked up by deer mice, juncos, and solitaires, and woven into warm nests. Small troops of gravid caribou came walking up the valleys to disperse and to seek refuge on high ridges where they would relieve themselves of their spunky youngsters that now kicked in their bellies. Once the warm days and the mud were there, the first green appeared, the catkins bloomed, the blue grouse hooted in the timber, and the willow ptarmigan courted on the brown meadows; then the life cycle was due for renewal, and the births would soon occur.

The grizzly roamed from his den searching for cadavers buried in the avalanches. More ducks winged in. The female sheep and goats looked for solitude in the cliffs. The cow moose moved to islands in the creek or dense timber. A young generation began to see the light of day. They frolicked sure-footed in the cliffs, though only hours old. They ran clumsily on the ridges, while their mothers rested from exhausting

births and milk production. Soon mothers and offspring
emerged from hiding and formed nursery troops. On other
mountains the rams gathered in large groups and played and
fought, invigorated by spring. Quickly the country turned a
lush green. The dwarf birches sprouted shiny leaves, the aspen
quaked their dress, and the willows soughed in the breeze.
Mosquitoes hummed through the mild evenings. Summer was
around the corner, and the water rushed from the snow and
glaciers and made raging torrents of the once meek creeks.

Then summer arrived. The willow thickets were filled with
the song and babble of sparrows and warblers. Mosquitoes
filled the days and nights and tormented sheep and caribou
even to the highest snowfields and the windiest peaks. The sun
never seemed to set, but hung on and on, finally dipping for a
few hours behind the mountain peaks. In winter the sun briefly
rose, only to dive back behind the same jagged walls. The
meadows stood lush in sedges; the bunch grass grew its long,
thin leaves as rapidly as it could; the mountain meadows began
to blossom on the rubble slopes, the moss campion unfolded its
delicate pink flowers. Everything was in a hurry to grow, to
bloom, to feed, to nurse, to grow new hair or fur, to grow new
feathers, to get the last vestiges of winter out of bones and
flesh, and to eat and live, while living and eating were good.
Everything hurried to mature, to set seeds, to grow bulbs, to
ripen fruit, to reproduce or get ready for it, for summer would
be all too short. The first frosts would soon come; the first
snowstorms would soon dust the mountain tops; the green
would soon turn to red and gold and yellow and purple and
brown and black. The short summer had hardly visited when
the first snow began to trim the peaks, to warn that winter was
not far off.

The mountains glowed in fall when Indian summer came
and bathed their flanks in autumn colors and sunshine. The air
was crisp. The caribou bulls had grown fat, feeding on dwarf
birch in the valleys. Their antlers were towering velvet-covered
racks, and their white necks told of the rut soon to come—of
combat and of breeding. Soon they would thrash small spruce
trees and rub the velvet from their antlers. Soon the antlers

would be white jagged bone, covered with streaks of red blood and rotting velvet. Then the bulls would rub their antlers some more, turning them brown in color. They would spar with each other, testing the strength of their massive necks, and then move slowly on to distant breeding grounds.

When Indian summer came to the valleys the ptarmigan broods formed into large flocks. Black bull moose with shiny antlers began to wade through the willow and birch thickets. On the slopes, the Stone's rams began to form bands. The sharp crack of their colliding horns echoed in the canyons. Fall was rushing in and so were the first snowstorms. Soon the creeks began to freeze. Ice built up on the rocks, growing into pillars as the creeks froze from the bottom up. The creeks rose. For a few days the water rushed around these ice pillars, and in its hurry, toppled them, dropping the level again. And the water went on.

Such was the land where the little cabin stood, oblivious to all this activity. Its walls were made of thick logs of white spruce that once grew where the cabin now stood. The man who cut them had mused at their age, for some of these trees had shaken the snow from their branches and bent under the force of the chinook when Newton and Leibnitz developed calculus, when Voltaire tickled France to laughter, when the French Revolution ran its bloody course, and when Napoleon's fate was sealed at Waterloo. These trees had stood here in this mountain valley while the cycle of seasons took its course, long before the first white man had seen this country, when Indians still went to Mount Edziza to mine its black obsidian and chip it into sharp knives and arrowheads or trade it to their neighbors. Now the trees rested, cut and peeled to become snug walls for the cabin. They are sheltered from rain by a roof and may last a century.

The cabin was built when the land was still wild, still unadorned by surveyors' ribbons, and free of ugly road cuts, of logging operations, or of mines. When the trees in the cabin walls were still standing, native Tahltans had lived down the valley at the base of the Spatzisi Plateau. Here the natives had fished in the lake, netted mountain goats in big rawhide nets which they stretched across gorges, or had clubbed sheep after driving them down into deep snow in midwinter. In summer, the people gathered berries and preserved them for winter in marmot skins by pouring hot marmot fat over the berries. The native people were gone now. They lived in Telegraph Creek or along the highway at Kinniskan Lake. The white people stayed in summer and fall only, till the snow and the cold came. Then they brought their horses down to Hyland Post where the Spatzisi meets the Stikine. Here the horses spent the winter under the watchful eyes of men hired to look after the animals. The horses had to be in good shape in summer and fall when they carried hunting and fishing parties through the mountains. But the land was still wild. The wolves still roamed the valleys; the caribou still gathered in large herds at breeding time on the upland plateaus; the black sheep and white goats still lived in small populations as they had done before, grazing the small patches of habitat cleared of snow by the chinook winds. The cycle of seasons went on as ever, and nature still reigned supreme over the wild, harsh land.

Of this, the cabin was also oblivious. After all, it had no soul and no mind of its own—although the man who lived in it thought differently at times. The cabin shed the rain and the snow; it was cool on blistering summer days and filled with warmth and comfort when cold arctic air froze the valley in winter. It whistled and screeched when the chinook winds tore at its roof as if threatening to lift the cabin from its foundations, and it sang with each drop when unending summer rains poured on its shining tin roof. But the cabin stood on, impartially sheltering the table, the stove, and the mouse, the man, and the weasel that were so often inside. It belched smoke backwards a few times, making the man cough and curse it loudly, but otherwise it behaved and stood as a promise of safety and comfort, shaded by green spruce, surrounded by dwarf birch and willows, unless the snows covered all and gave it a white coat.

On a winter day, the cabin's depths would stir to life before dawn had captured the darkness. Red sparks would fly from the stovepipe and die a few feet after gaining their freedom.

The airtight stove would throb to flickering life. The windows would glow as a lamp was lit. There would be footsteps inside and the clanking of dishes. Soon the smell and noise of frying meat and bubbling coffee would seep past the cabin walls. There would be the splashing of water in a washbasin and some loud and bad singing. As dawn advanced, the cabin door would open, and the man would come out, bundled in parka and mukluks against the cold. He would axe some wood on the chopping block below the cabin's overhanging roof and carry the chunks indoors. He would take the saw and cut a slab off the frozen quarter of moose that he took from the meat house. The meat would rest and melt on a plate on the window sill all day from where the man would pick it up in the evening, unless of course the weasel came first, in which case the man would pick it up from underneath his bed—the meat, that is, not the weasel. As the man sawed through the meat, the whisky jacks would come and land on his shoulders or head, or wait beside him, then dart forward to pick up a bill full of meat meal, or a piece of meat the man handed to them. By tradition, the meat trimmings were theirs, as well as the scraps of fat and sinew or whatever else the man handed them. A few scraps of melted meat were kept for the weasel, if and when it chose to show up and run to him for a free handout. It came often.

As the light grew brighter, the man emerged from the cabin. Sometimes he appeared with a pack-board and rifle and took off on his snowshoes down the trail to the frozen lake, or up the trail to the high valleys, and was not seen again till night. Sometimes he emerged with a spotting scope on a tripod and took off in the same directions. When the days grew longer in late winter he might be carrying a fishing rod as well and would return in the evening with a few lake trout, rainbows, Dolly Vardens, whitefish, or a rare grayling. Sometimes he carried a white rabbit or two on his return. In fall, he puffed back on some days carrying quarters of caribou or moose which were hung in the meat house. But usually he returned with nothing, still holding his spotting scope or camera, and always tired and glad to see his little cabin. On many days he did not leave at all but sat outside the cabin, looking at the mountains through binoculars or through his spotting scope, cursing the cold that reddened his nose into a painful burn, that made his eyes tear and crippled his fingers inside the gloves till he could write no more in a black book he held on his lap. It was then the man went into the cabin, held his hands over the stove till they were pliable again, and returned to resume his vigil once more.

The day wore on. If the man was away somewhere, the cabin interior was almost silent. Perhaps a white-footed mouse scratched and nibbled somewhere but that was little noise. The whisky jacks called and fluttered about; occasionally some rabbits came out in the sunlight and hopped to the ash pile where they nibbled ashes that were once wood burned in the stove. It was a rare day, indeed, if a big moose came to the cabin, or several caribou went by, or if the wolf that roamed the other side of the lake paid a visit and sniffed the man's tracks. He was a curious fellow, the wolf, but also a cautious one as was his nature. On some days a flock of willow ptarmigan cackled past the cabin; they fluttered into the willow bushes and pecked the red buds off the twigs. The ptarmigans were round and fluffy, and in the willows they looked like big balls of snow. They peered up at the eagle soaring high past the cliffs of the sunlit mountain as it searched for flocks of the white-tailed ptarmigan. An eagle must eat to fly, to soar, and to build a nest on those high cliffs, and to care for his screaming young.

When the man returned in the evening he shook the snow from his snowshoes and hung the webs on the cabin wall. He opened the air intake on the thick-bellied, black stove and allowed the flames to jump into throbbing life. He reached for the coffeepot nestled up against the stovepipe, and poured himself a mug of warm steaming coffee, closing his cold hands tightly around the warm mug. The little cabin had so much meaning, then, for it meant comfort and warmth and food and shelter and happiness and security and so much, much more. Again began the clattering of dishes, the slapping of water as the man returned from the creek carrying a full pail, having chopped a hole through the creek ice to reach water. As darkness fell, the cabin stovepipe again streamed sparks, the windows lighted up once more, and the long icicles hanging from the roof shone and sparkled in the glow from the window. Outside, rabbits were scurrying to the ash pile where they first fought each other—their fur flew in bundles—before nibbling the ashes' salt. They were a quarrelsome lot, these snowshoe hares; they had reached unusual abundance and had girdled trees and shrubs all around. Their trails were everywhere, as were their little round droppings.

By the time the moon rose the cabin's occupant could be seen writing or calculating on sheet after sheet of paper, or reading a book, one of many stored on several shelves. The cabin's daily cycle was coming to an end. The man yawned and went to bed, first arranging the bearskin under his sleeping bag. Soon the cabin was dark again; the stream of sparks from the stovepipe died down; the wood in the stove whispered softly as it glowed into coals, and the man's breathing was barely audible. The wind played in the branches of the tall spruce, a great horned owl hooted, the sad sound of a timber wolf drifted to the cabin, while northern lights danced in the sky and clouds raced past the moon heading into infinity.

He was a funny one, that man who lived in the cabin. At least the Indians thought so. They called him the crazy white man. Their logic was unassailable. After all, did not all sane white men leave the country in the fall? Did not all sane white men come to this country to hunt and kill big game, and to cart off the horns and antlers so that the heads of the animals might be stuffed and hung on walls? The crazy white man, however, showed no interest in this. The Indians had seen him arrive with his wife. They had helped build the cabin; they had kidded with him; and each winter they came by dog sled for a few visits. They could take much with a straight face, but to see a man who was not interested in shooting sheep, but watched them instead, day after day, month after month—well, that was too much. When they came for a visit in winter, it was to see if the crazy white man was still all right. Not that there was much that could happen to him, or anything one could do if something did happen, but a neighborly visit was a welcome diversion in winter for all concerned. On their arrival, they would shout loudly while still a quarter-mile or so from the cabin—

following good wilderness custom—for knocking at a lone cabin door after a silent approach is to invite suicide. They never stayed longer than overnight, and then packed their dog sleds and returned to Hyland Post. When they came for the last time, before the man left at the end of his stay, it was just to say goodbye. To utter these little words, they had to travel four days through unspeakable cold, and when they had departed, and the barks of their dogs had died in the distance, the crazy white man wiped an eye with the sleeve of his parka, and swallowed hard, for he realized how few of his tribe would have come so far only to bid farewell.

The man was a scientist, although no test tube, lab coat, oscilloscope, or microscope betrayed his profession. He was a type that was hard to pigeonhole in his outdoor clothing. He suffered from a lack of identity. Not that one could *not* find a label to pin on him; there were labels available, but there were too many. One could call him a zoologist since he investigated animals; or a biologist since he was interested in life processes; or a mammalogist since his interest narrowed to mammals; or an ecologist because he investigated relationships between animals and their environment; or an ethologist because he specialized in animal behavior; or a "wildlifer" since he studied wildlife. One could also label him a "fieldworker," since he worked, not in a laboratory but out in the field (which is not to be confused with farm laborer, although he often looked like one).

Yet it would be so easy for the man to gain identity and instant respectability. He need only don a clean, white lab coat and grab a microscope with one hand and a molecule with the other. Of course he should add a serious expression. He should also clatter about with a slide rule, or unfold a few rolls of crackling computer sheets. He might well utter some unintelligible profundities—or, better still, an occasional prophecy of gloom and doom. Everybody would recognize him, then, as a scientist and gaze at him in awe. Everyone would be convinced of his importance. Some might even think he could turn a blonde into a gorilla, and as such he obviously would command respect. Instead of playing the part of Scrooge in a lab coat, the man in the cabin chose to watch sheep. Maybe the Indians had a point after all.

Yet this particular crazy white man was not the only scientist of his kind. There were others. Some followed lions on the African plains, others watched seagulls in the dunes, or apes in the tropical forests of Africa and Asia; some stalked wolves in the timber of eastern North America or elephants in Ceylon; others studied ibex in the Alps, chamois in Switzerland, or red deer in Scotland; some followed sandpipers in America, caribou in the Arctic, or antelope in the Serengeti, and so on. These fieldworkers, who used primarily field glasses and notebooks, were less than credible to fellow scientists. They were so old-fashioned! Worse still, these field men insisted on ridiculous, heretical notions. They claimed that the best computer was the one between two ears. They hinted that under the microscope the most unimportant things look great. They encouraged their analytical, reduction-minded friends with cheerful thoughts; the more their analysis revealed about less and less, the more certain they would win a Nobel prize. They might even make the local newspaper. To the general public, the field men were also less than credible—but for other reasons.

Consider the thoughts of a weather-tanned rancher out on the lone prairie who spots a man holding a fishnet in one hand and a ladder in the other. Even a hard-nosed westerner cannot resist asking what one would do with a ladder and a fishnet. The fellow with the fishnet and the ladder was my friend, Tony. He was studying buffleheads—small ducks that nest in hollow trees. One catches buffleheads by placing the ladder against a likely-looking big tree in the coulee, then locating a likely-looking woodpecker hole, placing the net over it, and then kicking the tree heartily with the boots. The little frightened duck will then jump out of its nest hole and into the net— provided the right hole was covered. But the rancher could not know all that.

In general, field biologists, or ecologists, are not hard to recognize—even those who carry no fishnet or ladder under their arms.

If you were to see an ecologist returning from a week's counting of moose droppings, or from other challenging tasks, you would probably look at an unshaven face, and old coat, faded blue jeans with a few frayed holes here and there, and a pair of rubber boots. You would suspect, correctly, that this person is neither a bum nor a logger—such persons do not carry binoculars around their necks. That he is no tourist you would deduce from the binder twine—knotted binder twine—from which the binoculars are suspended. That he is no hiker you could tell from at least three clues: first, this man does not look as if he escaped from a Sears catalogue, nor from that of Eddy Bauer; second, his pack is far too small for that of a hiker; third, he is clad in rubber boots. Ever see hikers in rubber boots? Or with a packsack smaller than that befitting a well-trained mule? These considerations narrow the choice of possible identities considerably but not entirely. He could be an alienated student, or a professor on the lam from society. But, look again. The man does not have a beard—he is just not shaven. Besides, alienated professors hope to grow rich first on their alienation and then practice it somewhere, like in Australia or a South Sea island. Alienated professors are not found in the bush—only in society.

No, there is no escape from it. This something-more-than-shabby figure is a scientist—an ecologist. The rubber boots are not due to an exercise of free choice over other footwear but to a realistic appraisal of research funds and private income. You would suspect, correctly, that this man is not in collusion with the military and industrial complex. However, in these times of the awakening ecological conscience, and "environmental consultants," one cannot be dogmatic about this point, nor about the rubber boots, either.

Since ecologists are open to scrutiny by the public eye, they are past masters at making themselves inconspicuous. Heaven forbid if someone were to draw such a man into a discussion. A scientist's innermost thoughts, and the greater portion of his day, deal with professional matters, and professional matters deal with such thoughts as: how to determine virginity in moose, the incidence of ulcers in squirrels, or the rectal temperature of hibernating badgers. Imagine what situations an ecologist could get himself into if he were recognized and asked about his work. Try to explain to a business executive, a luscious blonde, or a darling, white-haired old lady why you were studying, say, the love life of Columbian ground squirrels! If you do not wish to lie, *and* yet still want to maintain some semblance of respectability, take it from me—play deaf or reply in Sanskrit. Try any other strategy and you are in a losing game.

You don't believe? All right, try ducking that question and speak about the land you work in. You can tell of its splendor, the snow-covered peaks, crystal-clear lakes, the morning mist over the meadow, the babbling trout stream, or the camp at day's end. You may then have to explain another question. How come, sir? Are you on holidays at government expense?

Nor are you any better off by emphasizing some of the less romantic experiences of a scientist's work in the wilderness—like breaking through the ice at 20° below zero, being caught in an unseasonal storm far from shelter, escaping being caught by an avalanche, a grizzly bear, or a bull moose, or lying helpless beneath a leaking tarp, too ill even to ward off mosquitoes and black flies. With such incidents as part of your story—and most field men get into such troubles sooner than later—you will be no hero in the eyes of the beholder but a fool or, at best, a ridiculous show-off. At the worst, you may meet a rich wilderness hunter who compulsively proclaims his manly deeds during guided hunts such as killing ferocious grizzlies, raging bull moose, or crafty mountain sheep at a quarter-mile or more. Then you will be in for some tales for which euthanasia would be a merciful cure for the teller.

Anyway, it is quite evident why ecologists prefer to be unrecognized by the public. However, this disinclination for recognition extends also to fellow scientists, since they tend to remember ecologists for deeds for which they would gladly be forgotten. Scientists would be more than human if their memories worked in a fashion other than remembering the embarrassments. My good friend Chuck was remembered at the university (where we obtained our doctoral degrees) for crawling

into bear dens and sticking thermometers into the unmention-
ables of hibernating bears. Chuck had, indeed, crawled into
numerous dens to discover if hibernating black bears were in
deep sleep. They were not. Every bear would awaken and
groggily look over his new den companion. Chuck went ahead,
anyway, and tagged the ears of the bears. A few of them re-
sisted. They would either chase him out or try to escape themselves—flooring Chuck in the process. This competent, silent
man, working without flamboyance, without an audience on
nationwide television to hold its breath and applaud, and without the slightest pretense, produced a memorable study of
black-bear biology. He was no self-styled or drummed-up hero,
yet he had the courage not to kill a wild, awakened bear, but to
embrace it.

One may wonder what scientists have to offer besides ridiculous facts that neither help one to get rich nor to ascend the
social ladder. If you still have some faith let me shake it a little
more by illustrating how human these eggheads can be.

It all happened at Elkwater, a little sleepy community at the
edge of the prairie in southern Alberta, close to the Cypress
Hills. One day an archaeologist came from the big-city university in search of Indian graves. An archaeologist can be recognized as the man who goes into ecstasy over bones which no
sane dog would touch. He searched hard and diligently (the archaeologist, not the dog), and dug industriously in various
areas around the little town. Finally, his search was rewarded—
he found a human skeleton and gleefully sent it off to the university for identification. Shortly thereafter he received two let-
ters: one from the university advising him that the bones had
been buried for all of 15 years, at the most, and the second one
from the skeleton's enraged widow.

Then a team of meteorologists came to this same little town
on a dry, dusty summer's day. It had not rained for weeks, and
the tall prairie grass stood brown and withered in the oppres-
sive heat. The men of science shot instrumented rockets into
the atmosphere to study high-altitude weather patterns. Unfortunately, their rockets set the prairie on fire. The flames

quickly spread and only by good fortune barely by-passed the town and its less-than-delighted citizens.

This prairie community was next favored by a visit from another archaeologist. He, too, wanted to dig. All archaeologists want to dig. It's compulsive with them. In order to reach his selected digging place, the archaeologist dammed up the creek to reroute it and allow access to the creek. He rerouted the water all right—right through the town. (No engineer he— just a scientist.)

But little Elkwater's ordeal was not over; not yet. A biologist arrived. He was lured by the tame, white-tailed deer that frequented the little community. Elkwater lies at the edge of a provincial park, and deer, protected from hunting, learned long ago to live in harmony with the town's citizens. The good scientist wanted only to study the social behavior of deer, and to do this he felt it necessary to mark several deer with neck collars—a procedure he had used in previous research. Two deer were fed a tranquilizing drug of a dosage prescribed by the manufacturers—it killed the deer. Two deer were injected (using a syringe gun) with the prescribed dosage of another drug—it killed the deer. When the good man ceased his experiments, in view of the town's sensitivity about their pet deer, his spaniel escaped from his departing car, rushed a deer, and killed it in the middle of town. I would predict little profit in going to Elkwater and proclaiming one's intention to do research in the name of science.

It is a pity that those who are ignorant of science look upon scientists with fear, regarding them as witch doctors dealing with dangerous mysteries. At the very least, they could regard scientists as average human beings—more or less. Some do get a little carried away by their work, as did the curator of a big museum, but it was still harmless stuff. The good man lived a colorless life among faded, moth-eaten skins, dirty skeletons, and grotesque skulls. He toiled diligently in that house of dusty death, and it left its mark. When the curator's daughter asked him for a cat, he gave her one, a stuffed specimen.

Take pity on these scientists. In plying their trade they have

Dall's sheep ram from the St. Elias Range, a thinhorn sheep, smaller in horn and body size than the bighorns from the Rockies

forsaken the world of power and riches. They are not free to act eccentrically, since they are employees depending for their livelihoods, their laboratories, their working space, and their money, on industry and public bodies. These benefactors look askance at any behavior seriously deviating from established norms. Even tenured university professors are not free to indulge in public behavior that is tolerated, condoned, and excused in artists. Moreover, scientists have forsaken any claim to lasting fame. There cannot be lasting fame in science. If one is searching for lasting fame, one should become a novelist, a poet, or, better still, a philosopher or composer. The works of these men live on after their death, continually enriching the lives of others, and are discussed and appreciated anew by every generation. An unknown artist can draw inspiration from the hope of posthumous discovery. He can reflect on Rembrandt, Spinoza, Delacroix, or Thoreau, and, thus inspired, accept hardship and grief. He will work and perfect his art without immediate reward but in the hope of future recognition.

For the scientist there is no such hope; if he fails to gain fame during his lifetime, he generally fails to acquire it. The reason for this is not that scientists work differently, in principle, from artists. They do not. A good scientist lives as much by the fruits of his imagination as does a good painter or poet. The difference arises because, unlike the masterpiece of a painter or a poet that is not tampered with, the masterpiece of a scientist is soon improved upon. An important discovery is but a stepping stone for someone to improve it, and soon it becomes public property. Moreover, if the scientist is a successful teacher, he only hastens the obsolescence of his own work, for he leads others on to improve upon his discovery. As long as he works, he gains eminence. He may be asked to comment in public on questions well outside his competence because he is a famous man, and obviously famous men know everything. He becomes a banquet speaker, societies honor him, prime ministers and presidents consult him. In the meantime, his scholarship slips a little. Old age knocks at the door. In panic he gathers his strength and writes his lifework into a resounding volume—his swan song. His fellow travelers note the new milestone in passing. They chuckle about its splendid contribution to the knowledge of yesterday—and are sometimes right. They say a few kind words when death overtakes him (obituaries are always nice). In a decade or two the book is out of date and of historical interest at best. Lesser men will comment on its weakness in the wisdom of hindsight. They will remember the once-great man by his errors. Finally, his contribution is absorbed into the general pool of knowledge and becomes anonymous public property. His name is forgotten.

This sounds terribly sad, does it not? The reader will probably protest and point, for example, to Darwin, Mendel, and Einstein. These are famous scientists, are they not? Certainly. May I ask, when was the last time you mulled over the intellectual contributions of these men to human culture? Did you enjoy the encounter in the manner of a novel by Agatha Christie or a story by Voltaire? Did you experience it as deeply as a symphony by Beethoven? What is left of Darwin's general discoveries that have not been thoroughly improved upon? Scientists who go on to lasting fame often do so for reasons other than science. Have you ever heard of the father of modern botany? His name is Johann Wolfgang von Goethe. Yes, the one who wrote *Faust*. Goethe was a pretty good playwright, too. As for power and wealth, science is not the road toward these goals. A scientist's power is like that of a jackhammer, good only in a manipulator's hands. A scientist's day must not be concerned with the use of his knowledge toward gaining power, nor does he study or intellectualize about its use as do scholars in the humanities. Scientists must be free to pursue the ridiculous, as it is only by means of this freedom that significant knowledge is gained. If he follows this route, then he is less than adequately equipped to deal in the realm of politics and business, unless he abandons the pursuit of knowledge and his profession as a scientist. There is no possible compromise. For this reason, scientists concerned with developing knowledge are not likely to become rebels or leaders of popular causes, although one may assume that their efforts ultimately alter the course of humanity. Their work affects philosophies, and, through this, they leave their mark.

Let us leave the philosophizing and go on with the story. You may wonder what there is left in science, and you may discover it by reading on. This is a book about science. It tells of a scientist's odyssey through various adventures, including some scientific ones. It speaks of the land in which he lived, the people whom he met, and the animals that he studied. It relates how discoveries were made, without recourse to the little white lies that fill the introductions of our scientific treatises. The setting is the wilderness of the Cassiar Mountains, the Rockies, and the St. Elias Range, in western Canada, as well as the Yukon roads and the Alaska Highway, and the little settlements along them. I will not make the claim that this book is a modest contribution to anything; my critics will be quick to point out its modesty, anyway. Nor will I be satisfied if it just stimulates discussion— only if it ends them once and for all!

In June 1961, Renate (my wife) and I left for the Spatzisi in northern British Columbia to study the life history of Stone's sheep and mountain goats. The science of animal behavior had begun to blossom in the 1950s, and we had been captured by this intriguing subject. We had planned to build a cabin and spend one year studying the animals in their native haunts. But the best laid plans of mice and men. . . .

2

On Yukon Roads

✐ The Greyhound bus was nearing our destination: Watson Lake in the Yukon Territory. It was an early morning in June 1961, and spring had just embarked on a comeback. Renate, beside me, had also awakened from a none-too-refreshing sleep, and we spoke of the eventful days that had just passed and the intriguing ones ahead. We would ultimately arrive in the Spatzisi, the unknown land, called after a river of the same name which translates into "the river of the red goats" in the Indian vernacular. We knew little of the land, beyond the promise that it could be a fair study area for the black thinhorn sheep or Stone's sheep. Otherwise, we were putting our faith in J. A. Walker, known more familiarly as Tommy, the hunting guide and outfitter in that land. He was expecting our arrival in the Spatzisi, along with part of his own provisions for that year. His supplies, as well as ours, were on a big semitrailer truck somewhere behind us on the Alaska Highway. We were to wait at Watson Lake till the equipment and provisions arrived and then drive on to Dease Lake, from where we, and the supplies, were to be flown to the Spatzisi.

Watson Lake is a little Yukon settlement displaying all the charms of that distant land. There is the dusty gravel road winding in search of a town. There are the hotels, motels, churches, schools, garages, stores, a police station, a post office, a community hall, and an airport. And, of course, there are four beer parlors and the inevitable jail, all five overflowing—in season.

Seasons are very important. Life in Watson Lake ebbs and flows with the seasons. In spring, the geese and ducks wing in from the south, and hard on their heels are the geologists, prospectors, camp cooks, heavy-equipment operators, engineers, and administrators. The charter aircraft and helicopter companies awaken to full activity. Soon the long summer days and the tourists arrive, and the race is on for the almighty dollar. It must be a race, for the bonanza will not last long, and the motels, hotels, shops, and other human enterprises, must make enough money in a brief two months to cover the expenses of the remaining ten. It is no different for the wildlife. The young must be raised while the summer lasts, their fur and feathers grown, and their fat stored and antlers developed—for the first frosts are not far off, and winter will again follow. So life goes on at Watson Lake: feverish in summer when a grubstake is earned, sluggish in winter when it is spent—bolstered often by government unemployment premiums and welfare checks.

Like the rest of the Yukon, Watson Lake has many surprises, and, when Renate and I left the bus with our hand luggage and headed for the nearest café, we encountered the first. It was 7:00 A.M., our time, but the café was closed. Surprise! It was only 5:00 A.M. Yukon time, and the residents were still sleeping it off. So, we gathered our belongings on the veranda of the log-house hotel and entered the deserted lobby. A car pulled up, a couple emerged, and headed for the café, only to be as surprised as we were. They, too, entered the lobby. We sat in hungry unison and then struck up a conversation—misery loves company.

We had not talked long when heavy footsteps, sounding on the wooden staircase leading from the second floor, diverted our attention. A barefooted, half-dressed man came stumbling down, gesticulating and cussing, while trying to stick his shirt-tail into his pants. It was evident that he had something to tell us, but he was slightly out of breath. He told us to shut up. We

were waking the whole hotel. The walls were so thin here. . . .
Indeed, the walls were thin. They would rob a mouse of
privacy. In the next room, one could hear one's neighbor
scratch himself, as was soon discovered. When we were assigned a room several hours later and proceeded to rid ourselves of Alaska Highway dust, we received another surprise.
After stripping off her travel clothes, Renate had taken soap
and towel and opened the bathroom door. At least she thought
it was the bathroom door. Instead, she found herself in an ad-
joining room which housed several sleeping men stretched out
on two beds. She beat a hasty retreat and barricaded the door
with two chairs. I forget where, or indeed if, we bathed.

The motels and hotels in the Yukon often provide innocent
adventures. Years after our initiation at Watson Lake, my
friend, Bob, and I were headed in happy anticipation toward a
small Yukon settlement in a helicopter. We had spent several
days in the mountains, exploring their ecology. The weather
had been quite bad, and we were dreaming of the luxuries to
come: a shower, a night's sleep in a clean bed, and a change
from camp cooking. There was but one hotel in town, and we
were soon ushered in. Our rooms were small but reasonably
clean. The blankets perforated by many cigarette burns were
no novelty to me, as I had slept under the like in other hotels.
Bob headed for a shower room and was soon singing and
scrubbing. I entered an adjacent shower cubicle and turned the
tap. A trickle of cold water emerged from a spout above and
dropped to the floor, less than an inch away from the wall. No
matter how the taps were turned, the trickle remained the
same size and temperature. Have you ever succeeded in taking
a shower in cold water which trickles one inch from the wall? I
waited for Bob to finish. Stepping out, he commented, "Not
much of a shower." Still, it was better than the one I left. From
four pinholes in the spout, the water emerged in graceful arcs
about eight inches from the wall. Moreover, it was warm—
lukewarm.

I slept soundly that night, but Bob did not. A noisy party was
in full swing in the beer parlor below. The whole settlement
had turned out. The floors were throbbing with rock music till

about 2:30 A.M, and Bob did not close an eye. I was awakened at 5:00 A.M., but not by rock music. The toilets were located directly across the hall from my room, from where, I gathered, a competition was being conducted between two truckers. Shouting encouragements back and forth, they tried to outsound each other—not by mouth, but from the opposite direction.

Up and dressed, we headed for a little restaurant one block down the street from the hotel. There was only one block to the town, anyway. It was early, the establishment had just opened, and customers were munching. It was a simply furnished, clean restaurant, run by two Indian ladies, one of whom caught my attention at once, and I noticed that Bob was also duly impressed. She was a young girl with firm, but friendly, manners and resembled a reincarnation of Sitting Bull. The girl was hefty and muscular, with a broad face and a prominent nose—hardly feminine, but eye-catching, displaying spirit and poise. Bob was impressed by her muscles, as apparently were all the customers, and not only the sober ones.

We ordered breakfast from this courteous Brünnhilde and settled behind our morning coffee to watch the show—in a welfare town, unspoiled by civilization and quite earthy. Another customer entered, obviously still bearing the effects of a night of gaiety. In particular, he was not quite sure of his steps. He was a small, elderly Indian, wearing thick glasses, and dressed in faded blue jeans and an old woolen shirt. After a moment's hesitation, he homed in on a table next to ours that was filled with construction workers. He insisted on shaking hands with all.

"My name Jo John." He paused and looked around the table, as if to make sure that all were duly impressed.

" 'Tell you something." He paused again, and looked around.

"I am going to Calgary." Pause. Another look around.

"My son is getting married." Pause. (Ditto.)

"Then I am flying to Vancouver." Pause. All nodded and went on chewing. The story seemed not unfamiliar. Jo John looked around, then turned and headed for the next table. He stretched out his hand.

"My name Jo John." He paused and insisted on shaking hands all around.

" 'Tell you something." He paused and looked around.

"I am going to Calgary." Pause. (As above.)

"My son is getting married." Pause. (As above.)

"Then I am flying to Vancouver." Pause. (Ditto.)

Jo John made his way to a third table, stretched out a hand to the guests, and, "My name Jo John." . . . The reader may fill in the details that followed. Then Jo John headed for the next table. Repeat. Follow script as at table 1.

The kitchen was his next destination, and here, too, he proclaimed the good news. (For details, return to table 1.) When he came out again, he stopped, gazed around the restaurant as if searching for someone he had missed telling the good news and discovered us. On he came. I wondered if I should not say "Hi, Jo John! 'Tell you something. Your son is getting married, you are going to go to Calgary and then to Vancouver.' Have you heard of it already?" But I held my tongue and went on eating instead. Alas, Jo John blew his lines. He discovered that we were strangers. Pausing in deep indecision, he finally weaved his way out of the restaurant.

Poor old Jo John. He was anticipating the big adventure of his lifetime: a long journey to exciting distant cities—maybe his first and, just as likely, his last one. The news was too good to be kept secret, too good not to be repeated again and again and shared with one and all. This attitude was no different from that of the little European peasant village where I grew up, where news, good or bad, was shared news.

We returned to the hotel after breakfast and met Jo John stumbling from the lobby with a case of beer clutched under his arm.

"Hi!" he said, stretching out his arm, "my name Jo John.

"And how are you this splendid morning, Mr. Jo John?" I asked, and shook his hand in Teutonic fashion. That upset the applecart again. Jo John once more lost his lines and, despite some struggle, failed to regain them.

"Hunting?" he finally questioned.

We shook our heads. Embarrassing silence.

"Want a beer?" and his face lit up.

We shook our heads again. Mystified, Jo John turned and stumbled on.

Just then, we noticed two figures on unsteady feet further up the road. Each clutched a case of beer. Both reeled, discussing and gesticulating. Two "gay" braves! They pulled up short in front of us. Strangers were an interesting novelty, and, after asking what we were doing in this ---- country, and in particular this ---- town, and on such a ---- day, they staggered on down the ---- road.

Morning was well advanced by now, and we entered the lobby to pay for the lodging but found no one to accept our money. We searched but in vain. An eerie silence had settled over the town. The residents were sleeping it off. The party had taken its toll. We finally left a note at the post office before departing that morning.

Our first day in the Yukon, at Watson Lake, was no less unusual for Renate and me. Our supplies were to arrive that day, but there was no sign of them—not that day, nor the next—and we settled down to an enforced stay, the first of many such compulsory stays at Watson Lake. It lasted only three days, which is short by Yukon standards, very short.

Watson Lake is a busy place in spring. It is an aviation center, out of which several charter airlines and helicopter services operate. Prospectors, geologists, miners, and various workers, along with the first tourists, were congregating in town. Most were waiting to be flown out for a summer's work in the mountains. As a result of all the usual delays, the now-busy beer parlors were booming, filled with customers waiting for their flights, searching for jobs, and renewing old friendships or making new ones.

We were a bit of a curiosity. Why had we come? To study sheep. Our reply was obviously somewhat surprising and unexpected. Were we doing this for the government? We shook our heads. This was also unexpected; apparently, had our reply been affirmative, all would have been well, for the government can be expected to indulge in such crazy things. We chatted finally about our common experiences, a necessary retreat in many human conversations. An old Austrian camp cook, glad to speak again in his mother tongue, told us all about the polar bears he had seen in the mountains and confided to us that no one had taken these observations seriously. We nodded gravely; mountain goats and polar bears do share a certain likeness. A half-sober prospector took a liking to us and looked us up daily. Stoned or half-sober, he helped us at every turn. Like many lonely men, he was grateful to anyone who would only sit and listen. In front of the hotel, I ran into an old school friend who was taking a degree in geology and was on his way up north. Then I met the prospector-father of an assistant who had helped me on a moose research project. Time passed as we awaited the arrival of our stores.

If one has no patience, Watson Lake will teach one to acquire it. There is little diversion for a stranger—particularly in winter time at Watson Lake. Beer parlors are not very exciting, and if they did become exciting places, the Royal Canadian Mounted Police would see to it that they did not remain so for long. Girls? You must be kidding! Reading matter is of the kind found in any small Canadian town, but a steady diet of reading from breakfast to midnight can depress one's appetite for even the best of books—let alone *Playboy*. Going to bed early is restful for one night only. There may be a movie show in town, once a week, but one must know of this. As a stranger, one is excluded from all the soul-refreshing entertainment such as the feuds between the Catholics and Presbyterians over the shape and cost of the town's recreation center; one is not caught up in the latest money-raising project like baking cakes to be sold along the Alaska Highway; one knows nobody to gossip about and knows too little of prospecting to harmonize with someone on mining stock. To kill time, one may stand and stare out of the hotel window, into the ice fog that blankets the area, and watch the big ravens wheel and flop over the houses—chasing dogs away from choice morsels in the frozen streets, or pecking happily at some piece of garbage they managed to drag to the top of a telephone pole. In the streets, cars

hum past, trailing huge plumes of white smoke in their wake.
The throb of idling motors is heard everywhere, for who would
shut off an engine he was lucky enough to get started at 20°,
30°, 40°, 50°, 60°, or even 70° below zero? One can watch the
goings-on in the beer parlors, count the number of drunks as
they stumble back and forth between beer parlor and restaurant, enjoy the frustration of others trying to get stalled vehicles started, and wish the hell one were down south.

There is not much one can do when temperatures remain at
50° below zero. The cultural centers are somewhat underde-
veloped, since earthy sins are the preferred entertainment. If
the local sample of churches has shown little impact, it may be
that preaching hell and damnation to overwintered sinners
merely stirs their desire to reach so warm and entertaining a
place. One pines here for diversion and perks up the ears when
the entertainment begins, such as a drunken brave battling his
squaw (or vice versa) in the adjacent hotel room. One knows,
then, that it is Friday night, the welfare checks have come, and
beer and romance have begun to flow. The latter is of rather
uncomplicated style, at least that witnessed publicly. A sample
of romance, performed at 2:00 A.M. in a hotel, would run as
follows:

"Marie? Open the door. I want to ---- you."

Silence.

"You hear me? You dirty bitch. Open up!"

"What? What did you say about my mother? You rotten,
dirty bitch. I'm going to kill you! Open up!"

One hears fists banging on the door and a rattling of the
door handle.

"Open the door. I want to ---- you. Only I ---- you! You
hear?"

This will suffice. It is the dialogue of the male partner only,
since the replies of the female are raw, even by modern standards. Despite the apparent coyness of the female, courtship
may succeed, or at least a fight may break out. If it's a dilly, one
may follow it with one's ears, down the stairs into the lobby,
then out into the frozen street. Here the eyes pick up the action. There is a merry chase around a taxi. She escapes inside.

He hits the car with his fists and boots, causing a couple of hundred dollars' worth of damage and performs a spirited dance with appropriate vocalizations. Then a member of the Royal Canadian Mounted Police appears and takes sides, ending the fun.

Getting stuck in Watson Lake is another hazard. In 1968, I drove into Watson Lake on November 7, since I had a flight booked with Stan's Beaver on November 8. We were to fly down to Skook Davidson's home. On the morning of the eighth, Skook asked Stan on the radio to search Lower Post for Jack No-see-um and ask Jack to come and work for Skook for the winter. Stan drove off to Lower Post, a small Indian settlement near Watson Lake, where he located Jack and found him agreeable to Skook's offer. It was arranged to pick him up on the following morning, postponing the flight by one day.

Stan drove down early next morning but, alas, not early enough—our wanted man had also been "wanted" by the Royal Canadian Mounted Police. The Mounties had gotten their man and locked him in jail. I heard something about a drunk and a few faces being punched in (including that of a girl), but this is hardly news if it comes from Lower Post. Upon Stan's return, we radioed Skook, and he asked us to look for Harry Moosenose, who also resided at Lower Post. Luck eluded us that day, also, for we failed to locate Harry, thus postponing the flight a second day.

Stan had no luck the following day, either, and for the third day, the flight was postponed.

On November 10, Stan finally discovered Harry's whereabouts and found him willing to work for Skook. However, it was too late in the day to fly out, and a fourth day's postponement was necessary.

The next morning a snowstorm struck, effectively grounding us, and postponing our flight for a fifth day.

Stan's aircraft had been booked for the following day. Despite the questionable weather, Stan took off with the party but returned without reaching his destination. No second flight could be made that day. This postponed the flight for a sixth day.

On the next day, the snowstorm continued to rage, and the seventh day of postponed flight was chalked up.

Finally, on the following day, November 14, 1968, the internment ended. Stan picked up Harry from Lower Post, and we flew off. We had been lucky, indeed, because when Stan returned without Harry and me, he was greeted by the Royal Canadian Mounted Police. This time they wanted Harry Moosenose.

Yet Watson Lake has a second face also. It is the home of a few men and women of considerable experience in worldly matters who stay in the north by choice. By this I do not mean the legendary prospectors who struck it rich and blew it all. Watson Lake has those, too. For example, the current school principal was an English diplomat whose past had spanned a long career in Arabian countries. The town harbors big-game outfitters and guides who sit with princes and gangsters at common campfires. There are businessmen who see the wide world down south if, and when, they want to, but who rarely fall victim to such desires. Take my friend, Hal, a businessman who has made and lost fortunes. His spirit of adventure was refreshing. Once he gambled his whole estate on three barges that were tied up in Whitehorse on the Yukon River. If he could get these barges down to the Arctic Ocean, then up the Mackenzie River and use them for freight service, he could make a fortune. He hired captains and crews and went ahead. It was an incredible journey down the river, a trip filled with toil, excitement, and one mutiny. Once at sea, the barges were anchored for a few days to give the crew some rest. A fire broke out on one barge and spread quickly. The crew was saved. Hal stood in a boat and took pictures as his fortune went up in flames. One drum of diesel oil after the other roared into a pillar of flames. In those days, no one had as yet sent trash into orbit, but Hal may have scored a first with his oxygen bottles. Like rockets, they burst into the sky with a swish and a bang, to disappear forever. And Hal stood in the dinghy and filmed. That's a Yukoner for you.

In summer one may encounter other scenes in the Yukon. It is a Friday evening in late July in Whitehorse. The Royal Canadian Mounted Police have barricaded the main street to vehicles, and pedestrians surge across the unobstructed spaces. Shopowners have pulled out their ware on the sidewalk, and there are cake sales and open-air hamburger stands as well. At one end of the street, at the Taku Hotel, a group of long-haired youths are singing and strumming guitars; a group of middleclass American tourists have gathered around them. July is tourist season after all. At the opposite end of the street, some three blocks away, a fiddler and guitarist, aided by microphone and loudspeaker, are pouring out old-time tunes. They don't play badly. Around them the sidewalk is crowded. In a small square, fenced off with yellow barricades, one can see dancers and hear waves of loud laughter.

On stepping close, one can see the cause of the mirth. Old Teepee Johnny is dancing. He is drunk, very drunk, as he is expected to be. He reels, on his old, thin legs, stumbles, weaves, jerks, stomps, flaps his arms as if he were a bird about to ascend. He grimaces a toothless grin. His eyes are small, gray, dull, and lifeless, as gray and dull as his gray-bristled face, his old hat, his ripped, dirty pants and floppy coat. He is an attraction all right, old Teepee Johnny. A young girl slips up to Johnny and dances with him; a middle-aged lady dances with him; if nobody dances with Johnny, Johnny dances alone— walking, stomping, grinning, croaking, clapping, turning.

In the opposite corner of the ring an elderly tourist couple, a bit stiff and painfully self-conscious, have taken heart and are dancing. An Indian brave and his squaw have entered the ring and are having a good time. A tall, rugged fellow, rough hewn, dirty and rude, dances with a paunchy, old Indian gal. Can she dance! Her movements are precise, a little leopardlike, an inkling of the fine performance her heavy-set body can command. In a corner a balding, elderly man dances with a baby clutched to his breast.

Onlookers are all around. Many are young teenagers; none of their age class participate except in laughter. Couples come and go; only Johnny hangs on. He misses no dance. A man tells me that Johnny is the Yukon itself, that he has roughed it for so long nobody can remember him otherwise, and that he is an English lord.

We knew nothing of all this in June 1961, when we waited for our freight to arrive from Dawson Creek. We marked time for three days, remaining, for the most part, in, or in front of, the hotel and listening for the sound of the big Freightways truck that was yet to appear. When it did arrive, we left for Cassiar, an asbestos-mining town in British Columbia. There were the usual crises before we had everything repacked onto another truck in Cassiar and headed to Dease Lake. Ken Pryor, who owned and drove the truck, was a bit worried. A bridge had washed out, and its makeshift replacement was good for ten tons only; we had a dead weight of sixteen. Ken looked the ersatz bridge over before we drove onto it and slowly creaked across. The green foamy water below was not one bit inviting. When we did reach the far side, Ken pulled a case of beer from its hiding place and insisted on celebrating. We celebrated.

The "highway" we were on, the so-called Stewart-Cassiar road, was then incomplete and barely reached past Dease Lake. The northernmost end, from Cassiar south, was particularly rugged. Its condition reflected the work of an incompetent contractor and a political scandal with a most unusual upshot: a minister of the Crown was convicted and sent to jail for accepting a kickback. The contractor friends he had served so well had constructed this end of the road. While we rode on it and suffered agonies, we deliberated on the lack of appropriate punishment meted out to the minister and his cronies. Not just a jail term should have been decreed (he was released for good behavior after only three years), but he should have been ordered to drive that road daily in a truck (at his own expense) for one year, at all seasons. He should have had a taste of the job for which he was responsible: he should have been made to wind within inches of gorges and lakes, to twist through devilish curves, and over deep holes and big bumps.

We reached the ghost town of Dease at the end of Dease Lake at midnight and drove down to the lakeshore. It was eerie—facing the dark, boarded-up houses. We heard the waves lapping gently on the shores and against a broken boat. The moon's reflection danced in the water. The wind whispered in the willows on the shores and sang in the crowns of the aspen in the forest beyond. The clouds raced past the moon. Then the sound of someone clearing his throat was heard in the distance. We held our breath. Gravel was gritting somewhere up the road in the darkness. Then a figure emerged into the moonlight from the shadow of the houses and moved toward us. Some "live ghosts" were obviously present in Dease.

The "ghost" turned out to be a surveyor who was waiting for a helicopter. He was glad to see us and helped us to unload the truck. He then led us to a deserted house, where Renate and I stayed for the next few days, while Ken left for Cassiar after sharing a cup of coffee with us.

Again we learned to be patient. We visited the small weather station close to Dease and met two delightful families who lived there and looked after the station. It struck us then, as it has many times before and since, that people in such outposts are often ambitious and hard-working, pursuing feasible goals. It is not akin to the prospector's struggle for riches, which Lady Luck may but usually does not reveal. It is not an irrational craze that drives men from their homes and breaks them slowly on the unforgiving mountains but a thoughtful striving toward personal enhancement, in pursuit of education, knowledge, and improved work skills. We encountered two prospectors about to depart for the summer, one of whom had just killed a moose. When I suggested that the hunting season was still months in the future, he insisted that as a prospector he could kill game when needed. We met a helicopter pilot. We chanced upon a forester and went with him to visit Laketon, a ghost town once populated by gold miners in the late eighteen hundreds. In those days Dease was small, but prosperous, since Dease Lake was part of the water route over which freight went past Laketon (located on the west shore of Dease Lake) which then had stores and a post office which also served as a jail. The latter is particularly well preserved and must have had its share of excitement, for two murderers were hanged there and their bodies buried at the crossroad to serve as a warning to all.

Much of that crossroad is not recognizable today, so over-grown has it become with aspen, birch, and spruce. Grave-stones are tipped by tree roots; the log cabins are largely col-lapsed and covered over by moss; the gold-digging works have rusted away; skulls and antlers of moose and caribou litter the ground. Once, four thousand people lived there, and the town was considered prosperous.

While Renate explored the remnants of the town and found some old newspapers, a baby bottle, and an old axe, I took the .22 and shot a couple of snowshoe rabbits and collected a few morels (a type of mushroom) for supper. It was a good rabbit year, an event that repeats itself every six to eight years in that land. We also went fishing during the few days we stayed at Dease. I caught a nice lake trout, and Renate hooked into something that we still wonder about. It only gave a couple of tugs and broke Renate's rod and line and that was that.

On the morning of the seventeenth, Herman Peterson ar-rived in his yellow Beaver. It was our first meeting with this leg-endary bush pilot of northern British Columbia. No one would suspect his fame by looking at this modest man with the blond, curly hair falling over his forehead. I flew with him a number of times and am grateful for his help and advice, with-out which I could not have reached destinations that, by the laws of chance, I should not have reached. Of that, more later.

Herman and a second pilot, Bob Grant, transferred our equipment and stores to Cold Fish Lake in their two Beavers, and showed us first a bird's-eye view of the land which we were soon to call home. We stayed in Tommy Walker's main camp at Cold Fish Lake. He took us on the following day out to the small lake and the surrounding mountains where soon our cabin was to be built and where I was to do my work. A grizzly followed our tracks that morning but spooked when he saw us. Caribou females had gathered with their small young on top of Goat Mountain; we saw a gathering of Stone's rams on Sanctu-ary Mountain and among them the rams which I grew to know as individuals and whose memory is burnt into my mind. We had finally arrived, although it was not an end but just the

Band of large rams on the range in springtime

beginning. We had left Vancouver on June 1, shortly after our marriage, and that first month of our married life was everything but dull. Before we reached Watson Lake we had a few exciting moments—for instance, when we camped at Six Mile Lake at Prince George. During the first night a Mountie shone a flashlight into our faces and wanted to know if we had seen a "wild party." We hadn't, and cussed him for the disturbance—after he left. The wild party came the following day. The graduation classes of '61 were having a jolly time with beer and liquor around a roaring bonfire. Unfortunately, their mood turned sour. They discovered our little tent, and silence fell. Then a murmur arose. We heard a voice bawling, "Let's beat them up . . . crack their heads with a beer bottle." A number of bottles arched over our tent. Then another voice shouted, "Leave them alone." Again the mob's murmuring arose. In the meantime, Renate and I had readied ourselves. She was gripping an axe and I a rifle. The minutes ticked away, while the mob swayed in indecision. Suddenly a Royal Canadian Mounted Police car appeared, and a mad rush of kids sought escape in the bushes. A struggle erupted at the bonfire. Meanwhile, an officer came running toward our tent, and we met him part way. How grateful we were to see the very man we had cussed the night before. The party was broken up, arrests were made, and, as the sky grew light in the east, peace returned again to little Six Mile Lake.

The trip was hard on Renate, however; had we known what still lay ahead, nothing would have gotten us into the Spatzisi. At times, it seemed as though nature herself had turned on us, but that was yet to come.

3

Our Wilderness Home

We needed a cabin. We were to stay here in winter throughout the study period and had to prepare accordingly. The site for our cabin was chosen with care, taking certain factors into account.

During the previous winter, while making a flight past the jagged massive that we came to know as Sanctuary Mountain, we had spotted six Stone's rams. Because an occasional ram had been seen here in previous falls, it was felt that a small group of rams might remain all winter. Since this was the best and only knowledge available, we built the cabin opposite the mountain. It was a gamble, and we knew it. We had to wait till winter to find out if the gamble had paid off or not, and a certain tenseness brought on by this uncertainty never left us that summer. We could not hasten time, so we proceeded with cabin building, cutting winter wood, and exploring the land.

The cabin was erected beside a nameless little lake where a grove of tall white spruce furnished the necessary logs. We also needed drinking water and that was supplied by Connors Creek—a stream that rushed past about fifty yards from the cabin. It was imperative that we have access to the lake, for here small floatplanes could land—our most important link with the outside world. The cabin was raised on an elevated

52

spot, just in case Connors Creek should flood, or the little lake should rise. Tommy Walker dubbed the unnamed body of water "Gladys Lake," and so it is called to this day.

We pitched tents and unloaded our stores at the site of the cabin-to-be on June 20, 1961. There were two tents, one for sleeping and one for cooking, since Renate had to look after not only ourselves but our crew of helpers as well. In total, there were seven of us, plus three horses. Rusty, who acted as foreman for one of Walker's outfits, brought in a crew to frame the cabin in rough; I was to finish and furnish it thereafter. That is how we met Alec (the old chief among the Tahltans) and Charlie Abu, one of my Indian friends from Hyland Post, our nearest neighbors, who lived about forty miles from us in winter. Robert, a big-game guide who served as a cook for hunters, had come from Telegraph Creek. Cliff and Pat were big-game guides who had worked several years for Walker. These helpers were all seasoned bushmen and knew how to construct cabins, a claim I could not make.

We cleared and leveled the land and procured large rocks to serve as cornerstones on which the logs of the cabin were to rest. This kept the bottom logs off the ground and extended their useful life. We cut spruce trees, skidded them to the building site, peeled them, rough-hewed them, and, with our combined strength, placed them round by round into position. It was sweaty work, made by no means more pleasant by the resinous surface of the logs. While the men toiled with axes and saws, Renate cooked meals and made tea for us. Her small tent was terribly stifling in the heat of the sunny days. She probably perspired more than did we.

The men kidded each other as the work progressed, or told tales during the short tea breaks or at lunch around the camp-fire. At day's end, the boys would saddle their horses and ride off to their camp, situated about a mile along the lake, returning for work again at about 7:00 A.M. each morning.

The cabin was not very big. Its inside measurements were 12 x 14 feet. At this elevation, the spruce grew thick butts, but provided hardly more than an 18-foot log due to the rapid taper of their stems. By July 2 we had installed the last round of logs and made preparations to put up the somewhat unusual roof.

On this day Renate fell ill, and her condition quickly deteriorated, to everyone's distress. When she failed to improve on the following day, there was nothing we could do but get her out to civilization. Since she was weak to the point of helplessness, we built a stretcher from aspen poles and carried her to Cold Fish Lake, where she was placed in a boat and ferried to Tommy Walker's main camp. Mrs. Walker took care of Renate until a plane arrived to fly her to Prince George on the following day. After spending a week in hospital, Renate took a job in Prince George as a receptionist while she waited several weeks for an opportunity to return.

After Renate was settled comfortably in the boat, and on her way to Walker's camp, we returned to Gladys Lake and cabin building. It was lonely now, and the work provided welcome diversion. The cabin was designed with a somewhat unusual roof construction. We put up a framework of logs, but, instead of covering it with boards, we used a skin of aluminum. Two big rolls of the material were flown in as part of our supplies, and when the shiny roof was completed there was still ample aluminum sheeting left over to furnish the cabin's inside. Just prior to their departure, the boys cut boards from a standing dead spruce for the furnishings and the door, and whipsawed a number of logs that were to serve as the floor. Then they rode off.

There was a lot of work still to do. First, I laid the floor, split log by split log. After that I constructed a ceiling from peeled, green spruce and pine poles, leaving space between the ceiling and the roof large enough to cache all our equipment. I covered the resulting "platform" with a layer of cardboard, salvaged from all the cartons in which our food and supplies had traveled. After nailing a layer of tar paper over the cardboard, I then stored the equipment. The cache was reached through a hole in the ceiling, located above where the bed came to stand.

Next, the windows had to be installed and secured in the log walls. Rusty had cut the openings on the last day of the crew's stay. The windows had been prefabricated in Vancouver and had traveled up the Alaska Highway with our other goods.

For several days I searched the land around the cabin for straight, thin poles, to nail on the inside of the cabin between the logs. Their function was to form a backstop for the moss that later was hammered into the clefts between the logs, from the outside.

A remaining piece of aluminum was used to cover the section of floor where the stove and heater were to stand later. I also covered the walls of that corner, hoping that the shiny surface would reflect the heat toward the cabin's interior. This aluminum application, again an unusual feature for a cabin, was insurance against a few hot coals falling from the stove door, perhaps dropping through the cracks in the floor and setting fire to the shavings below the cabin.

Next came the furniture which I built from green spruce poles and the shrinking boards cut from the dead, but not-dry, spruce, a fact that became increasingly evident as time progressed. The furniture turned out to be crude but solid and comfortable. Nails were avoided as much as possible in the construction; the emphasis was placed on interlocking units that were inserted into holes cut into the poles with an auger.

I built two tables, one of which I placed at a window from where I could enjoy a view of Ghost Mountain. The second table was built into the left-hand, distant corner of the cabin and served to hold my writing material, the radio, and camera equipment. Above it were fixed two bookshelves on which I kept my reading material, well aware of its value during the long winter nights to come. Then I made an armchair on which I placed two cloth-covered, foam-rubber cushions, one as the seat, and the other as a backrest. After the green wood shrank, the armchair creaked and shifted when I turned in it, but it held. Below the second big window, a shelf rack held our clothing in boxes. A red-checkered blanket concealed the rack and its contents from sight. Two grocery shelves filled the space above that window, while my rifles were racked over the other. The bed was built high enough to allow storage of tins and

The cabin in the Spatzisi

boxes beneath it. The final piece to be constructed was a stool with a foam-rubber seat cushion. In the right-hand corner of the cabin, just beside the door, a frame stand was made to hold the washbasin and shelves for first-aid kits and toilet articles. The water pail was placed on a block below the washbasin. The camp stove went into the opposite corner, and the airtight heater stood beside it, close to the door. The camp stove was elevated on four blocks of wood and stood at a height requiring little bending over when cooking. Furnishing the cabin kept me busy with axe and auger, saw, knife, and plane for several weeks, usually working with a net over my head to discourage eager mosquitoes.

Then came the great day when Renate finally returned. On the morning of July 29, Bill Smith flew her in, roaring down the narrow valley in his Cessna 180. The cabin was not quite furnished, the cracks in the log walls were not filled with moss, nor was the winter wood cut. Renate quickly saw what the cabin lacked: those little touches here and there that make a cabin not just a shelter to live in but a place to remember and yearn for. One day she dressed the windows in red-and-white polka-dot curtains and screened the grocery shelves with curtains of similar material. From somewhere she uncovered a little green earthenware vase, filled it with late summer flowers, and displayed it on the shelf rack in front of the window. Under her hands, the little cabin adopted a cheerful, tidy appearance with much room, surprisingly, despite the furnishings. With time, the poles on the ceiling turned greenish with a peculiar mold and retained that color from then on. After chinking the walls with moss, I banked the cabin with earth and dug a shallow ditch around it to keep the bottom logs dry. Then it was completed. Our castle was built.

It was lush summer: the fields of dwarf birch on the mountains and the stands of tall willows on the alluvial flats along the lake were covered in rich green, shiny leaves. While the first rounds of the cabin were being laid, there had been a few half-hearted snowstorms and night frosts. Then came the long days when even at nighttime the light outdoors was sufficient to read by. Mosquitoes were plentiful, alas, but one can become used to them. Within a week of Renate's return, the first frosts hit the valley, and the aspen, birch, and alpine flora began their slow change from green to yellow, gold, red, and purple. Alpine barberry and dwarf birch painted the mountains red. The first snowstorms dusted the mountaintops with white. One could stand outdoors and smell the fall coming. It is a scent that sends shivers down the spine and awakens a primaeval fever to hunt and provide. One morning you step outside, and there is that scent, and you know that fall has arrived.

Before Renate's illness, we had taken several long hikes through the mountains and, on her return, we again began exploring the land about us to provide a welcome break from cabin building and wood cutting. In the evenings we sat in front of the cabin, listening to the mountain sounds, the creeks, and the forest, and watching snowshoe rabbits emerge from the underbrush to nibble on the horse droppings left from the early cabin-building days. A pack rat paid us a visit one night and almost scared us witless with its loud rattling. With regret I removed the pretty but smelly guest. When the little poltergeist first startled us, I thought a grizzly had ripped into the cabin.

I took a male mountain goat, whose skin and skull were later to find their way to the Moscow museum, while the Russians returned the courtesy with a pair of saiga antelope.

On August 19, 1961, we were finally ready to begin our studies.

4

Our Initiation to the Spatzisi

The great day had arrived. With pack-boards on our backs we hiked along the old moose trail that follows Connors Creek, on toward Bates Camp. Here, we had been informed, a band of rams could be seen regularly, and we looked forward to observing them. About a week before this date—August 19— the autumn colors had begun to appear. It was as beautiful a day in Indian summer as I had ever seen, so full of extravagant colors, so crisp and fresh, a day that made one wish to live forever. We stopped to look at tracks of caribou, moose, grizzly bear, and wolf on the trail. Flocks of willow ptarmigan burst from the lush meadows in the subalpine. The cocks warned of our approach from gray boulders or peat hummocks in the heath. On the ridges grazed caribou bulls with big velvet-covered racks. Their body contours were soft, filled out by a load of fat accumulated during a summer's idleness and abundant forage. The white manes were beginning to sprout on their necks, a certain sign that rutting time and unrest were a mere few weeks away.

We crossed the high plateau that separated Connors Creek from Bates Camp and soon saw the long grassy slopes stretched out in front of us. The slopes invited, nay urged, one to pick up one's glasses and look for sheep. And there they were. There was a group of rams with dark gray coats, white rump

Three rams in a social interaction, all displaying their horns. The ram in the center performs a "present," the one at left a "low-stretch," and the one at right a "twist." These are all dominance displays and are different signals with the same meaning.

patches, and amber horns. It was the first group of Stone's sheep we had seen since June 19, when we saw the rams on Sanctuary Mountain. In short order we picked out six more rams scattered on the slopes. For the first time in months my nagging doubts began to ease. Perhaps we had not gambled in vain.

When dawn crept over the mountains the following morning, we were out glassing the slopes again. We had pitched camp in a small clearing of alpine fir, beside a gurgling, lively brook that came from a rock glacier behind camp. Broad, lush, wet meadows surrounded us, alive with ptarmigan broods. The previous evening I had taken two young ptarmigan with my .22 for dinner. Renate was less than happy with the bed of alpine fir boughs I had made, and she let me know of this while the campfire heated water for coffee and mush.

In the gray light we soon began to discern the dark shapes of the rams on the opposite mountain slopes. They were widely dispersed, feeding low on the grassy slopes. I opened the notebook and began keeping track of how many were feeding, standing, moving, or resting, at five-minute intervals. These data, routinely taken, record the activity pattern of the animals during each observation day and allow one to state with some precision how predictable such activity is, and how it is affected by weather or by social events. The rams did nothing exciting. They slowly fed their way uphill and reached the cliffs by late morning. Here a few, as yet mysterious, social encounters took place, with the rams stretching their heads forward when passing each other or twisting them in a peculiar fashion. Soon they bedded down for a few hours. In the afternoon, they again began to feed, but toward evening they started to race and frolic through the cliffs, bounding exuberantly, zigzagging, and running after each other, or freezing suddenly and standing statuelike. There were a few clashes, then the rams came together into a tight knot resembling a group of football players in a huddle, their heads facing into the circle and their white rumps pointing out. It was all very puzzling. Something was going on in the group of rams out there, but what, and why? Eventually some rams lay down, and others started to graze. Then darkness fell.

The next two days revealed the same basic pattern of activity for the rams. I noted that the peculiar actions rams performed in front of each other were recognizable, and I began keeping track of these postures. There might be some rule which these actions follow, but this only the future could tell—provided we had sufficient opportunity to observe these sheep.

Once a black wolf appeared below the rams and trotted across the slope. The rams grouped around the largest-horned ram and followed him without haste to the base of the cliffs where they resumed watching the wolf. Then two young rams left the group and followed the wolf, keeping well above him. Soon sheep and wolf rounded the ridge and slipped out of sight.

Thus far, we had seen no female sheep anywhere, and we began to search for them in the surrounding region. These forays revealed that wildlife, although present here, was widely

A huddle in an April snowstorm. The rams have grouped together for a session of nuzzling, horning, and playful clashing.

dispersed and very scarce in much of the area. Although we failed to find female Stone's sheep on these trips, we did see, from camp one evening, a group of forty females and lambs on a distant mountain. They appeared and vanished within minutes.

Seven days after we arrived at Bates Camp we had to leave. A hunting party was to arrive to shoot rams, and our presence was pointless and unwelcome. However, we left our tent standing since we hoped to return after the hunting party had left. As we were departing on August 26, a storm descended, and the first blanket of snow quickly covered the ground. The temperature was mild, and soon every branch was dripping. By the time we had waded the first half-mile of dwarf birch thickets we were soaked and remained that way till we reached our cabin. We were not to have respite from this weather for some time to come.

Five narrow valleys radiate from Gladys Lake. Four bring in water from distant cirques or small glaciers, while one guides the waters from Gladys Lake down toward the Spatzisi. In the two weeks following our return from Bates Camp, we explored these valleys and climbed the mountains surrounding them, searching for sheep or signs thereof. The weather remained dreary. Snow chased rain, and rain chased snow; the snow line on the mountains descended, the shrubs were soaked, the moss was soaked, the creeks ran high, and fog often covered the mountains and hugged the valleys. The days had grown noticeably shorter. The trips brought little cheer, for I saw sheep only once in those two weeks. On one occasion, I had crossed a ridge in the fog when two small rams appeared ghostlike in front of me. After noting my presence, they turned and moved downhill without much haste. We saw a few caribou and the odd moose, but discouragingly few. Renate had a little better luck. On a few days a small band of mountain goats remained in sight of the cabin, and Renate observed them. The trips did not uncover much sign of sheep. We found abundant clam and trilobite fossils, picked mushrooms, took a few blue grouse, ruffed grouse, ptarmigan, and rabbits, and wondered if and when the opportunity would again present itself to study mountain sheep.

On one day I shot a mountain goat male which we canned as meat supply for the following summer. For a whole day we toiled, cutting meat, searing it, preparing barbecue sauce, filling cans, and finally cooking it. One day Renate discovered a large patch of black currants on an alluvial flat close to Connors Creek. She made a jelly from them that far surpassed any commercial product. Fishing in Gladys Lake and the surrounding creeks proved completely futile, despite the presence of a pair of American mergansers on Connors Creek which suggested the presence of fish. Then one day we noted swarms of slender fish, each fish up to a foot long, migrating into Gladys Lake. These were whitefish, as I discovered much later.

Since the days around Gladys Lake proved rather unproductive in observations, we decided to leave for the Spatzisi Plateau in the hope of observing rutting caribou. A return to Bates was not yet possible. On September 17 we set out on the fifteen-mile hike.

Rams following the largest-horned member of their group, in this case a 20-year-old ancient ram

During our first day on the plateau we saw almost forty caribou, including a small herd of bulls, whose antlers created the impression of a moving forest. They were big creatures, these dark, Roman-nosed Osborn's caribou, the giants among caribou. How big they were I realized only after standing beside a big bull I had shot. The rut had not yet begun, although the bulls and many cows had scrubbed their antlers free of velvet. The bull was fat, and we stripped the fat off his back to render it down for cooking and baking. It was fortunate that we got him so early in the season, for he was not only in excellent condition, he did not smell as caribou bulls eventually do during the rut. This animal was not much smaller than an elk; one haunch, cut off at the hip and including the skin but without the metatarsus and hooves, weighed sixty pounds. This indicates that the bull must have been close to five hundred pounds live weight, yet he was far from the largest we saw.

I carried the haunch and skull with antlers back to the cabin, while Renate toted the fat. By the time I returned to the site on the following day, a pack of wolves had found the carcass, and all I could recover was part of a front shoulder. Imprints in the little snow that had fallen showed clearly that a small pack had come, eaten, and moved on again.

For a few days we hiked over the plateau, watching caribou as the weather permitted. Then it came time to leave, for soon no hunting party should be present at Bates, and I could again gather data. Three months had passed, and all I had had were four days of continuous observations on Stone's rams. We assembled our pack-boards, loaded meat and antlers on top, and returned to our cabin. On our hike, we had to cross a shallow river where it emerged from a little lake. Here we saw a large bull moose, a cow, and a calf in the water. It was the first time that Renate had seen a large bull and heard his peculiar, low rutting call; it sounded a little silly coming from so large an animal as these big mountain moose of northern British Columbia.

We had to wait a few days at the cabin, for Tommy Walker was to pay us a final visit for the year. He came with Bill Smith of Northern Mountain Airlines. Tommy left us a camp stove and a radio with which we could remain in contact with Bill and Marge Smith in Prince George, or with Merv Hess and his wife in Fort St. James. If an emergency threatened, they could be relied upon to fly in and help us out. No one anticipated how soon we were to make use of that service.

We talked and joked, and relished our mail along with the latest news. Tommy brought us a large package and made us promise not to open it till Christmas, a promise that was kept. I had almost missed seeing Tommy and Bill, for that morning I had hunted for moose close to the cabin and found a big bull with a cow. Five careful shots seemed of no avail, and, dumbfounded, I had tracked the bull without even detecting a drop of blood or any other sign of having hit him. Later I found a couple of loose screws on the scope mount and also noted that the stock had warped away from the rifle barrel after being soaked for weeks. These faults were soon taken care of.

When Bill and Tommy left us, Renate and I decided to separate. I was to go to Bates Camp, and Renate was to remain at

Band of female bighorns and young in the rocky terrain at high elevation

the cabin. There were goats now about Gladys Lake, and Renate could work there. On but one day did a ram appear briefly on Sanctuary Mountain, and then it vanished again, so there was little left but to hike to Bates.

It was winter now. Snow covered the ground, and Indian summer was but a pleasant memory. How ironical fate had been. There had been no hunting party at Bates. The group had canceled out at the very last moment, and we could have stayed in our camp all of September and thus have been well along in understanding the Stone's rams. Instead, the animals were still a mystery. When I arrived at Bates Camp that evening I spotted the rams. They stood widely dispersed in several groups over the mountain slope.

It was difficult to get a fire started. The wood in the tent was damp, and it took me some time to find a dry fir pole in the snow-covered, wet thickets nearby. I put the camp stove Tommy had left with us in the tent and got a fire going to dry the damp tent and wood. I cleared the snow from the tent roof to prevent it from collapsing. The snow began to fall again as darkness closed in. It was the thirtieth day of September.

There were more rams at Bates now than there had been in August. I recognized several of them as being the same individuals we had seen earlier, but there were also some strangers. One was a four-year-old ram whose right foreleg was missing; only a stump of his upper leg remained. He hobbled about but was spunky and clashed with other young rams that day. Another stranger was a ram with an incredible set of horns. I named him Curly. His horns did not appear thick, but they made up in length what they lacked in mass. They swept down and back in a graceful arc, forming one-and-a-half windings.

I sat all day behind the spotting scope, observing and recording the actions of the rams. The rams had fattened visibly, probably both because their hair had lengthened and because fat deposits had expanded their contours. They had darkened in color, because the hair was more fully grown. Most individuals looked almost black. Their social actions made as little sense as they had six weeks earlier, but I recorded each action after having classified it, in the hope that an analysis of which ram did what would help me solve the puzzles.

The following day a group of five rams and a group of four mountain goats moved away from the mountain and cliffs and headed to a gravel outwash where they fed on frozen herbaceous vegetation and seed heads. Although the day was cloudy and punctuated by small snowstorms which occasionally obscured vision, my eyes barely strayed from the rams and goats when they were visible. It turned dusky, signaling that evening was not far off. Suddenly, from behind, I heard a voice calling my name. It was Renate. She was wet, tired, and dejected, and had not slept for two nights, since heavy scratching at the cabin door had robbed her peace. She was uncertain of her skills with the rifle, and the noises were strange to her. During the day, clouds obscured the mountains, and she had not been able to gather data on goats, so she shouldered her pack-board and came to Bates to join me. The next morning she was too ill to rise and remained stretched out in her sleeping bag. I continued to observe the rams but returned periodically to keep the tent stove going and cook meals. Renate's condition improved slowly toward evening, and she got up, pale and weak, but eager to handle camp chores and then observe mountain goats.

We decided to take no chances but return to the cabin the next day if Renate's condition would allow it. On the following morning, she felt well enough to go. At dawn I went back to the observation point for an hour or so. Barely had I settled when a black wolf appeared in the valley. All the rams were up in the cliffs. A quick search with the field glasses showed a black speck I had not seen earlier, and a check with the spotting scope showed it to be a dead ram. The wolf had killed it. I ran to the tent to fetch Renate, but the wolf had gone before I had a chance to show her. We walked to the wolf kill: it was a five-year-old ram, apparently in good physical condition. I recognized him as one of the five that spent all day yesterday in the valley. We autopsied him and noted his injuries and physical condition, and I packed the ram's head onto the packboard, for it would be a good specimen for the osteological museum of the university. We took our sleeping bags, then, and left the tent as it was, for we hoped to return soon, once Renate was well again.

A few miles down the valley we saw the black wolf again. It had spooked a small band of caribou which fled toward a second band on top of a ridge. A couple of instants later two big bulls engaged in a fight. The larger pushed the smaller one with mighty leaps straight downhill. Both went over a ten-foot cliff but landed well, and the fight continued all the way down. Here, the loser disentangled himself and fled.

We reached the cabin in the evening. The next day, Renate took a turn for the worse. When sickness strikes at home it is no pleasure. It is even less so when one is helpless in a corner distant from civilization. Renate's condition worsened each day, until it became evident that a call for help must be placed to Prince George, for she needed aid I could not give her. On October 14, Merv Hess flew a Beaver in, and Renate left the Spatzisi. For a long time, I stood beside the little lake—long after the aircraft's roar had vanished. Renate and I were not to see each other until ten months later. Within twenty-four hours, the lake was frozen over, and it would have been impossible to land the aircraft and take her south to safety.

The day after Renate left it snowed heavily, and I delayed my return to Bates. It snowed the following day no less. Again I delayed. Visibility was next to nil in the blowing snow. The storm continued during the following day. Finally my patience became exhausted. I loaded the pack-board and left for my distant camp.

The snow lay deep. The willows and dwarf birch were bent low by its weight and blocked the trail. I had to unlimber my hatchet and chop my way through the heavy bushes that grew close to running water. Half an hour after leaving the cabin my clothes were drenched from the arms down, and water gurgled in my boots. Thin ice, covered by snow, concealed deep puddles and slippery mud on the trail—neither a boon to sure footing. The snowstorm kept up, and the flakes whirled around me. Once, a short lull set in, and glancing back I saw my path winding like a dark snake through the snow-covered dwarf-birch flat down to timberline. I had cleared a lot of snow from the bushes.

Connors Creek was swollen. This time I did not bother to remove my boots, socks, and pants, but waded through in my clothes. They were wet, anyway, and getting wet with creek water instead of meltwater would make precious little difference. It was difficult to navigate in the storm, but when I felt the land begin to rise sharply I knew that I was not yet halfway to camp. The snow became deeper as I entered the alpine region. Bog and peat hummocks now lay below the snow, and each step became more difficult. The feet had to be lifted high to clear the snow. Then cramps set in, and I was forced to rest.

At this point it dawned on me that I had acted foolishly. I was wet and very tired. The snow was quite deep now, and my progress had been very slow. The snowshoes on my pack-board were useless in the soft, damp snow. Even if I reached camp, I could not likely get a fire going in the camp stove, for, by this time, the dry kindling in my tent would have absorbed plenty of water. Dry kindling would be very difficult to find as I had removed much from my camp's vicinity, and I wondered whether I would have strength left to search for it. Moreover, it was almost certain that the tent had collapsed by now under a load of more than two feet of snow. Should the storm continue, it would be unlikely that I could ever plow my way back. So I wearily arose and turned back to the cabin, determined to go out again once the storm had passed.

In the flying snow a shadow appeared and drifted across my path. It was a rutting bull moose. He took no notice of me but moved on and hid behind a small fir to watch me go by. A caribou cow appeared from a clump of alpine fir and disappeared again into another. My feet splashed in a puddle, and the hard branches of dwarf birch swished against my parka, scraping the cloth thinner with each scratch. One day, this parka would disintegrate, and the wool pants would become shredded beyond repair.

I was about to descend into the timber when I noticed that it had stopped snowing, and one could look below the cloud blanket across the valley. My eyes wandered to Ghost Mountain, habitually searching the slopes and cliffs for any sign of life. Then I noticed something. Sheep! A ewe and a lamb. They moved in deep snow at the edge of an aspen bluff and disappeared. Again a snow squall set in. Maybe there were more sheep there? Had we not seen half-a-dozen sheep once before on Ghost Mountain when Tommy and Bill Smith had come to say goodbye to us? A flicker of hope arose. How I loathed the land at this moment with its clouds and rainstorms, its endless dwarf-birch flats, its endless wetness, and its bitter disappointments. However, after I had reached the cabin a good supper of roast moose and hot tea, and a change to dry clothes turned me into an optimist once more, and I wondered whether the sheep would be on Ghost Mountain next morning.

I was out at sunrise. A beautiful day broke. The sky was blue, the sun shone on a brilliant winter landscape, and there on Ghost Mountain stood twenty-seven Stone's sheep! I was not dreaming. In addition, there were eight mountain goats. In front of the cabin, I sat on a block of pine behind the spotting scope, observing and recording. These sheep were all ewes, lambs, and subadults, the first I was able to observe after four months in these mountains. I dared not move for fear the dream would vanish, but the sheep stayed—they stayed the whole day. Maybe everything would be all right still? Maybe there would be sufficient opportunity for observations right in this valley? Maybe the sheep would stay on Ghost Mountain?

I was out early the next morning. The sheep were gone. The sky was still clear and blue. The sun rose from behind the jagged peaks and lit a beautiful winter landscape, but the sheep were gone. I saw their tracks on the slopes. Feverishly I searched the cuts, the cliffs, the aspen bluffs. Not a sign of life. Suddenly a movement caught my eye, low on the mountain, in the place where a small group of ewes and lambs had been gathered the night before. This was no sheep, however; it was a wolf. A big wolf. A yellow wolf. My insides began to boil. Now I knew why the sheep were gone! Angry, depressed, and yet curious, I reached for the spotting scope and focused on the wolf.

He lay in the snow, his paws stretched forward, his ears cocked, and his big tail waved slowly back and forth. He was looking at something just in front of him. Suddenly, he lunged forward and threw a small dark object into the air. He caught it again and then dropped it on the snow and allowed it to roll downhill. He pounced after it and tapped the object with a paw, sending it on a diagonal course below a small bush. Then the wolf sat down, stretched and yawned, stood undecided, and finally trotted over to the creek where he inspected some tracks and beds left by sheep. Then he trotted downhill and pulled at something in the dwarf birch. He turned a little, and I could see a black object beyond, and then something red ahead of the wolf's muzzle. No doubt about it, it was a sheep killed by the wolf.

No other thought was in my mind but to get that wolf so that the sheep would not be chased away again. I walked into the cabin and took my old rifle from the hook, screwed on the scope sight, and pushed five rounds deliberately into the magazine. Hurry would be to no avail. It was an hour's hike to that wolf, and I had to make sure where he rested after his feed. The wolf was still busy with the sheep; then he jogged away into a small aspen bluff. There he lifted his leg alongside a tree, obviously a male. He trotted on until he was in the open again, among some boulders. Suddenly, a second wolf, a small black one, stood beside him. Both wagged their tails; a game developed. They romped like puppies in the powdery snow, jumping at and around one another. Then the big yellow wolf lay down beside a boulder so that I could see only his ears and back. The black wolf moved a little way off and finally disappeared from sight in a depression.

My time had come now. I went for them. In my haste I had forgotten to shed some clothing, and soon I was wet with sweat and half blind because my glasses fogged constantly. Every fifty yards I was forced to halt and wipe my glasses. It was a long time before I ascended the slope and reached the wolf kill.

The tracks told a plain story. The wolf had surprised the sheep from above and chased it into the dwarf-birch thicket. A bare fifty yards where the sheep and wolf tracks joined on a common course, beside a small alpine fir, the sheep had been caught. I only glanced at the old ewe and moved on. I estimated the wolves must have been about two hundred yards further on. A quick check of the rifle showed that its muzzle and scope were free of snow. I advanced, slowly, very slowly, and still my glasses fogged, and sweat rolled down my face. "Now," I thought, "I should be in sight of my prey." The slope was empty. I could see no signs of them. Further up the slope I moved—still nothing to be seen. I turned and scanned the slope below. Had the wolves left? Again I turned, and there they were—both about eighty yards distant—padding up the slope. My first shot was hasty and missed its mark. Both wolves broke into full run. The cross-hair swung ahead of the big yellow wolf, and a split second later he rolled in the snow. Up he came again and rushed downhill toward me. I could see a red patch on his ribs. Another round clicked into place, and I bided my time with this shot. Just as I raised the rifle, the wolf suddenly collapsed and slid into the snow—dead. The second wolf was a long way off by this time but still in range. I dropped on one knee. The wolf stopped. The cross hair swung over, and, as the shot broke, I thought it was too low. Still, the wolf jumped up, turned a somersault, and then dashed from sight into a depression. I heard a short howl; then all was silent.

I remember walking slowly to the dead yellow wolf and staring down on him. I felt no satisfaction, no joy, and was surprised at this. It had been different, very different, on all other occasions. My thoughts drifted to that bright autumn day in northern Saskatchewan when I shot my first big game, a bull moose; I had skipped high school to go hunting. After a week of crawling through wet forests and camping in the rain, a clear day had come. It was in the morning, at sunrise, when I saw the bull fifteen paces away in the tall timber walking slowly toward me. A few seconds later I fired, and soon, still incredulous and shaking with excitement, I stood beside his big body. To me, he was the king of the forest, the animal of song and ancient saga of the German tradition in which I was raised. When the time came to dress him out, I cut his belly open but could not move the huge gut. So I dropped everything and ran for help to a farmer I had befriended. I experienced the same thrill when I picked up my first white-tail buck by its antlers a few weeks later; and when I stood beside my first mountain goat. It was, after all, hunting that made me a zoologist, that had first dragged me into the woods and made me stalk and observe wildlife. Yet, while I paused beside this large wolf that lay at my feet so very dead, I felt different for the first time. Had I not come here to study the normal life of sheep—a life which included live wolves, and sheep kills? It was a rhetorical question. Then, remembering the black wolf, I slowly ascended the slope.

There was the wolf track, and there was the blood and plenty of it. I thought, "The wolf must be dead in the depression beyond." But it wasn't. Nor was it in the second, or in the deep cut beyond. The tracks went on, and I followed. The trail led me from one cut to the next, and still there was blood in the tracks. The prints disappeared into a patch of alpine fir but emerged on the other side, as I found upon circling the patch.

The wolf had already run half a mile, when its tracks moved

into the cliffs. It was easy to follow them visually. They led into a little cut, and from there I surmised they probably went over the top of the ridge. I could see everything plainly in this cut, and the tracks terminated at its end against a rock about three feet in height. "The wolf must have jumped on top of that rock to leave the cut," I conjectured. "I shall find its tracks beyond." I noted that a small detour would allow me to stay on the level instead of crossing the cut, and so I went in along a narrow band of cliffs toward the spot where I had last seen the tracks. Curiously, there were no tracks on top of the rock where I expected them to be. Where had the wolf gone? At this point I noticed three tiny, scrawny, alpine firs growing on the ledge, standing about ten feet in front of me. Could the wolf be in there? There was hardly any cover. Nevertheless, I raised the rifle and advanced. With the rifle barrel I pushed the first fir aside slightly. There was black fur. It rose and sank slowly. The wolf lay flat under the branches. Without aiming, I fired. It was the end of the wolf.

I skinned both wolves. It was difficult lifting the big yellow male, but I did get him up on a tree. The black wolf, a female, had caught my first shot in the brisket, and the bullet had disintegrated, spraying lead upwards. The sheep they killed was an old ewe which had already lost her front teeth and was at least thirteen years old, an animal way past its prime. I recorded all that was to be taken note of, loaded the wolf skins onto my pack-board, and returned to the cabin, depressed and very tired. My thoughts roamed over the recent past. Would the future be as painful? More than four months had gone by, and on only nine days had I been able to accomplish what I had hoped to do almost every day. And although my intent had been to protect my study animals, the sheep, killing the two wolves would probably deprive me of future observations of some importance. Indeed, to my knowledge, no wolves visited Ghost Mountain that winter, although one big yellow one did roam the other side of the valley. When, to my delight, wolves appeared again at Gladys Lake the following fall, they went unmolested. Yet that twentieth day of October, in 1961, was a turning point, and it was a turn for the better.

This has been the history of the first four months in the Spatzisi. I went intending to stay for twelve months and stayed twenty. I went in the hope of finding many sheep but found few. I went in search of sunshine and an open land and found rain, fog, and thickets instead. Renate and I had planned to stay together and found ourselves apart for a long time. And yet it was not all bad. The cabin was built—by accident—in the only worthwhile locality for watching sheep within two days' hiking distance in any direction. It turned out that the cabin was surrounded by four small wintering areas of sheep and mountain goats. I was able to observe directly from the cabin, often from dawn to dusk, and thus had no need of camps and lost no time in useless travel. The few sheep available, at first a cause of despair, offered unprecedented advantages. I came to know almost fifty of them as individuals, an impossibility had there been twice their number, or had they been Dall's sheep or bighorns. Since Stone's sheep are very uniquely marked, I had little difficulty keeping track of the various individuals and getting to know their lives and fate. Individuals they were—unforgettable individuals.

5
Life and Death in the Wilderness

✒ The first ram I got to know was D-ram. He came to Sanctuary Mountain a few days after I had shot the wolves, and, on October 27, crossed to Ghost Mountain where he stayed for the duration of the rutting season. One of the very dark rams, D was black of body and neck with a brownish face, a large Roman nose, and circular, narrow horns quite modest in size and mass for so old a ram. With some difficulty (aided by my spotting scope), I discerned a minimum of eleven age rings on his horns, so I knew he was older than eleven years. In fact, he had reached the age of twelve and one-half that fall, but I discovered this much later when I held his head in my hands a few hours after he suffered the death of most sheep. Wolves had killed him.

Old D had his eye on S-ram, a dark gray animal with flaring horns and a light face and neck, who was five years his junior. When S returned to Sanctuary, whether in fall from the summer range, or in spring from a distant wintering area, D soon noticed and from then on followed S like a shadow and would not leave him in peace. He insulted S-ram at every turn, before and after almost every resting period. If S were walking on the slope, D was never far behind.

S-ram had a "double" whom I marked down in my notebook as S^1-ram, and so this "name" stuck. S^1 was a year younger than S, but otherwise very similar, differing only in a few minor marks on the face and neck. This "double" was of no interest to D; in fact, he led a rather unremarkable, normal life.

E-ram's life was different. This was a splendid ten-year-old, full-curled animal, with horns larger than those of D, and yet he was a nobody. He was a coward, in the best sense of the word, declining to enter the lively melee around an estrous ewe despite his large horn-and-body size. E was content to let others breed and fight, merely looking on as others fought a hot contest for the prize of the rutting range. If the action moved on, E followed—and watched. He, too, had a "double," C-ram, who was, however, younger than E. C was seven years old in the fall of 1961. Both rams appeared similar: in the way they held their heads, in their walk, and in their coloring—but there the similarity ended. C was a calm individual who dominated others in his age and size class. When he returned in the fall of 1962, one year older and heavier of horn and body, E meekly submitted at once.

I had climbed the rain-soaked, foggy mountain the day C returned, dark and sleek from a summer of fattening. He walked along the old diagonal trail that led from Sanctuary Valley, at an angle along the rugged cliffs, and through the deep avalanche chutes of Sanctuary Mountain. I expected E to fight when C came at him, displaying his horns, and insulting E by treating him like a female. However, E simply turned and continued feeding. C followed him that day and the next, but I saw no sign of E having changed his mind. He remained subordinate to C.

My favorite among the Sanctuary rams was Peter. He was small in body, bearing a set of unexceptional horns that formed a good three-quarter curl—normal for a seven-year-old ram. Peter's body was light gray, and his neck and head were white. His legs were short, and he was as turgid as a knackwurst. Although small, Peter had the heart of a lion—some achievement for a sheep! When the rutting season came, Peter crossed the valley to Ghost Mountain. He could be seen in almost every

A very old ram. He was a minimum of 20 years old that spring, had been miss-
ing all his lower front teeth since age 16, but was still a dominant ram. He had
been tagged as an adult and must have been at least 4 years of age at tagging.
He is the oldest ram known from the wilds. The following fall he could not be
found, nor the following spring, which means that he died.

scrap. Larger and superior in horn size and strength as the
breeding rams were, Peter gave them no respite. Again and
again he attacked. Sometimes he skillfully shot between the
guarding ram and the female in heat, and then chased the
female into the cliffs. There he mounted once or twice before
the breeding ram arrived and knocked him flying off the female. Peter was not overly impressed. He continued to work
hard and accepted punishment for truly marginal success.
When I returned in 1965, after three years of absence from
Gladys Lake, I again searched for Peter; but, although the rut
was in full swing, fourteen days passed, and I left without
seeing him. Maybe the brave little soul had taken up courting
behind Ghost Mountain, successfully defending ewes in heat
and perpetuating his kind. I wished it were so but with little
hope. He would have been eleven years old that year—an age

only half the rams reach, at best. Maybe he had been shot, and his stuffed head was staring with eyes of glass from some wall; maybe the wolves had killed him after he returned exhausted from an earlier rutting season. Spunky little Peter was an individual I missed greatly. I wished for his silhouette to appear where Ghost Mountain runs into Lick Mountain. He would surely stand and stare from a pinnacle at the slopes and cuts below, and then run to a rutting group and make life miserable for some larger adversary. However, Peter never came.

Shortly after D's arrival in late October 1961, an old silver-headed, black ram, with full-curled, flaring, amber horns followed. He was larger than D and ultimately went by the designation "f.c." in my notebook—short for "full curl." He was supposed to be B-ram, but somehow "f.c." continued to crop up whenever I was taking notes on him, so he became "old f.c."

Old f.c. was exceptional in that he had almost no white hair on the belly. His black coat closed in from all sides, reducing the white belly markings to the size of a hand. His body features revealed his age, shown by a back that sagged slightly and a belly that was quite generous—yet his movements were firm and spirited, and he was undisputed master of the rutting range on Ghost Mountain. F.c. did not hesitate to approach if he spotted a ewe coming into heat and under the tender care of some other ram. At his approach, the rival left. F.c. might not keep his prize in peace, but his dominance was uncontested, and the braver of his subordinates only attempted to cull the ewe from him, not to fight him. He rushed and butted them mercilessly during their daring attempts but ignored them if they fed or rested. Once—maybe due to exhaustion— he voluntarily left the female in heat to an eager rival and fed and rested for two hours. After the rest, he reclaimed the ewe, uncontested as ever. D chose to leave for some other locality whenever old f.c. arrived.

Of all the rams I observed, f.c. taught me most about the rutting behavior of mountain sheep and was the only one who disclosed in detail the fate of an old sheep when misfortune becomes its lot. In early December 1961, before the rut had ended, old f.c. became noticeably slower in running. Something appeared to be amiss. One after the other the Sanctuary rams left Ghost Mountain after the last ewe was bred and returned to Sanctuary Mountain. Old f.c. remained. He began to lead a lonely life. The big rams had left, the ewes had no interest in him and vice versa, and the young remaining rams stuck with the ewes. Old f.c. usually lay on a pinnacle, looking across to Ghost Mountain where his sharp eyes must have seen his former companions and rivals. He acted as though he intended to cross, and yet he did not do so, and the days passed. Christmas and New Year's day came and went, and f.c. was still alone on Ghost. On the morning of January 11, 1962, he finally did cross to Sanctuary. Now I could see what was wrong. Old f.c. held up his left hind leg when he stood, and he limped when walking. That day his limp was noticeable, although not strikingly so; but it rapidly worsened during the following week.

For a day or two old f.c. attempted to follow the other rams, but he gave it up and reduced his activity to the base of the lower cliffs that circled Sanctuary Mountain. Within ten days of his return he settled into a predictable routine. During the night he would rest in the cave at the bottom of the cliffs, together with other rams. In the morning, if the sun shone, he moved out in front of the cave and exposed his body to the thin rays of the winter sun. He would be the last to leave for feeding, hobbling down the trail that led from the cave to the grassy west-facing slope below. Here he would paw in the soft but deep snow for forage, alongside the other rams.

A sheep must dig for its forage in winter and does so with powerful strokes of its front legs, throwing the snow back and downhill and opening a crater in the snow blanket. The hungry creature must work very hard—at times at rates of 1,800 strokes per hour of feeding. The forage it retrieves during the coldest period of winter, in January, is generally not sufficient to cover its energy expenditure, and the animal must supplement its energy requirements by burning its body fat. The cold, the wind, the heat-robbing winter sky at night, the hard work of clearing forage, and moving in deep, soft snow, drain body heat from the animal and steadily reduce its energy resources.

A sheep that has little fat to burn is already at a disadvantage, and old f.c. had probably little left to burn after squandering his resources guarding ewes, fighting, and neglecting to rest and feed during the rut. Once rams have entered their period of dominance, of high social success, of guarding and breeding females, they begin to age and die rapidly. Mortality increases five- to eightfold over that of younger, subordinate rams. Once they become breeding rams, the males have not long to live. Old f.c. was a breeding ram. Worse still, he was an injured breeding ram. He was handicapped. He could remove snow from forage only with great difficulty, and he had a sick leg to heal.

When a sheep paws snow, it spreads the hind legs and lifts one foreleg, thus giving it a solid three-legged stance. Old f.c. gamely tried, but his sore hind leg gave way under him, so he attempted to balance himself on one front leg and one hind leg while digging. That he had difficulty obtaining sufficient food was apparent, for he never paused to rest while feeding during daylight hours. He fed as long as possible on the slope and then ascended the trail to the cave at night.

Old f.c.'s misfortune had not escaped his subordinates. In particular, it had not escaped G-ram, a seven-year-old. He, more than the others, took advantage of old f.c.'s condition and followed to insult and clash with him. The old ram still retained sufficient vigor to defend himself, however, and within the course of two weeks he was left alone by G and ignored by the others. He followed his routine, and every morning I checked to see if he were still there, observing him and the others during the day.

As the days passed, I noticed that old f.c.'s routine was not quite invariable and that his appearance was not that of the other rams. He moved further downhill now; his movements lost the crispness I had become so familiar with, his haunches grew thin, and his backbone protruded. The other rams looked round and turgid by comparison, and their spunky actions contrasted with that of the lame, old ram, whose return journey to the cave at night became ever longer. Old f.c. paused now and again for a rest and then slowly climbed on. His limp was as

Yearling ram pawing a crater in the snow to reach the meager forage below

bad as ever. I hoped for his recovery, not only because he was
so well-marked an animal and so easily recognizable, but also
because he had become more than just another ram to me.

January passed into February. Old f.c.'s routine was broken
for a day when he limped up the cliffs and roamed over Sanctuary Mountain as if searching for something. I could not tell if
his search were successful, but next day he was back at the cave
again. One evening, when old f.c. was painfully hobbling back
to the cave, he encountered an eagle sitting on a stunted fir beside the trail. The old ram stopped and stared at the great bird.
In better days, he probably would have rushed the bird and
tried to hit it with his horns as other sheep did, given the opportunity. But the old ram only stood and looked, and the
eagle looked back, and the old ram limped on.

Then one day old f.c. failed to return to the cave. He simply
bedded down in the snow, low on the hillside where he last fed.
It was cold then, more than 50°F below zero. He had given up
the cave, his last hope of conserving a little heat by shielding

himself under the rock from the cold, black sky, by getting out of the wind, and by absorbing the body heat radiated by his healthy companions.

I toyed with the thought of killing old f.c., of terminating his slow death with a quick one, and relieving his suffering. I did not do it. I had come to see and study the "life" of sheep and that included their "death." Yet old f.c. hung on to life. He braved the icy winter—despite being little more than a skeleton covered by a shaggy, black coat—and moved lower downhill each day.

March came. Now old f.c. had reached the bottom of the slope and fed on a little knoll, just barely above Gladys Lake. On March 10, 1962, I saw him alive for the last time. It was evening, and I had shouldered the spotting scope and snow-shoed out onto Gladys Lake to check the position of various sheep on Sanctuary, Shady, and Cliff mountains. The sun was sinking slowly behind the jagged backbone of Mount Will. Sanctuary Mountain was bathed in the soft light one finds at the end of a clear day. Old f.c. was resting on his knoll, lying broadside to the rays of the sun, soaking in its warmth—the life-giving power so cherished by all who must suffer the freezing winters. I mounted the spotting scope on the tripod and looked at old f.c. He was watching me, at a distance of almost half a mile, his jaws moving slowly as he ruminated. He turned his head again toward the dying sun, and his horns shone in deep amber. As I looked at the black ram with his silver head, once more my hopes for him were renewed. Maybe he would live. Was it not March already? Were not the days lengthening? Was it not warmer even now? Maybe old f.c. would gain strength. So far, the wolf that lived across Gladys Lake had not crossed to Sanctuary. Perhaps the old ram's luck would hold. I returned to the cabin.

During the night a storm struck and did not let up for two days. Fierce gales howled and blew in from the Pacific. The spruce trees were bent mercilessly by the warm wind's mighty hand. The snow was blown as one blinding wall down from the steep mountain slopes, from the tree branches, from the lake, sweeping down those narrow valleys. The cabin yelled, screeched, and creaked—God knows what prevented it from being blown away—as it moved with each relentless blast.

Then, the storm was gone. A new layer of soft snow had fallen, and the cold snap was on again. It was early on March 12 when I left to check for various groups of sheep, including the rams of Sanctuary Mountain. The individual sheep were soon accounted for, except for old f.c., and by noon I decided to look for him in the small hills that were an old moraine at the foot of Sanctuary. Old f.c. could be hidden in a dip, or behind a little hill, and I could possibly find him. The search, however, proved futile. The storm had removed all tracks, and I found no fresh ones. Could the old ram have moved up again into the cliffs? The thought made me happy, and I continued my search, concentrating on the cliffs above. By chance my eye fell on two whiskey jacks, not far below me, and they had obviously found something interesting. They hopped to the foot of a big willow bush and tugged at their find in the snow. A rabbit, perhaps, I thought. Then they pulled up some black hair, and it dawned on me that my search had probably come to an end.

A wolf had killed old f.c. There were some frozen tracks in the snow on a windblown area, showing his last run and the elevated tracks of the wolf. He had been dead a couple of days now, well buried by the snow, and still not frozen. After ripping open the ribcage and sampling some rib meat, the wolf had abandoned the carcass. I could not blame the wolf; old f.c. was incredibly thin. His hide was so weak I could rip it with my hands; his bone marrow was as red as jelly. His left hind foot was swollen above the joint, and about a cupful of yellow pus ran out when I opened the swelling. The joints between the hoof bones had completely dissolved, and the bones gritted against each other when I moved the hoof. Old f.c.'s ailment had been hopeless from the start; he could not have recovered.

I skinned out the carcass of the old ram and made the necessary notes, such as: the site of the fatal teeth marks (behind the jaw) indicating how he had died (by suffocation); the distance he had been dragged by the wolf (about five paces); and that he had died after he had been dragged (since he defecated where he lay). Mundane information, all. Then I took old f.c.'s head, skull and all, secured the flaring horns I had so often admired onto a pack-board, and left for the cabin.

Before I removed the skin to clean the skull, I took out my drawing pad and sketched old f.c.'s head. I directed the shine of life to his eyes which gave him the appearance of looking down the mountain—as he had done so often in his lifetime. A year later I reproduced his head in color, using pastels on a gray, rough sheet of paper, for I did not want my memory to lose the image of the black ram with the silver head and the flaring, amber horns.

Several days later, when I passed the spot where old f.c.'s remains had lain, I found that a wolverine had dismembered the body and dragged the pieces away. Only hair and gut lay around. In the following summer, a patch of plants, slightly greener than the rest, marked the spot where old f.c. had died. As I paused for a moment, a junco came down, picked up the hair, and flew away to build his nest.

6

Animal Combat and Communication

In the fall of 1961 I received my first insights into the lives of mountain sheep. Some were uncomfortable to contemplate. Distinct rules govern the conduct of these animals, and—as I discovered later—they applied not only to sheep but to men as well. These rules appear to be universal in animal societies, and man has not escaped them any more than he has escaped having his blood pumped by a typically mammalian heart, his food chewed by classically mammalian jaws, or his skeleton moved by mammalian muscles and nerves. The very disdain one experiences when reading such comparisons is probably biological, not cultural, in origin. This aversion, based on our desire to be something special, unites us with the mammalian stream of life and does not segregate us from it. Our tendency to disclaim evolution and to ridicule our humble primate origins, and our desire to model ourselves after gods (that we first made in our image) and to look upon ourselves as fallen angels rather than as extraordinary animals—these are all due to biological rather than cultural motivation. I shall argue this case later.

For the present, suffice it to note that there are principles operating in the social behavior of vertebrates, and these principles apply to sheep as well as to committee chairmen. Some familiarity with the behavior of animals is not undesirable when studying committee chairmen.

In the fall of 1961, I knew nothing of such heresies and was only puzzled by the horns of those rams. They were pretty extravagant outgrowths, ridiculously large in size, and simply begged an explanation. They were not likely to be a joke of nature, I realized, for by that time I had already learned that little has been left to chance in the process of evolution and that those large horn cores could be there only for a very good reason. Ultimately, it turned out that much of sheep biology rotated about them. Neither the behavior of sheep nor their evolution can be fully understood without a knowledge of the functions and the consequences of their horns.

The primary function of the horns of a ram is to serve as a weapon. That, of course, is not a new insight. What was new was to learn that, in fighting, rams focus the whole force of the clash on one horn heel by every available means. The rams' horns deliver blows with the combined effect of a sledgehammer and a karate chop and thus achieve the most forceful clash possible. The attacking ram not only rises on his hind legs, races at his opponent, jumps into the fray, and flicks the heavy horns forward to hit with one edge, but he also employs gravity by moving above the opponent and racing downhill at him or even by jumping down on top of him from a cliff. Although the latter is not a common occurrence, I have seen rams do this a number of times, and on each occasion the defending ram caught the attack skillfully with his horns. Hence, the massive horns serve not only as weapons, but also as guards, as defenses; they are part of the head armor with which a ram shields itself from injury in combat by catching and neutralizing its opponent's blows. Examination of the horn and skull structure bears out these contentions.

The horns of a large but unexceptional bighorn ram weigh about twenty-five pounds, inclusive of the massive skull, and, of the Stone's rams I studied, the weight was about eighteen pounds. Here is your eighteen- or twenty-five-pound sledge hammer. On its outside edge is found a prominent ridge which in most rams shows signs of chipping. This is the ridge that

Ram's head, showing damaged horn. During fighting the ends of the horns are broken off; in this ram the left horn has been damaged, while the right horn tip is still largely intact.

first makes contact with the opponent. The horns grow from massive horn cores which are hollow. In fact, the bones at the front split into an upper and lower level, forming a double roof of bone—a bone helmet—over the brain. The upper and lower roofs are connected with cross struts, thus creating a honeycombed network of bone between the upper and lower skull roof. This network is about one and one-half inches thick at the most and extends from the nasal bones to the back of the head. This sturdy helmet is covered beneath the horn cores with a tough layer of skin up to a quarter of an inch thick, and upward from the horn cores by a deep, resilient, mass of horn (the horns themselves) up to two inches thick. This is only part of the defensive structure, however.

No matter how well armored the head, it must still remain on the spine and not snap backwards or sideways under the impact of a 250-pound ram rushing full speed into the clash. Thus, the skull is anchored by massive articulation surfaces on

the spine and tied down by many strong ligaments. Probably
more important, however, is the thick elastic cord—the nuchal
tendon—that runs on top of the spine to the skull, from where
it broadens into a wide mass that is fused to the bone immediately behind the horns. The function of this structure is, apparently, to neutralize the effects of severe blows. In a clash,
the head of the ram is positioned so that the force of the encounter pushes the nose into the chest; that is, the head rotates
forward against the tension of the thick elastic bands and masses
that tie the top of the head to the top of the spine.

In order to explain why rams usually escape serious injury in
combat it need not be postulated that they fight in such an altruistic manner as not to harm each other. This would be akin
to saying that in duels with sabers, in which the combatants also
usually escape serious injury (at least for a time), the duelists do
not "really want to hurt each other." Anyone who fences will
admit that this is nonsense, and that each tries to cut or hit the
other but is prevented by the opponent's skill in deflecting the
blade and by his evasive actions. Fencing consists of compo-
nents of attack and defense, and the resulting action, a ritual-
ized fight, is the consequence. In principle, combat consists of
attack and defense.

Why is so obvious and mundane a point raised here? Because
much of the recent popular writing on animal behavior has not
only overlooked it, but has created the myth that animals have
evolved "bloodless" combat in which the participants seek not
to harm each other despite being able to do so. I was familiar
with this view and even believed it when I first began my studies in the Spatzisi. Then I had a traumatic experience. It was
early in the morning of November 14, 1961, and I was searching the slopes of Ghost Mountain for signs of sheep and goats.
Low on the mountain stood a lone male goat. His stance was
awkward, and he held up a hindleg. Then he slowly hobbled
forward. I could see a big red blotch on the neck of his white
coat and his unusually dirty belly. All mature male mountain
goats in the Spatzisi have dirty bellies during the rut, caused by
pawing rutting pits and throwing muck against their bellies in
the process. This male, however, was exceptionally dirty. Then

A butt. The larger ram on the left lunges, but the smaller ram pivots and catches the blow, thus neutralizing the attack.

my eyes caught a movement in the cliffs above. It was a second male mountain goat, and one foreleg was red. He moved down the slope toward the wounded one, who hobbled away, pitifully slowly, and obviously in great pain. There was little doubt they had fought recently. The second male returned to the female group and courted.

Because it was a beautiful clear, sunny day, I felt I had to remain behind my spotting scope and watch sheep. The few such days there were had to be used to gather behavioral data. As much as I wanted to know the extent of that goat's wounds and body damage, I had to stay where I was. But I could watch him, at intervals. The badly wounded male stood all day, low on the slope. The victorious male visited him several times and made him hobble along; other males came, looked over the unfortunate one, and they, too, made him hobble along. Evening came, and still the wounded male stood there with his back arched.

During the night I heard a storm tear at the cabin's roof, and when morning came it was snowing and blowing. Since no observations were possible that day, I took my rifle from the wall and headed out for the mountain. I found the wounded male. He had not moved much during the night. When the snowstorm eased for a moment I saw him barely thirty paces away on the slope above me, but before I could shoot, the snowstorm obscured him again. I moved closer and shot him when the wind slackened. Minutes later I saw the second male and took him also, for the purpose of autopsy in order to determine the damage caused by fighting. The two warriors fell into the snow-filled trench below, where they lay about ten paces apart. On my way down the cliff I slipped and fell, and landed in the deep snow of the gorge between the two dead goats.

After I had examined both goats externally and had skinned and performed an autopsy on the badly wounded one, I was emotionally shaken. According to every rule of animal behavior I had learned up to then, animals did not do to each other what these males had done. Only human beings maimed one another like this. There was no escaping the obvious fact that the belly, groin, and chest of the badly wounded male had been perforated ten times; that his undersides had been beaten to reddish-black pulp; that his sides and haunches, shoulder, and neck were discolored yellow-green; and that the only untouched part of his body was his back. There was blood in the body cavity, a leg muscle was ripped and torn, and the liver was cut. Dollar-sized red spots covered the flanks and shoulders where the horn tips had hit but not penetrated. The hair on the lower part of the body was caked with blood and dirt from the rutting pits. In later years I was to see worse damage on goats—inflicted by their sharp, black horns—but for a first time, the wounds of these two males were quite enough. That night I called Prince George on the radio and excitedly I told a puzzled Marge Smith to relate the tale to Renate, that the improbable had happened in complete contradiction to ethological theories.

The eulogies of some behaviorists who claim it is the stronger who "saves" the weaker in combat, so that the weaker may breed some other day, sounds somewhat improbable. Of what

The clash. The attacking ram (and the ultimate loser in this encounter) is on the left, attacking from uphill.

disadvantage is a dead opponent? What does a victor gain by sparing a defeated rival except another fight in the future with the chance of defeat, of loss of dominance, of reduced breeding, of injury, sickness, or even a shortened life? These are rhetorical questions. Close observation of the truly dangerous combatants, such as the horned ungulates, shows quite clearly that the first and major reason, though not the only one, that combatants escape injury, is their great skill in defense.

The collection of tricks used by animals to reduce the effectiveness of dangerous adversaries is the same employed by man: holding onto an opponent's weapons is one; evading blows is another; stepping so close that the opponent cannot strike is a third; and neutralizing attacks against body armor is a fourth. As long as an adversary's horns, jaws, or claws are held immobile, they cannot be used to inflict damage; as long as attacks can be deflected or avoided the opponent's efforts are in vain; as long as an opponent cannot bring his weapons to bear on his rival's he wastes energy to no end; as long as each attack can be neutralized against an armored head, a shoulder, or a haunch covered with a thick, gristly skin shield, nothing is resolved. As long as one remains on guard and feints, and waits for that little mistake by the rival, everything is to be gained.

And yet, in observing fights in large mammals, one notices only too often a reluctance on the part of dominants to press charges, to gore when chance presents a golden opportunity, or to kill an opponent who momentarily loses his guard. Killings do occur, and the chance of death by murder during the lifespan is quite high for some species. Nevertheless, for those armed with extremely dangerous weapons, such as our mountain goats, potential combatants avoid fighting as much as possible. Why? The reasons have little to do with altruism but can be explained much more simply. In a dangerously armed species, that is, mountain goats, bears, and most carnivores, the opponent who is heedless about launching into battle faces prompt and certain reciprocation. The moment his weapons pierce the opponent and send jarring pain through his body, the aggressor is subject to instantaneous and very damaging retaliation. By the time the fight is over, the victorious aggressor is hardly in better shape than the vanquished and is just as certain to sicken and lose out in breeding. Why? Because his is a pyrrhic victory. To have won is a useless exercise if it has so weakened him that he can no longer successfully oppose his other daily rivals. Hence, the hesitation of even dominant individuals to grapple with an opponent is not so much a sign of altruism as of naked self-preservation. As long as a rival with dangerous weapons is likely to get tit for tat there is natural selection for those individuals who settle dominance by means other than the use of their weapons and who relegate fighting to extreme occasions only. There is, then, selection for the "coward" rather than the "brave" individual, for the cautious rather than the foolhardy, for the bluffer rather than the fighter. In place of fighting, one sees elaborate displays of strength and might; but this is true only where dangerous weapons are matched against poor physical defenses. Where such defenses are excellent—be they armored heads in sheep, or shield, helmet, and chain mail in knights—fighting can again

One-year-old male rubbing and nuzzling the horns of a large old male (young rams begin to pacify dominants early). The animals are shedding their winter coats and look untidy.

flourish. I have seen rams fight for up to twenty-five hours and reel in exhaustion from the strenuous combat—not from injury. The sagas tell of armored knights flailing away at each other with swords in chivalrous matches till they too reeled from exhaustion—not from injury. Fighting in which dangerous weapons are skillfully neutralized takes on a sporting, playful flavor—be it in rams, deer, or in human society—in the form of jousting, fencing, and fancy weapon plays. In mountain sheep, gazelles, antelope, cattle, or deer, the males spar after dominance is settled, or among territorial species sparring goes on either outside or inside the territory, or sometimes in well-developed ceremonies there is sparring between territorial neighbors. In the mule deer, large bucks, for instance, work patiently—at times for days—to get on sparring terms with a smaller buck. Once on sparring terms, bucks may remain together, with the smaller parasitizing the larger's dominance by insulting bucks larger than he is: in case of trouble the

larger friend will rush to the rescue. In these sporting engage-
ments, the males learn—for mammals are learning machines—
the proper orientations and actions so that the "fight" is a testing of strength, obviously a pleasurable event to the larger as
well as the smaller, for it is the latter's option to start and to terminate the "fight."

In these sporting, sparring, or clashing matches, the rule is
that, although the dominant may solicit the fight, it is the subordinate who starts and ends it. Why? Because it is the only way
such contests could exist; with a reluctant subordinate, no combat can develop, and a dominant forcing a fight will only
frighten off the subordinate. One consequence of sporting
jousts is that dominant-subordinate relationships are reinforced, serious combat is reduced, and the animals may be *con-
ditioned* to attack into the defensive system of the opponent.
What reward is there for the subordinate in such sporting
events? Why do they search out these violent encounters? My
answer is, admittedly, little more than an educated guess, but
the essential elements to the answer are known scientific facts. I
suspect that there is a sexual physiological reward system.
Fighting is satisfied, at least in some large mammals, by stimulating sexual reward centers in the brain, and it is known that
these centers exist. It is possible to implant electrodes in the
brain centers of rats and see them sit and stimulate themselves
steadily. Further examples are the erections evident in fighting
or sparring ungulates, in the dominance displays of such mammals or of many primates. Notable also is the swelling of male
genitalia in dominant cercopithecine primates and the wither-
ing of scrotum and penis of the defeated animals. When deer
horn or spar, one can see signs of sexual arousal, including, at
times, ejaculations. Violence can bring about pleasant sexual
arousal, a peculiarity well noted by the Marquis de Sade and
Casanova, who knew that exhibitions of blood and gore, execu-
tions, or fighting were perfect preliminaries to orgies. Havelock
Ellis has also dwelt on the connection between the performance
of violence and sexual arousal, whether in the form of sadism
or masochism. In life forms in which overt aggression is possible as a result of good physical defenses, rewarding of aggres-

Two large old rams on good terms. The older of the two is about 16 years old.
He nuzzles the nose of the massive ram on the right, to which he is subordinate.
Nuzzling is a sign of his subordination.

sion with sexual arousal insures that males interact aggressively
and perfect their combat techniques, so that each is trained and
ready when the need to fight arises. It also insures that mild
pain is not a physiological punishment but a stimulant to continue the aggressive engagement. We know that sexual arousal
dulls pain. Why not use it as a painkiller in combat? For the
human animal, erection in agonistic situations, as well as in
sadism and masochism, may only be relict adaptations akin to
our persistent appendix; we reward successful aggression socially with praise, medals, and public eulogies. In those forms
where such is not the case—as in deer, sheep, or nonhuman
primates—reward could well be by sexual arousal.

During later studies I was to discover that sex and aggression
were closely linked in sheep: they matured in parallel during a
ram's development; rams were stimulated to sexual acts after
fighting; females used aggressive behavior on exhausted males
to stimulate them into copulation; in highly evolved sheep it

was not only aggression which was increased, but also overt sexual behavior. The two systems (male courtship and female-courtship) appeared to be linked. In essence, during female-courtship, when it is the female which courts the male, the ram acts the masochist.

There is one important point to consider in fighting. If members of a species can kill or maim an opponent instantly and thus escape retaliation, the species experiences no selection for inhibition in the use of weapons. A male mountain goat, using its daggers on a rival, has an excellent chance of getting ventilated seconds later; a human, hitting someone over the head with a club, piercing him with a sword, lance, arrow, or bullet, is usually safe; even if the opponent rises to a last attack, the aggressor is usually protected by some sort of shield—or by distance. Therefore humans, due to cultural processes (weapon and shield technology), have freed themselves from the natural selection which curtails lethal aggression in other animals. For a bear or mountain goat, murder is so dangerous as to border on suicide; for a ram, it is next to impossible. For a human, it is easy and safe; no wonder we punish it via cultural means. In animals, the victim punishes its murderer; in humans, the in-group decides the punishment.

The realization that there was no need to consider altruism as a factor in animal combat came less as a shock than as a disappointment. I had demolished—for myself, and ultimately for others—a little golden animal story, a little myth that was simply too good to be true. We were, after all, no worse or better than other animals. The little golden myth that upheld, for all to see, the theory that animals fight bloodless combat and do not kill each other, had pictured animals a little better, a little more innocent, than ourselves. I did not feel elated in disproving the theory; I would rather have proved my intellectual heroes to be right.

The realization that there was little altruism in the combat of rams and that each one looked after himself was sad but not shocking. However, my discovery that the dominant male treats a defeated subordinate male like a female was a different matter. I still cringe at the memory of seeing old D-ram mount S-ram repeatedly. D-ram had been using S-ram the way a breeding ram would use an estrous female. This insight came when I witnessed breeding activity, and later saw how an estrous female acted toward the breeding male. Hers was the prerogative to butt and rub on him, to excite him by coquettish runs, body contact, and aggressive displays. She used aggression and teasing to elicit sex from the male. In principle, subordinate males acted like estrous females. True to form, and incapable of absorbing this realization at once, I called these actions of the rams *aggressosexual* behavior, for to state that the males had evolved a homosexual society was emotionally beyond me. To conceive of those magnificent beasts as "queers"—Oh God! I argued for two years that, in sheep, aggressive and sexual behavior could not be separated; that one was just the reverse side of the same coin; that one must call it aggressosexual behavior and nothing else, and so on. I never published that drivel and am glad of it. A little truth at a time is wonderful medicine; too much at once shakes one's very foundation. Eventually I called the spade a spade and admitted that rams lived in essentially a homosexual society. They are not the only species to regularly practice it. Homosexuality is based on female mimicry. The smaller, weaker animal fakes a female and consequently redirects aggression by the dominant into sex, and this in turn allows him to remain in the group and live. If there were *no* selection for intense gregariousness, there could not be selection for female mimicry either—the two processes are linked—although it must be understood that female mimicry is only *one* adaptive strategy. There are others, as we shall see later.

Female mimicry is based on taking advantage of, or parasitizing, the inhibitions of males to thrash or injure females. Males that hit and injure females cannot be expected to do much breeding, nor to leave those females they do breed healthy enough to raise big, vigorous offspring. In other words, a male so abnormal as to beat up the weaker sex only assures that he will leave none of his own kind to torture future generations—at least in animal populations this is true.

It would have been very surprising, indeed, if sheep were the only social animals that had evolved female mimicry. At the time of my studies, Dr. Wolfgang Wickler, then a research associate of Konrad Lorenz, had, in fact, suggested the very same thing for baboons, where female mimicry in the males included the evolution of the atrocious red swelling below the tail, typical of females in estrus. Even rainbow trout make use of this deception. Thus, while the dominant male courts the female that is about to spawn, his rivals lurk nearby in *female coloration* ready to dash forward to participate in insemination once the female lays the roe and the dominant male ejects the milt. The successful female mimics thus insure the perpetuation of their kind; while the dominant, lying alongside of the spawning female, fertilizes the eggs on one side, the female mimics spawn on the other, unoccupied side.

In the cichlid fishes, sexual behavior is used to stop aggressors short. It works because a signal is flashed that the aggressor must not attack, at risk of reproductive failure. He who attacks conspecifics that act like spawning females is just as likely to attack females that spawn, or that are about to spawn, and thus chase them to some rival's territory. Spawning is so rare, and faking it so common, that it would tax a mind greater than that of a little fish to tell the difference between mimic and model.

The behavioral system of rams thus has two parts: that which is used toward smaller animals, including the female, and that used toward larger animals. Therefore, there is no behavior used exclusively toward the female. Large rams treat everyone smaller than themselves in a like manner, although they are not equally interested in all size classes of sheep. They can clearly differentiate sexes, but they do not treat other sheep on the basis of sex but on the basis of size. To us, this is, of course, a little odd—if not mind-boggling—that conduct in a society is based on rank (or size) and not on sex. We shall return to some of these consequences a little later.

Also emblematic of fighting by rams is that they use their horns as rank symbols, akin to insignia in an army. In fighting, right after a clash, the rams freeze into statues for a minute or so, and show each other their horns. Thus immediately after each ram experiences a certain blow, he sees a certain size of horn. Horn size or weight is the greatest variable; while a ram doubles in body size from one to ten years of age, his horn weight increases twenty- to thirtyfold. After each clash, the rams are able to compare the force and the size of every sledgehammer blow. We can infer that the rams are thus conditioning each other to associate a given combat potential with a specific horn size. Hence they must learn to treat strange rams in accordance with their horn size, which is indeed what they do.

Furthermore, dominants flash their horns on meeting subordinates, which insures that the subordinates are reminded of the blows that go with the greater horn size of their superiors. By displaying their horns, the dominants thus reinforce the lessons the subordinates have learned earlier. Such reinforcing behavior in Stone's rams accounts for almost ninety percent of all behavior patterns of the dominant. This horn display is, of course, the converse of the salute in the army, something like rank pulling. Thus, horn size as a rank symbol, and horn displays that emphasize horn size, insure predictability of social relationships even among many strange rams and confine fighting to those of equal horn size. Clearly, the only stranger a ram will fight is the one he is uncertain about: can he safely accept his blows or should he shun him? Such a stranger will have, of course, horns of the same size as those of his uncertain opponent. Thus, each behaves as though he were the dominant and attempts to treat the other like a female—which is an insult, of course—and then they fight till one gives up and accepts the female role. All uncertainty is then resolved. In this connection, rams fight to clarify "uncertainty," the consequence of which is the assumption of one of two social roles. We call the consequence of many such clarifications in a band the *dominance hierarchy*. Rams do not necessarily fight for females but for superiority.

I noted that rams deem it an insult to be treated as a female. Dominants can take very energetic steps against subordinates that direct female behavior at them. Therefore, subordinates learn not to insult—except when they are safe from prompt and certain punishment. For example, a small-horned ram passing *uphill* from a dominant, and just far enough out of reach, often gives him a horn display in passing. Better still, when a dominant is defeated, the victorious ram will shower on him an orgy of courtship patterns. Then smaller rams may join in and, in turn, insult the defeated ram with impunity. Woe if the defeated ram rises against his inferior tormentors. The victorious ram will at once send him sprawling. So the defeated ram grazes and allows the insults to proceed. A sick or injured dominant may also become the target of insults by subordinate rams. Little boys are not the only ones to thumb their noses.

The principle to be noted here is that an insult is an act implying lower-than-actual status (an honor is, of course, the converse). Our insults equate the opponent with something lowly (creep, scum, scab, monkey), with a wish for his premature end (go to hell, jump into the lake), with insignificance (scram, kid), with impotency, or with males who show female-like, inferiority-implying attributes. As you may note, in principle, our actions are no different from those of sheep. Insulting behavior by subordinates occurs when the dominant cannot see it, or know it, or—better still—if he does see it, can do nothing about it.

For the sake of completeness it should be noted that juvenile mimicry—playing baby—is another way in which subordinate animals can escape persecution by dominants. In sheep we do not find it. Juvenile mimicry as submissive behavior can evolve only where male and female raise their children together, and where the result of a dominant attacking childlike images would be to select against his own brood. We can expect to find it in carnivores in which all adults raise the young, as in wolves, for example. As we shall see later, rudiments of this type of submissive behavior can be found in ourselves.

The courtship behavior of sheep tends to be strikingly cautious; it is tender—by sheep standards—and includes a lot of showing off. By showing off, one understands that the ram uses behavior that correlates with his rank as a social superior. He shows off his horns. Indeed, as Professor G. H. Orians, professor of zoology at the University of Washington (Seattle), has pointed out, the female should be attracted by such show-

Young ram charging at a defending ram. The ewe is in heat, and is hotly contested.

ing off, because only dominant males are at liberty to do so, and in selecting such a male for her mate she unconsciously ensures social success for her offspring. Here, choosing to mate with the largest, most handsome male perpetuates a successful genetic trait. This, in turn, ensures that there is a payoff in sex for bragging males. Of course, they can brag only if no superior male is present to stop them. If one observes the melee of a rutting sheep band on a mountainside one wonders, indeed, how the female can exercise any choice of all—but she does. She encourages large-horned suitors most of all, and, if chased by small courtiers, may run to large males where she is least molested. The carefulness of the ram's courtship is easily explained. The less attention he draws to himself when he is courting, and the less frequently he notifies wandering rivals, or superiors that happen to pass nearby, of his possession of a female in heat, the more likely he will be to sire an offspring. A ram that is rough, and causes the female to flee quickly, cap-

tures the attention of all rams in the vicinity and has an excellent chance of losing the female to a rival.

Evidence of the excellent defenses of the ram is that females
barely protest obnoxious rams, but flee instead. The activity is
different in species in which male and female are similarly
armed, and even more so if the female is aggressive. None illustrated this better than the mountain goats which lived side
by side with Stone's sheep around Gladys Lake. Both sexes are
similar in size when fully grown—the male a little heavier than
the female—and they look so much alike as to confuse even an
expert at times. Both carry short, black, needle-sharp horns,
which rest on a thin fragile skull and function only as weapons.
Goats do not catch the opponent's blow with the head, and thus
do not fight head to head, since their vulnerable skulls would
hardly stand it. The goats' defenses consist of evasive maneu-
vers and reliance on the dermal shield on their buttocks, because it is here where most blows land. Their fights are very
rare and terribly damaging, since they stab each other in the
belly, groin, chest, neck, throat, haunches, legs, ribs—in short,
everywhere but on the head or back. On top of it all, it is the
female that is more aggressive than the male. What happens
when boy meets girl? He prostrates himself before the
"weaker" sex and crawls on his belly to the lady. He has to work
hard at it before he becomes accepted, and then, but for only
two weeks of the year during the rut, the male becomes dominant over the female.

This brings us to how communication between animals is
achieved and the principles that it follows. The preceding
pages touched on a good number of attributes of communication, albeit not in a manner designed to clarify how it is
made possible, which form it takes, and what it communicates.

In looking at the actions of rams we can quickly pick out several patterns that are defined as threats. Threatening actions
are simply the first movements of an attack, or in other words
they are an uncompleted attack. The animal signals what it may
do (attack) by performing a part—sometimes only a very small
part—of the action. Since sheep have only one weapon, their

Old ram delivering the full clash force with one horn. He has managed to get ahead, swings around and clashes heavily on the challenging youngster.

heads and horns, the threat takes the form of an intended movement to butt, or, if the intention is to clash, it takes the form of rising on the hind legs first, inclining the head, and dropping again on all fours. We can call this the category of weapon threats. Animals with several kinds of weapons, such as moose, who may fight with antlers, front legs, or hind legs, have appropriate threats for each weapon. Another very general weapon threat is the rush threat, in which the animal makes a short rush in the direction of the opponent, again implying grievous harm. The weapon threats, excepting perhaps the rush threat, are probably recognized as such after a recipient has experienced the consequences of not heeding them. They are sharp threats and usually draw quick responses. The rush threat may take advantage of the emotions of fright generated by a large, rapidly approaching object—like the feeling of standing close to a track and facing an onrushing train or being buzzed by a low-flying aircraft. The threats, in addition to being visually terrifying, may be accompanied by sounds from the animal which are usually unharmonic, loud, choppy, and generally "startling" and "frightening." Odors may be noticeable during a weapon threat, but their effect in communication is far from clear as yet. The threats thus play a visual, auditory, and olfactory part, and, if not heeded, may terminate in a most painful and unpleasant tactile form of communication—a butt, kick, slap, stab, or bite!

Thus communication runs in channels—vision, touch, hearing, smell, heat sense, and, in some animals such as several families of fish, the electric sense. Each signal has modulations, and we find that opposite goals have opposite kinds of modulations. We call this, after Darwin, *antithesis* or *the law of the opposite*. For example, in addressing rivals, males use the opposite modulations from those used to address females. For the rival, the tactile message is likely to be a sudden, nonrhythmic, high-energy stimulus (the scientific description of a kick in the pants), while to the female it is a gentle, rhythmic, gradual, low-energy tactile stimulus (tickling, nibbling, caressing, licking). The auditory message to the rival or predator is likely to be loud, unharmonic, sudden, and arhythmic, but to the female it will be low in intensity, harmonic, and rhythmic. The visual message to the rival will contain elements of superior size and height, a display of weapons, pronounced movements—either very slow and stiff or very fast—but to the female the message is likely to de-emphasize height, size, weapons, or power. The motions of the courting male may well be the very opposite to those in threat. We know too little of odors in communication to make anything but wild guesses at the principles that govern their use. It may be that the pungent odors used toward rivals also attract females if used in small dosages.

Another group of actions, the dominance displays or rank signals, are so important that we must treat them separately later. Sufficient to say that such displays are stimuli that *remind* a subordinate of his position, and, by reminding him of the last beating he got, keep him in his place. These are by far the most common signals. They are pervasive through repetition, so that the message is not lost on the receiver, even though he may not react to it. They are also pervasive by virtue of being transmit-

Mounting by young rams; the larger mounts the smaller in asserting his dominance

ted simultaneously on several channels of communication. Pervasiveness makes the message unambiguous through repetition, or through saturation of the senses, by sending stimuli with the same meaning in support of each other. In case "dominance displays" does not ring a bell, "bragging" or "showing off" should; both are rank displays—so is humility.

A surprising attribute of animal behavior is the clarity of the signals. They are quite unambiguous—even the subtle ones. Even humans react with discomfort to someone who is neither hot nor cold, who cannot make up his mind and who frustrates any attempts to gain clarity of understanding. To a female elk in the company of a harem bull, ambiguous signals from the bull are suicidal. Picture the bull who does not signal clearly that he comes to herd the cow. The cow remains a split second too long and consequently is raked by the sharp antlers of the bull before she can escape. Such a blow can kill or maim. Even if the bull has bred the cow, if he herds sloppily he may wound the mothers of his own progeny. He would leave fewer offspring than a bull who herds clearly. Conversely, a bull that courts sloppily enough to raise doubts about his intentions may chase females for a long time with little breeding in return. He, too, will raise few offspring compared to the dashing, clearly courting male. A male who raises doubts about his intentions is likely to have to run much more after females—a process that costs him precious stored energy. During the rut, a bull feeds little, living mainly off his fat depots that he acquired in summer. Every extra run after the females costs additional calories and melts the fat off his back. However, every ounce of fat he can save increases the bull's chances for survival during the long, cold winter that closely follows the rutting season. Therefore, the less the bull runs, the less fat he loses and the better are his chances of living and breeding another year. The more sloppily he courts, the more he runs, and the less likely is his survival through winter. It is quite evident that a bull's chances of breeding and survival are increased if his courting intentions are unmistakable.

The elk accomplishes his courtship in a very direct manner, by showing the female what she is about to experience—namely, being licked. Flicking his tongue in and out of his mouth, the bull approaches, and, upon reaching the female, he at once begins licking her croup. Here, the same principle in communication is followed as in the weapon threats—the animal signals his intentions by performing part of the act.

Many principles as well as particulars in the rules of conduct of mountain sheep have been covered here. What we have not answered is, why there are all these rules in the first place. What is the behavior good for? It appears that the behavior forms and maintains a predictable social environment for the individual, effectively removing or at least reducing uncertainty, or anxiety. Uncertainty leads to stress and has produced ulcers in monkeys. Social uncertainty in chickens can be induced by creating huge flocks or by introducing strange chickens into a flock. This is also a good way to make chickens lose appetites and weight, to stop laying eggs, and to grow faulty feathers. And all these consequences can be the result of merely introducing *one* strange chicken into a flock once in a while. When rams meet strangers they, too, grow excited, and seasons of major movements such as spring and fall are excellent for observing severe combat among strange rams. Aggression does settle the rank of each individual; threats continue to remind the subordinate of the consequences of revolt against dominants, and appeasement signals allow the dominant to live in predictable security. All benefit from a rank order, whether the larger or the smaller, for all can convert essential resources into growth and reproduction rather than waste it in strife.

We can equate many actions of animals as being activities that create knowledge on the basis of which an individual may act in everyday life or in crisis. When a strange area is reached, the individual explores it; his "curiosity" is aroused, which means no more and no less than that he is exploring. In so doing, the exploring mammal repeatedly moves from the known to the unknown area, and ends exploration after having covered each nook and cranny several times. In "play," the young animal can harvest experience most worthwhile in later life, be it in learning how to evade pursuers, in learning how to scale cliffs or trees well, or in learning how to fight, and how to avoid pain and trauma. In short, the animal is *programmed* during play to do those things that can aid it to escape predators, to defeat rivals, and to act instantly on the basis of stored knowledge without having to figure out a new set of behavior rules when danger looms. Soldiers are drilled for much the same purposes, to make them obey and act—unthinkingly. The key phrase in all this is *predictability of environment,* be it physical or social. Human beings have not escaped such a need either, as the therapeutic value of an orderly, predictable, daily routine in the presence of friends and neighbors reminds us. A very tiny touch of uncertainty or unpredictability is stimulating and delightful; a little heresy is cherished; a major departure, however, from an orderly routine, from society, or from one's *Weltanschauung,* is upsetting. Why do some of us long for the place of our youth? For the forests, the village, the brook, the lake, the winding dusty road through the fields, the old church, the school, or what have you? Why do you think a transplanted mountain sheep released in unfamiliar mountains takes off and wanders on and on? He, too, is looking for home.

7

The Bear and the Bicycle

𝓘 It had been a long night by the time I laid down the philosophy book and turned out the lamp to go to sleep. I
stretched out my tired limbs in my big, down-filled sleeping bag
in happy anticipation of sleep to come. Then my ears caught a
sound coming from the darkness outside the cabin's wall. Footsteps! I froze instantly into immobility. The steps in the rustling
leaves came closer, directly toward the cabin. I quickly dismissed the thought of man. I was alone. My closest neighbors
were forty miles away, and they would hardly pay me a visit at
1:00 A.M. Moreover, no one would be fool enough to approach
a lone cabin without shouting from a quarter of a mile off.

The footsteps could only come from a bear. Grizzly? Black
bear? Neither was welcome. The cabin's door was flimsy. I did
not relish shooting in the dark, either. The muzzle flash was
certain to blind me momentarily, and no second shot would be
possible. I had no flashlight. Among all the packages sent by
the Hudson's Bay Company, the one with flashlights and batteries was missing.

Now the steps had reached the cabin. I yelled loudly, jumped
out of the sleeping bag, ran to the lamp, pumped it up,
searched for matches—continuing my yelling—lit the lamp,
grabbed the rifle, flipped a cartridge into the chamber, and
then headed for the door. I could see nothing outside, at least

as far as the lamp's light could reach. All was silent. The wind whispered in the big white spruce in front of the cabin—that was all. I looked around. Then I got up my courage and walked around the cabin. Nothing. Satisfied that the bear had fled, I went back inside, replaced the rifle on its hook, shut off the lamp, crept inside the warm bag, and promptly went to sleep.

Bang, crash, bang. . . . I jumped out of the bag and yelled. A thunderous crashing echoed from somewhere outside the cabin. I grappled for the lantern, pumped it up, fumbled for matches, lit it, grabbed the rifle, flipped a cartridge into the chamber, and again headed for the door. What a sight greeted me! My meat house, a small flywire-covered construction that stood below the big spruce, had been tipped over, and both moose haunches lay beside it. The big racket had been caused by empty naphtha cans I had stored on top of the meat house. They had come tumbling down as the bear tipped the house over, and the noise had probably spooked him.

It was clear to me that the bear would return—and I swore under my breath that I would be ready for him. First, I turned off the lamp, then I dragged my armchair in front of the door, donned my parka and insulated underwear, stuck my feet into felt boots—it was a chilly October night—put the loaded rifle over my knees, and waited.

The night was black. Even an hour later I could barely make out the outlines of the big spruce tree forty feet away. With that much light around, the bear would probably have to lick my face before I was aware of his presence. If I hit him poorly with my first shot, I would be temporarily blinded and for the next shot would not be able to aim in the proper direction. I felt distinctly uncomfortable. After two hours of vigil, the cold air was the only thing that prevented me from falling over from fatigue, and it caused me to shiver. Finally I quit. I stood up, walked to the meat house, placed a half dozen empty five-gallon cans on top of it and returned to the cabin. If the bear returned, he would have to move those cans to get at the meat. I removed my parka, crawled into the bag, and once more fell asleep. Since the bear had not come back for two hours, maybe he would not come at all.

When I awoke, the sun was shining from a blue sky through my little cabin window. I had slept soundly indeed. It was a beautiful morning. I stretched myself and—bang, crash, bang. . . . I was out of my sack like greased lightning and snatched the rifle on the fly. As I leaped through the door, the rifle bolt clicked, and my eyes caught a black object moving behind the wood pile. Three jumps further and I saw him clearly. A medium-sized black bear. "Bang" went the rifle, and the bear was dead. I breathed a deep sigh of relief and began to examine him. He was a young bear with an unusually thick and beautiful pelt. After I had completed my examination and skinned him, I looked at the carcass and pondered. Up to that time I had never eaten bear. The meat looked very good. Indians ate it. The Tartars prized smoked bear hams as a delicacy. Maybe I should save his meat as well. I had only two moose haunches left, and I was rapidly depleting them. So, I hung the haunches and massive forequarters in the meat house alongside the moose quarters. The bear had come to eat my meat supply, but I would now eat him—so I mused—and went on with my work.

However, I never did acquire an appetite for bear steaks. It was a strange meat. A deep cut would soon turn crimson—probably as oxygen molecules attached themselves to the myoglobin in the meat. When I cut off a steak, one side would appear normal in color, while the other looked crimson, as though painted with lipstick, and although the fried meat tasted all right, it was a bit greasy. Despite strenuous reasoning with myself, I could swallow only a bite or two before giving it up.

As the weeks went by, I looked with apprehension on my dwindling supply of moose meat. It would never last until February, when I would terminate my stay here. The moose meat had been the gift of American hunters in September and was packed about eight miles on horseback to the cabin. Moose were rare in the near vicinity of Gladys Lake. Although I could have taken a moose any day about eight to ten miles away from the cabin, it would have been very difficult to bring the meat back, and I would have lost many valuable days which I needed for the study. I kept my eyes open for a moose or caribou close to the cabin, but no favorable opportunity arose. Each day brought me closer to eating bear meat, and I knew that I would soon have to find an alternative.

I could not shoot a sheep or goat because these were my study animals. Besides, I knew each one as an individual, and they had grown dear to me; the thought of eating them was about as cheerful as contemplating eating a friend. Finally, however, I discovered two big strange rams and a small group of females that did not belong to my band of study animals. They had settled down about six miles from the cabin on a mountain rarely visited by sheep. About three days following my discovery, a snowstorm again interrupted my research, and I decided I might as well go and try to get one of these strange rams. It was a tough climb. The snow was deep, and it was a long way up to the sheep. Whenever my strength threatened to falter and tire, the thought of eating bear drove me on.

Presently, I reached timber line and waded out on top of the long ridge which curved around a cirque glacier and melted into the big mountain beyond. I had not seen the sheep during my climb, because the storm had been blowing without interruption. I wondered if I would even locate them in the flying snow. However, the snow did stop for a brief period, revealing the two rams about half a mile away on the ridge. They were moving toward me and went out of sight into a dip. I moved quickly ahead and readied my rifle. I had barely reached the big snowdrift where I expected to get a good view of the country beyond when the horns of the first ram emerged above the snowdrift. I raised the rifle and held the ram in the scope. It was an unforgettable sight. An old ram with rugged and massive, but not overly long, horns was returning my stare. He flipped backward at the shot's impact and scarcely kicked. Elated, I stumbled forward. However, with each approaching step the ram shrank in size. When I stood beside him I could not believe my eyes. I had taken a dwarf—a diminutive little old ram. Quickly I counted his horn rings. He was fourteen years old, an ancient fellow. Unbelieving, I took a tape from my pocket and measured the horns. They were undamaged and measured all of 32½″ in length, with a basal circumference of 12¼″. This was incredibly small! In the white snow dunes and blowing snow this dwarf had fooled me. Had he been of average body size only, this would have been a ram with enormous horns. Eventually I recovered from my surprise and began to take stock of the situation. It was now afternoon, and I was a long way from the cabin. The ram lay at the edge of a cliff. It occurred to me that I could save myself the trouble of packing the animal down to the level. A snow chute descended beside me. If I were to throw the ram into the chute, I could pick him up a couple of hundred yards below. So, I dragged the ram to the chute and dropped him, and he slid down as expected. As he gathered speed, he began to roll and bounce, and suddenly he flew up and sideways and landed on a small ledge beside the chute where he came to a sudden halt. He must have hit a rock which deflected his plunge off course into that snow pocket, and there he lay. I could find no way—up or down—to the ram despite intense searching. He had come to rest in an inaccessible spot. In short, I ate the bear.

That small, old ram, however, had started a ball rolling. Why had he lived so long? He had reached an exceptional age for a wild sheep. I had been puzzled for some time why I had no heavy-horned rams among my study animals more than eight years of age. Among the younger rams there were plenty with long annual segments and thick horns; why were such rams not present in the old-age segment? There was F-ram. At seven years of age he had horns at least forty inches in length, bigger than those of all the older rams. Could it be that rams with vigorous horn growth died earlier than rams with poor horn growth? At once I realized that that was my answer. Yes, indeed, and I also thought I knew why. Because vigorous, large-horned rams rut earlier in life, they spend themselves into bankruptcy chasing females and rivals, and, without adequate fat depots, they succumb to the harsh winter following the rut. In contrast, however, the less vigorous rams, prevented from breeding, are less active, feed and rest, save energy, and live to rut another year. If that were so, clearly the rams that die before the average death age should have larger horns than those that die after the average death age. That was a nice hypothesis, but untestable, since I had far too few skulls from rams that had died naturally; so I dismissed the theory.

I would probably never have remembered that hypothesis had it not been for the green bicycle that I took to Banff National Park. I had no car-driver's license, because there had been little use for a car in my life until then. At the university we lived in dormitories and, since it was only a short walk through the woods each day to reach campus, a car was superfluous. When out in the wilds, I relied on my legs to get me where I wanted to go, and a car was of no use anyway. In short, there had been no stimulus for me to use a car; consequently, I learned to drive at an unusually late age by North American standards. In Banff National Park a fire road bisected the study area and, since the valleys were much wider than in the Cassiars, and distances between the mountains were greater, I thought that a bicycle, a green one, would be just what the doctor ordered.

It was a nice bicycle. The moving parts were well oiled, and it was a delight to pedal—on pavement. My plans had not included several common attributes of fire roads, namely: deep mud after rains, deep ruts when it did not rain, and big stones that were designated as "gravel." The somersaults I executed when traveling that road on my sturdy new bike would have been welcome acts in any circus program. The spills would have mattered little, but the lack of progress in covering the big land did matter. In early summer, my sheep moved out, and I was stuck in the valley, for it took much time hiking or bicycling to reach the distant mountains, thus causing me to lose touch with my study animals. Had I owned a car I could have picked up contact with them easily. During one of my desperate cycling-hiking-searching sessions I suddenly came upon the scattered skeleton of a bighorn ram directly in my path. The horns were not very large for an old ram, and, following habit, I began counting the age rings. The ram was sixteen years old—a record! This was the oldest ram I had found up to that time and, curiously, he was a relatively small-horned animal. At once my mind flashed back to the time more than a year ago when I had taken the dwarf Stone's ram, and I knew that I had my work cut out. During the whole summer, I searched each cut and valley and accumulated forty-three usable ram heads. While I found many more remains of dead rams, most of their horns had split and rotted and yielded no measurements. I had to know if rams with poor horn growth died, on the average, later than rams with good horn growth. My friends in the Warden Service, in particular Frank Coggins, added several heads, which they found on patrol, to my collection. When fall came I did have the answer. Rams that died before they had reached the average life span indeed had horn growth superior to rams that lived beyond the average life span. It was the breeding rams that died early—the ones that exhausted themselves chasing females.

8

The Great Game

✎ The study of animals does show what animals aspire to most. It is not sex. Not by a long shot. That's second best, at best. Some would consider it to be a quite satisfactory second prize, which undoubtedly it would be, were it not that the second prize goes to the same winner as the first. So does the third, fourth, fifth, and so on. The rules of the game dictate that the winner takes the cake, and the losers get the crumbs— maybe. It is true that he who has, gets, no matter how much we may detest and cry about nature's injustice. It is all very sad.

The "best" is difficult to talk about. We identify it directly with no word in our language. This is less than helpful. We nevertheless recognize it in bits and pieces and attach all sorts of names to it: power, dominance, self-esteem, bravado, ego, rank, individual worth, status. . . . Maybe we cannot define the "best" adequately, since it is found in contradictory situations, and we recognize it in its diverse pieces without acknowledging that it is really one and the same. We may call it, "It." We find It in instincts of animals and in the culture of man; It makes saints and charlatans; It makes martyrs and murderers; It is the spoils of the victor and the final triumph of the vanquished or condemned; It can be arrogance and It can be humility; It makes leaders but also followers; It is the driving force of cultures, technologies, the arts, bird songs, philosophies, music, nuptial colors, the development of plumed helmets and frocks; It is the prerogative of kings and the achievement of paupers; It makes men choose death over life; It makes us deny reason, or use it for It's sake; It makes youngsters grow well and keeps adults vigorous, sane, and healthy; It is desired, ridiculed, loved, hated, sung about, cursed, eulogized, and hidden; It is common to mice and men, elephants, dogs, fish, and fowl, in short, to everything that runs, breathes, kicks, sings, stinks, and lives. One may throw up one's hands in despair trying to grapple with so messy, diverse, and all-embracing an entity. "It" will not be easy to pin down, but the effort may well be worthwhile. It is the essence of the game that living things play, including ourselves. At first, though, I must continue to talk in riddles.

There is a game that living things play—an ancient game, as old as life itself. In this game the players usually do not know the outcome. They have no means by which to adjust their strategies toward winning. They die ignorant of their success or failure as well as of their reasons for playing the game. The players—even the successful ones—do not maximize personal gain but expose themselves to mortal dangers and exercise diligent toil; and yet they play, and play, and play. . . .

The rules of the game are very simple: anything goes—as long as it increases the player's number of descendants. Note—the number of *descendants,* not the number of *children* born. This distinction is quite important, since a strategy that maximizes the number of children, but does not provide for their upbringing so that the children become successful adults, is a losing strategy. That's all there is to the rule.

Simple as the above may be, its consequences are everything but simple. The rule is manifest in countless strategies of life. Anything advantageous to the increase of descendants over *all* generations is incorporated into the genetic structure of individuals, be it related to body size, digestive physiology, coat color, antipredator strategy, combat technique, courtship display, bioenergetic efficiency, unambiguous communication, antigen response, mimicry, camouflage, healing mechanism, bluffing, deceit or whatever. The game is played with so many, and such diverse, means that the strategies are far beyond the mastery of any individual scientist. Myriad scientists are employed to develop knowledge of life strategies, or organisms and their systems, where they are formalized in many disciplines of the life sciences. Unfortunately, the elementary simplicity of the game is easily overlooked when studying the complexity of strategies designed to win in the game. Consequently, the major message that the life sciences have to make is lost in the din of noise generated in discord by all disciplines. One message that the game, the Great Game, has for us is that organisms—including man—are structured to compete with one another, and that they exercise their means of competition continuously. They have been *programmed* to do so and act unconsciously in line with the rule of the Great Game—unconsciously, because every unconscious heritable attribute that helped individuals win has been passed on in the genotype and has spread rapidly throughout the species. As a result, the unconscious heritable attributes of the various players have quickly spread and mingled to reinforce each other in the genotypes of their descendants, while the less successful heritable combinations remained behind in the dead bodies of the losers. After all, the genes of a successful individual are the combination of genes of 256 individuals eight generations ago, 512 individuals nine generations ago, and 1,024 individuals ten generations ago—assuming no inbreeding. Conversely, if an individual's descendants are just able to replace themselves, his genome is split 1,024 times, ten generations hence. From this it is evident how quickly a favorable attribute can spread and how quickly several heritable attributes can mingle in succeeding generations. For billions of years our ancestors have been shaped by the rules of the Great Game, and you and I are still slaves to these rules. No matter how outdated the means of intraspecific competition are for us, we continue to exercise them. Before illustrating how some of our actions continue to comply with the rules of the Great Game, we must look more closely at those individuals who are winners in the game.

Winners in the Great Game possess three attributes: the ability to insure continuous access to resources in short supply, to use resources in short supply frugally, and to choose only mates who are also likely to be winners in the Great Game. The rules of the Great Game dictate that females should fall for superior, dominant, males and be attracted by their displays of superior masculinity, for the females' male children will be more likely to be social successes than if they are fathered by socially inferior males. Conversely, in species which raise few children, males should fall for females displaying attributes of superior motherhood, be it in physical shape or in behavior. After all, it follows that a female whose hormonal mechanisms are mixed up is not likely to be feminine-looking nor likely to be anything but a mixed-up mother. Secondary female sexual characteristics, which are very sensitive to hormones in their development, attract males; this is fortunate, for, ultimately, such attraction presages good care for the males' offspring. The winner in the Great Game is one who insures for himself or herself more than an equal share of resources, who breeds only with a highly desirable mate, or who breeds and protects more than an equal share of desirable mates. The winner is an individual with better-than-average abilities to compete, to raise children, and to use resources efficiently—even if it means his own early death, or the death of those closely related to him. Altruism is well developed in some animal societies, but it is blind altruism, subservient to the rules, and is practiced on behalf of individuals closely related to one another—and thus of a similar genotype—and with decreasing frequency on behalf of individuals increasingly distantly related. By sacrificing themselves, individuals insure that "their" genotype spreads through the reproduction of their next of kin. For example, the honeybee: the little worker descends with thousands of co-workers from one queen and is of the same genotype, by and large, as her co-workers. Her sting is fatal to herself, for when she stings, the act of stinging tears out her entrails. But by stinging and dying, the honeybee usually insures life and success to the occupants of her hive, her "sisters," "brothers," and "mother."

The first requirement for success in the Great Game is the ability to insure a greater-than-equal share of resources. Generally, this means that the successful player somehow displaces the less successful one. Displacement can be accomplished by overt aggression, but overt aggression has many drawbacks. It costs a lot of energy, it risks wounding and even death, it weakens the aggressor, thus reducing his ability to tackle the next fight successfully. In short, overt aggression is not the best means to insure access to a scarce resource. Yet it is and must remain the ultimate means. Typically, we find that individuals sort themselves in the order of their combat ability, in a so-called dominance hierarchy. The most dominant individuals generally have almost unhindered access to contested resources and mates, while the most subordinate have lesser, if any, access. Dominance is achieved and insured by overt aggression, but it is maintained by other means. A dominant individual tends to use less dangerous means to solidify his status, such as the threat of violence and a variety of subtle, indirect means. Toward subordinates, as well as strangers of equal size, he employs signs that advertise rank. He acts like a "superior." He uses symbols to signal his status.

These symbols advertise the bearer's physical prowess, his ability to protect females from harassment by lesser males, his priority of access to prized possessions—such as nesting sites, feeding areas solely for his use as well as for the mate he will select—his willingness to stand battle if need be, and the fact that he is already a proven winner.

The means by which an individual signals its status are called dominance displays, and the rules in both animal and human societies are much the same. In animal dominance displays, size, height, mass, vigor, virility, and possession of weapons (as well as their noisy use) are pointedly emphasized. In addition, specific sounds, motions, and odors are associated with the dominance displays, the purpose of which—teleologically speaking—is to provide as many stimuli as possible with which dominance can be associated by the onlooker. It is most important to note that, in dominance displays, animals do not use weapons in threat. That is, they do not point weapons at the onlooker in a fighting manner. Instead, the weapons are put out for show; they are displayed to their best advantage. In human terms, positioning the tip of a sabre at an opponent's throat is a threat, but decorating the sabre with tassels and inlays and rattling it in a colorful scabbard is a display. This distinction between a threat and a display is vital; the first is direct aggression; the second is implied aggression. The distinction between the two is practiced in animal societies.

The most consistent trait of dominance displays is implication. It is seen when opponents shred a shrub or small tree with antlers, horns, or tusks, or when they horn the ground causing pieces of sod to fly high or dust to rise skyward. In such demonstrations, the subordinate or rival who caused the display, and to whom it is being addressed, is pointedly ignored by the dominant. This is a second rule of dominance display in higher vertebrates: the dominant acts as though he were ignoring the subordinate. He looks away from the subordinate and does not approach him directly; in short, he pretends to be unaware of the subordinate's presence—outside of an occasional glance at him. This characteristic of dominance displays has cost the lives of zoo keepers who were attacked because they were unaware that an ungulate was addressing them in a serious manner even when it looked away and did not approach them directly. Dominance displays are usually meaningless to the uninitiated. Since these displays imply aggression, they are often subtle signals which a novice human onlooker easily overlooks or misinterprets—despite the fact that dominance displays are anything but inconspicuous.

The emphasis on size is achieved by means of a body orientation in which the animal's outlines are made to appear largest to the onlooker. This is usually a broadside orientation. In addition, the silhouette may be "framed" by enlarging special skin outgrowths (such as dewlaps in cattle or some antelope); by raising special long hairs along the neck and back; by raising the tail to which long hairs are attached (as can be seen in the yak); by spreading the body (as best exemplified by the varanid, a large, lizardlike reptile which spreads its rib cage); by fanning feathers and fins (as is well illustrated in numerous birds and fishes); by inflating air sacs (as found in some reptiles and birds, and in camels and the Mongolian gazelle); or by rising as high as possible above ground on stiltlike legs and arching the

A dominant ram insulting a subordinate ram by kicking at him with a front leg. This is a pattern rams show to females they court. The larger is thus shown courting the subordinate. The latter accepts the insult.

back; in short, by using as many means as available to increase the apparent height, size, or mass of the animal.

In addition, the animal's colors, shade patterns, hair outgrowths and movements are such during the dominance displays that an artist would immediately recognize in them the very principles of attention-guidance and attention-fixation that he employs in painting. That is, the animal's exterior is structured so as to catch the onlooker's attention and to guide his eye unerringly over the animal's exterior in such a fashion that he notices the displayer's size and mass. If the animal assumes a broadside display, the arrangement of spots, stripes, and hair tufts, and the movement of tail, ears, belly, and feet may be such that an onlooker cannot fail to shift his attention back and forth from quiver, to spot, to stripe, to movement; in short, to look at the whole animal. Fritz Walther, a great ethologist and antelope expert, pointed out very well how stripes of color may be arranged in social antelopes to "frame" the body and, in so doing, make it highly conspicuous. Here we have, in essence, the biological basis of art. The "ornaments" and colors we so often admire are there to be looked at, not by us—mind you—but by the rivals and mates of the animal.

Since animals quickly habituate to common occurrences and thereafter pay scant attention to them, it is obvious that, in a dominance display, an animal must seek attention by doing something unusual. In some species, this takes the form of an exaggeration, such as an exaggeratedly stiff and slow walk, giving the appearance of a musclebound animal. Conversely, in other species, the individual moves exaggeratedly fast during the display—again, to catch attention with this unusual behavior. Normally, an animal's everyday motions are relaxed, as is its stance. By departing from this norm, by moving slowly, proudly, and ponderously—as well as by other attention-getting means—the animal in a dominance display stands out above its surroundings.

When weapons are emphasized in dominance displays— though not all such displays emphasize weapons—they are shown in such a fashion as to accentuate their size to the subordinate. In mountain sheep, the horns are displayed frontolaterally, that is, halfway between a side and a front view. In deer with palmated antlers, such as those of fallow deer, caribou, or moose, the palmated parts are shown to their best advantage to the rival or subordinate. The displaying buck or stag twists the head and neck so as to give the opponent the benefit of a very good look at the headgear. Indeed, this is beneficial to both the rival or the subordinate, for the combat potential of these animals is well reflected in their horn or antler size.

The weapons—horns, antlers, tusks, or teeth—may also be exercised for the benefit of onlookers. In deer, sheep, cattle, antelope, rhinos, and elephants a dominant male may shred trees and rip up soil in a display before a rival. As well as weapon exercises, the displaying males may also perform feats of vigor, such as the peculiar jumps and "bucking" of displaying gnu bulls, or the leaps and treetop-shaking performed by rhesus monkeys.

In addition, the male may combine implied threat in the

A large ram, left, blocking the way to a smaller ram. The smaller ram angles his chin downward in threatening to butt; the larger displays, apparently quite undisturbed by the smaller's threat.

dominance display with a sexual exhibition which takes the form of erections. In old-world monkeys, such erections lead to colorful, showy displays, partly because the genitals are well colored, and partly because displaying dominants make these genitalia conspicuous. In ungulates, only old-world deer and a few antelope have reasonably showy sexual displays during dominance presentations.

Thus far, the visual aspects of dominance displays have been emphasized, but there are olfactory (or odorous) and auditory (or audible) ones as well. In mammals, dominant individuals often mark themselves more than do subordinates, or vocalize in a characteristic manner. Thus a dominant often not only looks like one, he also sounds and reeks like one. Be it in daylight or darkness the status of the dominant is revealed to all companions, whether they like it or not.

We have met the "It." Crudely put, It is a psychic state, a value judgment of superiority that an individual animal possesses, and which he displays in many ways. It is, in every form, pure advertisement, but in the animal world, such advertisements are likely to be backed to the hilt with real performance. The animal unleashes all means to deliver the message that it is Number One: attention fixation and guidance; mimicry of stimuli associated with danger; use of many channels of communication; repetition of messages to reinforce them; use of actions that conspecifics do not habituate to; and employment of stimuli that rely on phase contrast, which are highly memorable to onlookers and can be associated with danger. The individual must use all these means so that his message rises above the noises and smells of the surroundings—above the "averageness" of his surroundings. In cases of doubt, that is, when encountering a stranger, the individual follows what is probably the best strategy—he acts as if he were Number One.

At the animal level, the advertisement of It is quite unsophisticated—by human standards. We recognize its value, however. We know from animal experiments that individuals of high rank are physically healthier than those of low rank and are less likely to fall victim to diseases. They grow better, and raise more and healthier offspring, but they may also die sooner, due to the wear and tear entailed in being superior—as in mountain sheep and ibex, for instance.

In humans, It manifests itself culturally, and, due to the complexity of human cultures, is difficult to recognize. Secondly, it is difficult to recognize the manifestations of It, that is, the superiority displays, when they are being performed, either by oneself or by others. To put it bluntly, if one is pissing, one knows it, but if one is "windbagging," "cutting up," or "playing a dandy" one usually does not. The more subtle the superiority display, the more difficult it is to spot—or to admit to oneself. Unfortunately, self-esteem and dominance displays are often so closely linked that to spoof a person's put-on may cut and insult him deeply. We have little difficulty recognizing It when it is displayed crudely, such as in military uniforms and mannerisms. The insignia, campaign ribbons, medals, orders, sashes, epaulets, plumes, tassels, salutes, goose steps, and so on, are there for an obvious reason and have an evolutionary history quite similar to that of display organs in animals. We owe this insight to the detailed, fascinating work of Dr. Otto Koenig of Vienna; he is our first "cultural-ethologist." He also recognized what we may call the "rule of the flip." Thus, by and large, the rank of an individual is directly related to the gaudiness of his dress. The more medals, tassels, plumes, and so on, the higher the rank of an officer. The rule of the flip sets in when gaudiness—or any attribute of a fashion—has gone to the utmost permissible limits, and when more medals, more sashes, more plumes, more tassels, add little to increase the visual distinction of the bearer and become a burden instead. At this point the real dominant, the top dog, or even the group of top dogs, abandons gaudiness entirely and flips back to simplicity. The real dominants contrast themselves with their surroundings—and in particular with their immediate subordinates—not by becoming more colorful, but by becoming the reverse.

Such a move is clever, Koenig points out. Does not the real leader look like the common man? Does it not indicate that a common man, or common men, are in charge of it all?

We can see the rule of the flip operate in fashions. The miniskirts rose to a level beyond which the word "skirt" lost its meaning. There was no further up to go. So, down went the hems of the skirts again, but not gradually. They zoomed all the way to the ankles to become maxis. The fashion flipped.

The rule of the flip is not the only screen that prevents one from seeing the manifestations of It at once. Common to the dominance displays of animals and men is demonstration of superior status by *implication*. In *all* instances it is implication of superiority. Sometimes, such as during military parades at which the latest functional military hardware is displayed, the implication is too obvious to describe. The space race, with its glittering technology and internationally acclaimed successes, is only slightly less obvious in its implications. Now that the points have been made by the space race, politicians are somewhat less convinced of the validity of the reasons they once gave in supporting the space venture. Less obvious still, yet recognizable to the initiated, is the implication in the following demonstration. After the Maxim's machine gun—the first dependable single-barreled gun used by troops on all fronts in World War I—was invented, it was demonstrated in England before the Chinese Imperial Ambassador. For His Highness's benefit and contemplation, a sizeable oak tree was cut off with the new wonder weapons. Thereafter, of course, the dignitaries had their picture taken with the fallen tree and machine gun. His Imperial Highness could probably not help but ponder what the new weapon meant to China's foreign and internal policies. In these three examples, military superiority in one form or another is implied. However, implications in dominance displays of our species may aim at a superiority in matters other than aggression, thus obscuring the manifestation of It somewhat.

International sporting events aim obliquely at superiority in combat but may aim even more directly at superiority in national life styles. Notable in this respect are the hotly contested Olympic Games where it is not so much individual feats which are publicized as it is the number of medals won by various political blocs. An innocent who accepts the expressed purposes of the Olympic Games literally may wonder what logical connection exists between these aims and the widely exhibited national flags, national anthems, and national dress. The question remains whether it should not be only the winners' names that are proclaimed and the individuals who are honored for their sporting achievement.

Superiority is also implied by an alliance with success—and with the convenient forgetting of failures, unless, of course, a failure can somehow be transformed in the public eye into success. We may name this kind of change the "principle of transferal" and will encounter it later. The weapons, dress, insignia, flags, and behavior of soldiers offer rich documentation for implied superiority by alliance with success. The battle flags of regiments are inscribed with past victories, implying more in the future, and conveniently create a regimental identity for the soldier. The uniform may be cut according to the style of an old, successful regiment or even the uniforms of militarily successful nations. Its colors and decorations may commemorate battalions that gained great distinctions. British rifle regiments take pride in their distinctive colors, their salutes, their rifle drill, their marching tempo, and the distinctions awarded them after historical battles. Often one does forget the reasons for some action, such as the salute. Who remembers that this military gesture of greeting was once the privilege of the feared, elitist Grenadiers and later spread to all troops? Dr. Otto Koenig's research on military uniforms produced myriad examples of how uniforms and military mannerisms follow successful examples, even those of former enemies.

Superiority is implied in life style, social systems, intrinsic worth, and so on, as when a nation, a region, a town, a village, or a family lists its famous soldiers, musicians, beauty queens, poets, writers, sportsmen, scientists, philosophers, philanthropists, and perhaps even its businessmen. At the individual level, superiority is implied in the famous friends one can allude to, the "contacts" one has, the well-known people one can invite to cocktail parties or dinners. We are only too familiar with "name-dropping." In Germany, a company turned this particular dominance display to its financial advantage: it rents TV personalities for private functions. In the display of one's friends, one sets the social level at which one expects to be treated.

Superiority is implied in the display—subtle or otherwise—of possessions, be it wealth, beautiful girls, race horses, or cars. In this we have developed considerable sophistication. We signal not only superiority, but also alliance to specific groups and their philosophy. "Keeping up with the Joneses" is a recognized phenomenon of middle-class North America. It is tied not only to a display of possessions, but also to orderliness and the possession of conventional skills, such as good lawn-keeping and gardening and expertise in house repairs and painting. At the highest levels of wealth—as at the highest level of political power—we again see "the rule of the flip" operating. Men of great wealth reduce their display and become quite inconspicuous. They may cherish this inconspicuousness—and the wide choice of camouflage their wealth permits.

The display of wealth may be tied to some sporting occupation, and competition for superiority may take place within specific, often exclusive, clubs, that is, clubs occupied with sailing,

horse racing, trophy hunting, trophy fishing, collecting of
various objects, sculptures, or painting. The competition may
reach irrational proportions—irrational and ludicrous to all but
the competitors: trophy hunting, for example, in which the
wealthy build museums to house their kills and great lodges to
hang the heads and hides of dead animals, write expensive
books for others of their kind on their exploits, meet in exclusive clubs to hobnob with politicians and princes, and make
films of their hunting trips. Some individuals, unfortunately,
are not even disinclined to break laws or pay high prices for
illegally killing endangered species that are protected on reserves or in National Parks. Some obtain trophies by shooting,
on private hunting preserves, aged animals bought from zoos
or game ranches.

In a similar vein, hobbies create opportunity for competition
and opportunity to be a recognized authority on something.
The subject matter is of little importance—what counts is the
recognition of others that one has achieved expertise and skill
in a particular area, whether it be rabbit raising, canary breeding, trapshooting, flower gardening, auto building, drag racing,
or what have you.

Superiority may be implied in many ways. There is alliance
with mythical powers to raise one's status; and there is alliance
with authority—be it with science, with ancient writings, or with
Dr. Spock. There is also alliance with age—a practice most
prevalent in Chinese philosophy—wherein alliance with an
older authority implied superiority. Somehow, these three
kinds of alliance are inseparable and reinforce each other. How
could anyone resist implementing practices proclaimed by the
Bible, verified by science, practiced by the ancients, and urged
by mature, world-wise men? Unfortunately, considerable mischief can be created by allusion to mythical powers. Although
priests and Jesus criers are obvious proponents of this, they
are, on the whole, rather harmless compared with other priests
who take advantage of the respect that ignorant persons have
for uncomprehended worldly abilities. What is not understood
is either eulogized or ridiculed; there is no middle ground. If
the uncomprehended is associated with complex, massive,

shiny machinery, or has been proclaimed as extremely difficult (or exceedingly promising) in a profound but obscure manner, then the uninitiated treats it seriously. Moreover, he is eager to climb on the bandwagon. The priests of the new gospel take the limelight. The bandwagon followers crowd in to be visible in the light of the stage, and the performance of human dominance displays, par excellence, begins. In the sciences, various cults, gospels, and fads appear and disappear from center stage. While the cult is on, social karma is gained by stuffing lectures, speeches, papers, notes, and articles with sufficient jargon appropriate to the cult, be it computer modeling, systems analysis, molecular biology, environmental pollution, or whatever. To keep an audience in awe, and in the dark, by speaking about something they could not possibly know or understand, is to make a display, to impress others with mythical powers. A company promoting its "systems capacities" does just that; an individual who says little about his work, but acts as if his audience fully understands him, also does it. Each listener is fooled into believing that the rest of the audience probably does know what the talk is all about, and he nods his head wisely. To ask questions would reveal one's inability to comprehend. So the game goes on. It is a good idea to cram one's addresses with the jargon of mysterious cults. Even better for one's prestige is to make a *minor* correction to one of the conventional wisdoms of the cult or, at a meeting, attack one of the high priests on a minor, quite insignificant detail of his gospel. All these tactics can frequently be seen at major scientific conferences. Persons unfamiliar with the new "wonder field" are led to assume that something incredibly important is happening, and those who ought to know better have a lot of vested interest in their social prestige, karma, and glory.

Some practice a minor version of the flip: they caution, they attempt to dampen extravagant hopes, and they point out the uncertainties. This is seen as modesty, becoming of great men, and is a demonstration of "superiority through humility." It may seem odd to consider humility as being a superiority display, but it is one, nevertheless, and as such becomes, of course, arrogance of a sort. Humility is indeed something only a very superior individual can afford. It can be observed in the actions of some very successful scientists of world renown and undoubtedly in other famous men as well. These humble individuals are exceedingly courteous and are very considerate and tolerant of the views of others, particularly of younger scientists. They will answer the most ridiculous questions with a straight face, will introduce students to colleagues as equals, are quick to admit their errors and will even dwell on their failings—in short, they are utterly charming, lovable, entertaining chaps. Why should they not be? Who is present to challenge their stature and achievements? These men are above and beyond meaningful challenge—and they know it.

Superiority, prestige, or social karma may be gained in any endeavor, either by winning or, if not by winning, then by having played the game right. This system rewards the loser as well as the winner, and the loser may maintain his sense of worth, if not his superiority. He lost, but so what? He played it right, fair and square. He acted like a sportsman. It was bad luck to lose; there were circumstances beyond his control; his wife had a baby; it was Friday the 13th; and so on. Adhering to some standards even in defeat, for instance, by performing feats of courage, skill, or endurance, can be used to turn defeat into a "moral victory." We may call this the rule of transferal; that is, by focusing attention on another aspect of the game, the loser celebrates a victory of sorts. Recent and past history records many examples. The British cherish Dunkirk as having been a great success due to the miraculous rescue of most of its army in a crushing defeat. The Germans have quite a few moral victories. They remember Stalingrad as having been a moral victory for their soldiers who went down to defeat against great odds and never surrendered; they recall the *Bismarck* for the heavy losses this battleship inflicted before she sank with flags flying; they eulogize their Luftwaffe for the hopeless odds it fought against; they laud the retreat from Italy in 1943–1944 because it was engineered by Kesselring and has become a classic of military strategy; they remember the "Great War" for the specialized armaments they developed too late for use in decisive battles and for the efforts of the civilian population under the stress of heavy bombing raids—moral victories all. Moral victories are the last glory of the vanquished, of the individual who is down, but not out.

Maintaining superiority by sticking to a role can be seen in another connection. The social karma of a person is enhanced by sticking to a role, be it ever so humble. If one is a servant, a cook, or a street sweeper, one can maintain a sense of worth and step up proudly if one's job is well done. Who is not likely to value and reward faithful servants, excellent cooks, or skilled artisans? This "role placement" requires that the individual adhere strictly to the mannerisms and dress of his role and that he play it unambiguously. A good cook is superior to a bad king, and infinitely more preferable.

The striving for status dictates much of our daily life. To be equal or better, to have as much or more, to be as daring as or more so, to be as wise or wiser, to be as humble or humbler, to be as feared, as admired, as attractive are hidden demands in many thoughts, words, or actions. Is it surprising, then, that journalists—in commenting on news and events—set themselves up as judge and jury over the words, concerns, or actions of men by far their superior? Is it surprising that reviewers of movies, concerts, operas, or books continuously find fault with what they review, and all too often criticize what they have not understood? Is it surprising that much of everyday conversation is concerned in harmonizing with someone on the faults of other persons, institutions, materials, performances, machinery, or games? By agreeing with a second party about the faults of a third, we reinforce our superior judgment and being, and satisfy our in-group requirement, as we shall see later. Even when we laugh heartily with someone, it may be at the expense of another's status. Humor is often status-degrading and, as such, is aggressive, is often a dominance display, and is worthy of closer attention in that context.

Wit and humor lie in the unexpected recognition of a familiar situation in which someone usually is short-changed. We are amused at oddly shaped people, who are then linked to something inferior. Our slick cartoons deform people in a manner that makes us chuckle; we laugh at the misfortunes befalling a circus clown and his ineffectual efforts to remedy a situation that, by normal standards, requires minimal mental and physical effort. Our mild jokes deal with small, excusable failings in others—excusable because we practice them ourselves, because we transgress on little taboos (the portly, well-married, older gentleman whose eyes stray a bit at the sight of pretty, mini-skirted legs). Our puns are amiable humor in which we suddenly recognize an absurdity (the priest, protesting to cannibals who are about to drop him into boiling water, "No, no, I am a friar"). Our ethnic jokes, debunking some unfortunate nationality, are hilarious to all but the affected nationality. Jewish jokes, of course, debunk somebody else and illustrate the cleverness of their own group. Our most ferocious jokes are reserved for enemies or persons hated for their great power, and relegate the despised to a status of contempt. Political jokes fall in this category. They allow us a chance to laugh at the stupidity and inadequacy of leaders. We cherish the surprise of seeing different symbolic situations reduced to the same level, pleased when someone of power and might whom we dislike is shown to be inferior to us. The famous Konrad Lorenz, Austrian ethologist, quite rightly recognized that there is something aggressive, even pain-inflicting, in laughter.

Our behavior is often intended to provide for us some kind of distinction or to reconfirm it. Some individuals, having failed to gain recognition in socially approved competitions, may switch to despised actions. If recognition cannot come through fame, then it must be attained through infamy. Just to capture attention—to be on everyone's lips, to see one's name in the papers, to appear on TV, to be discussed on radio—is a powerful urge. To hold some distinction is better than none at all. Being the local vagabond and greatest drunk is, after all, a distinction of sorts.

A reversal of values held by a dominant segment of society can be observed in countercultures and can also illustrate the law of the flip. The subculture, in rebellion against the dominant culture, gains distinction by adopting values diametrically opposed to those held by the dominant culture. This phenomenon could be observed in North America in the 1960s, wherein the subculture values adopted by youth were in strong contrast with establishment values. We can arrange them in pairs:

Establishment values	*Youth-culture values*
Short-hair styles	Long-hair styles
Clean-shaven faces	Bearded faces
Conformity in dress	Nonconformity in dress
Status-directed clothing, often expensive	Antistatus clothing, comprising cheap but comfortable garb
Sexual discipline	Sexual promiscuity
Aggressive, militaristic behavior	Submissive, antimilitaristic attitudes
Disciplined language	Undisciplined language; permissiveness
Family-oriented life	Solitary or commune-style living
Work ethic	Antiwork ethic
Artificially produced, prepared foods	Natural health foods, organically grown
Personal discipline	Personal freedom or permissiveness

These are superficial comparisons. The two cultures share more values than either is likely to admit. Nevertheless, there are sufficient differences between the two to be recognizable and to give a member of one culture distinction from the other. In so doing, identity and ego satisfaction are preserved, particularly to members of the counterculture which has, after all, no intrinsic values of its own, but derives them by inverting those of the dominant culture.

Where does this leave us? We began by striving to identify that which animals most aspired to. And It was the answer. All else follows. Bred into animals, and ourselves, is the command to compete with others of our kind, and we obey this command and will follow it to the end of our existence. We strive for status, recognition, and dominance, but due to the great importance of culture in the life of humans, our rank displays—our competition—have been shifted from the biological to the cultural realm. Consequently we have many, many channels in which to compete—and through which we may gain recognition. Nevertheless, our dominance, status, or superiority displays have a biological origin we can recognize in fellow creatures; they still serve a biological need that we may call ego satisfaction. Though we disdain any implication that threatens our status, we readily accept the most irrational claptrap that makes us look good or compares us favorably with some image our society applauds. Hence, we are biased by nature to compare ourselves to some idol, be it rational or not.

Ego satisfaction and superiority displays are by no means all negative. Distasteful they are, at times, and at other times, worse. The bravado displays of our young males, as witnessed in their use of noisy cars, cycles, offensive language, and signs, do belong to this category. True, these actions have far more than passing resemblance to the displays of chimpanzee males. It does not constitute unnatural behavior, however, blatantly offensive as such personal advertisement may be. These young males are only trying to "be somebody," and many will succeed in finding an activity in which they can make their mark. Again, dominance displays of a more subtle kind can be annoying at public meetings: when an egotist monopolizes the stage and pontificates on irrelevant points; when the critic plays opposition for the sake of hearing his own voice; when the "No" man, who believes this word is the prelude to his profound wisdoms, interjects an argument with no basis in fact. Of course there are other rules that govern meetings, but dominance displays are unfortunately an all too common phenomenon. Note that asking questions is confined to a few at such meetings. Understandably, most persons believe that asking questions could lead others to think that the questioner is a little simple-minded and has not grasped the argument. It is easier and safer for the ego to say "No." Agreement with the no-men—that is, disagreement—indicated by vigorous head nodding with a very serious mien, places one among the knowing, the wise. Agreement with a new point of view easily implies one's intellectual subordination to another. Convincing an opponent publicly is equivalent to his admitting inferiority publicly. Hence, one should not "convince" publicly. One convinces by befriending. Otherwise, one does not convince an opponent—one outlives him.

All in all, these are relatively minor inconveniences of ego satisfaction. There are greater hazards when ego satisfaction, in the form of face-saving, creates, maintains, and drags out wars, when it turns the toil of men to destruction, and when it falsifies and makes a mockery of their values.

As indicated earlier, we generally do not recognize or admit to ourselves the dominance we are putting on. However, once we recognize our displays it becomes embarrassing to put them on, for we know only too well that we are putting on an act. One cannot take one's own actions seriously. This does place us at a disadvantage, for far too often we are judged favorably on the basis of our dominance displays or put-ons. Despite the negative aspects, ego satisfaction is most worthwhile promoting, for it is central to what we can shamelessly cherish and enjoy.

Ego satisfaction is the reward of achievement and the driving force toward achievement. It provides cultural diversity and excellence; it stimulates the search for perfection by a search for recognition; it extracts the best in intellect and skill; it imposes discipline and the willingness to cooperate, and allows individuals to accept and endure hardships cheerfully. Without dominance displays there would be no art, no pageantry, no music, no architecture, no science, no poetry, and minimal courtship—if any. Of course there would be no wars, either.

If the actions of men are puzzling at times, it may still be comforting to note that they follow in their actions the laws that living things obey, and thus are not disobeying nature but are very much a part of it. Just as the nighthawk that buzzes over our well-lit cities on summer nights, as the bighorn prowls in the mountain crags, so are we bound to advertise our worth to those of our own kind. Man is very much a part of nature—a fact we may not be amiss to remember as we strive to alter the face of our sustaining planet.

9
Old Skook

ℐ The Canadian Rockies are home not alone to mountain sheep. For unexplained reasons, sheep have attracted the attention of a disproportionate share of peculiar characters, be they among the guides, outfitters, poachers, or biologists. The mountain sheep is, of course, hailed as North America's supreme trophy by big-game hunters, and its lore has long been steeped in an aura of mystique. This is one reason sheep attract men, and why sheep poaching now, as in the past, has been a profitable business. In years gone by, it sustained Banff poachers when the marten take was poor. For $50 a head they sold the horns of rams to a Banff museum, which in turn packed the heads into barrels and sent them on to New York. Today, sheep heads rate higher. One poaching ring in California netted about $150,000 during three years of operation. In Banff National Park the poachers were rugged men who plied their trade, in part, for sheer hellishness, and savored the pranks they played on the warden service. I knew several of them in years past. I had also met the man who headed the desert sheep-poaching ring in California just prior to the ring's exposure. He was the past-president of the Desert Bighorn Council, had been an active member of that society for the preservation of these relatively rare animals, was a taxidermist of notable skill, and a first-rate sculptor. His bronze bighorn rams will probably never vanish from my memory. The pursuit of the almighty dollar got him, that and the sleazy morality of the rich, influential clients he guided to the kill. One can only conjecture the fate of any of these poachers had they confronted one man of quite different mettle—a man whose name is legend in the North and who now lives, old and crippled, in a little cabin where the Rocky Mountains end. I do not think he would have shot them—not dead anyway—but he might well have given them a wholesome thrashing, which, according to his philosophy, would have straightened out their crooked souls. That man was a superb fighter, an exceptional soldier, and a fair, ruthlessly honest, and kind man. One of Canada's most decorated soldiers of World War I, he was awarded the Victoria Cross, the highest decoration for gallantry in the British Empire. Today, this old "warrior" outfits for sheep. That is, to sportsmen desirous of hunting sheep, he provides the gear— the horses, guides, wranglers, and cooks—which hunters take to the sheep ranges. Although he earns his livelihood from hunting, he hates it, but sees the income as the only means to remain in the land he loves, to stay with his horses, and to remain independent to his dying days. The man is "Skook" Davidson.

When we went north to the Spatzisi, Skook was already an old man, and the grapevine relaying tales about his past activities had begun to wither. Yet one still heard much about this crusty Scotsman—of his marvelous, well-fed horses that were the envy of other outfitters; of his lonely Diamond J. Ranch on the Kechika River; of the fine Stone's sheep that inhabited his guiding area; of the boys he raised; and of his idiosyncrasies, in particular his rough and ready humor. Years later, in November 1968, I met Skook and shared his cabin for three weeks while studying rutting Stone's sheep. The Indians had named him "Skookum," meaning big or mighty in their language. It was not that Skook was overly tall or massive, although he was not a small man. It was his fearless abilities as a fighter that earned him the name. He had also been a severe drinker and a hell-raiser at heart. When I saw him, his crippled frame betrayed little of his past, but his deep-seated blue eyes, which sparkled mischievously from behind his prominent nose and shady eyebrows, told a tale of their own.

He was no ordinary man, and he came to this land in no ordinary way. On his twelfth birthday, in Scotland, his father made him a present of a beautiful pocketknife. That was a long time ago, when a pocketknife was still a treasure dear to a boy's heart, and young "Skook" went off to school elated. The school day began as usual, with long prayers, Skook recalled.

"And so we stood there and prayed, and prayed. Then I noticed the beautiful red braid of the girl in front of me, and the devil just bit me. I took out my knife and carefully cut off the braid. I slipped it into my neighbor's desk, folded my hands, and went back to praying—but in earnest this time!"

He paused, shook his gray head, and waved a hand.

"It was of no use. It all came out. I was the only one with a knife."

Skook was thrown out of school for this prank. His stern father decreed that he would do better in the colonies than in Scotland, and Skook was shipped out. He was thirteen years of age when he stepped off the ship in Halifax and commenced his trip west across Canada.

"People were awfully good to me," Skook recalled.

He had ten Canadian dollars when he stepped off the ship, and he still had ten dollars when he reached British Columbia. Nobody would accept money from "little Scottie." He stayed at a ranch in the Cariboo district where he learned the trade that made him a renowned horseman, packer, and outfitter in later years when he guided expeditions of the Geographic Survey of Canada through the roadless, rugged ranges of northern British Columbia.

When World War I broke out, Skook volunteered for service and could not get to the front fast enough. When the Canadian Brigade landed in Great Britain he took time off to return to his native village in Scotland. The first soul he met was the red-haired lass whose thick braid had been the cause of his banishment. Although she recognized Skook, she stuck her nose in the air and walked right past him. Unforgiving souls, these Scots!

Before he left, Skook's mother presented him with a small Bible. She made him promise that he would read a certain psalm if he were ever in trouble, and Skook promised it high and holy. He stuck the little Bible into his pack where it stayed throughout the war. His activities at the front earned him many decorations, and he returned a hero to the little Scottish village after the armistice.

The first question his mother asked upon his arrival was, "Did you remember your promise?"

Skook was taken aback and feverishly tried to recollect which promise he had made.

"Did you read the Bible when you were in trouble?"

He nodded, but his mother seemed less than satisfied.

"Show me the Bible," she commanded, and Skook took his pack and removed the small book from its pocket. His mother leafed through the book, and her face became cloudy. Her gaze transfixed him.

"Son," she said, "you have lied to me," and, to the great sorrow of the already miserable sinner, she slowly raised a 50-pound note from between the pages.

Years later he still mused on what it had cost him not to read the Bible, particularly since he could have used that money so well on his leaves in Paris.

His departure from his home village was sudden and final. In a fight he punched his brother-in-law head over heels down a staircase and left.

Skook's years at war, his daring exploits on expeditions, his great skill as a marksman, his fondness for his shooting irons, his capacity for whiskey, his jokes, and his fairness and capable fists all helped to make him a legendary figure after his return to Canada. He never married but gave his affection to his horses, which are some of the tamest, friendliest creatures I have encountered anywhere. He kept dogs and cats in his cabin, and he soon learned to hide his true nature behind a gruff, crusty exterior, for others did take advantage of this good and generous man. He adopted homeless boys and raised them. When I asked someone who knew Skook how he had raised the boys, I received but one word in reply, "Rough!" A sample of Skook's educational methods may suffice.

The boys had knocked off work a little early, and, rather than being at their assigned tasks, they were squatted on the gravel beside a creek. Skook noticed they were absent and neglecting the jobs they were supposed to be doing, and he moved to set the matter straight. He took the rifle and went in search of them. The two hookey-players were rudely reminded of their faux pas by the action of a bullet splattering sand, stones, and water between them. They scurried back to their task.

Skook did have faith in rifles as educational tools. One of his Indian guides had the habit of occupying the outhouse for extraordinary lengths of time. The lesson was not long in coming. When the guide again disappeared in anticipation of a long sitting, Skook took his watch, laid it on the window sill, and placed the rifle beside it. After four minutes he took the gun, aimed, and sent a bullet screaming through the top of the "john," with the anticipated result of a startled guide hopping rabbitlike (his pants around his ankles) out the outhouse door and off across the yard. The lesson worked.

Skook's shooting irons spoke up when he rode into little settlements, such as Lower Post, and people knew that he had arrived. He shot some hotel roofs and bars full of holes, then magnanimously pulled a wad of banknotes from his pocket and paid handsomely for the damage. While he eventually gave up his jolly sniping, after a stray bullet clipped a man, he never did cease his practical jokes, which are not for tender souls.

On one occasion a priest in Hudson Hope complained to Skook that his church was so empty on Sunday. Skook lent him an understanding ear, and suggested that he could help. When Sunday came the church bells began ringing early and seemingly never quit. The prolonged ringing was unusual, and something unusual in a little settlement is soon noticed and draws the curious. There was Skook, ringing the bells with all his might, and urging the "heathen bastards" to get inside. He rounded up the half-willing souls with stern orders—which to ignore was fraught with danger. Skook's fists saw to that. When the church was packed, Skook took his ten-gallon hat and passed it around, while the service commenced. When he had finished collecting, Skook folded his hat and—to the surprise of all—walked out of the church. He soon returned, however, pushing a wheelbarrow on which rested a keg of whiskey that he had bought with the collection. He passed out the whiskey to a titillated congregation which then—so the story goes— drank to the health of Jesus Christ.

Although Skook was a hard drinker, he was a principled man who never drank on the job—that is, not in the bush. Whiskey was there to have a good time with in town, and nowhere else! Being a Scotsman, Skook practiced the expected forethought, making sure he had drinking reserves on each return to town, by purchasing a hearty supply of liquor before departing and caching it away. As a hiding place, Skook chose a spirit house in an Indian graveyard, and that for good reasons. Indians in northern British Columbia and the Yukon build beautiful, little houses for the soul of the departed right over the graves. These spirit houses are sometimes works of art, well built and gaily painted. Inside the house, the relatives of the dead place some of the deceased's belongings, and then close the door never to open it again. From then on the spirit of the dead lives in the house. Such a place Skook deemed a good hiding spot for his whiskey, and his success proved him right—for a while. On one return the whiskey was gone. Somebody had taken it. His secret had been uncovered. However, Skook went on to town, acting totally unaware of his loss. He got roaring drunk, made sure that everybody saw how much whiskey he bought before departing, then mounted his horse and rode off with his pack string into the bush.

He hid his whiskey in the same spirit house, as if nothing had happened, and rode on. A mile down the trail he tied up the horses and returned on foot to the graveyard. When darkness fell he crept to the spirit house, slid inside, and closed the door. He did not have to wait long. Soon there were halting steps outside, and slowly the door creaked open. "And then," Skook said, "a hand came in. So I took hold and shook it."

The scream of pure terror from the departing Indian must have been memorable!

That culprit got away lightly compared with one who could not curb his sexual assaults. Skook did not say where it was, but the man in question made a great nuisance of himself in a certain town, and appeared beyond reason. The law of the frontier can be rough in such cases: at a convenient time, a group of citizens performed an operation on the culprit that cowboys perform on bull calves at branding time.

"He became a decent citizen thereafter," Skook mused. "It sure quieted him down. A couple of days later, at the bar, the doctor said, loudly, so all could hear, 'Well, whoever did the job'—and he looked me in the eyes—'sure knew what he was doing!'"

The frontier people have a strong sense of what is right and what is wrong, and practice justice, if not always according to law. It is rumored that Skook never paid income tax, "not to that damned government anyway," but made up for it in his own way. On one occasion at least he distributed extra funds, beyond that needed for living, to children in a town. Another tale recalls his treatment of debtors. During a visit to town, he lined up a group of them in front of the hotel and addressed them in approximately these words.

"Well, you bastards, you ain't gonna pay me my debts anyway. So, I figure, I might get some satisfaction out of you." With these words he lit into them and publicly thrashed the whole bunch.

Fighting was so much a part of Skook that he made his last fling at it when he was well into his seventies. He had come to town on one of his increasingly rare visits. At a bar he befriended a big, hefty, young miner, and the two were soon celebrating their former feats of fisticuffs. They were both getting pretty high in spirits, when Skook turned to his newly found friend and challenged:

"Let's clean the place!"

The other apparently did not quite understand but nodded

anyway. At once Skook grabbed a full glass of beer and threw it over his shoulders, glass and all. It landed with a splintering of glass on the next table. Next, he took his partner's beer bottle and threw it at the light bulb—but missed. With a crash and a roar, old Skook rose and whirled, fists up and ready to "clean the joint." That's as far as he got. The proprietress of the bar marched up to him, grabbed him by the scruff of the neck, called him a damned old fool, marched him out of the bar, up the stairs, and into his room, and then locked the door. Women have been the downfall of Skook—even a tough old fighter can't slug a woman.

As an outfitter for big game, Skook met America's élite, if not the world's. He met with millionaires and gangsters, with politicians and royalty, and treated them all alike. Once an oriental prince was his client. The good man had a long flight behind him and was not feeling well at the time he climbed into the aircraft at Watson Lake that took him to the Diamond J. Ranch. He did manage to survive the landing on Skook's landing strip. Pilots insisted one did not land here but made a calculated crash. His Royal Highness emerged from the aircraft and was met by Skook, who shook his hand, told him to climb aboard the horsecart, and turned to the horses. The ranch, located a quarter-mile distant where the pack string was being readied, consisted of several small log cabins with earthen roofs, a small corral, and hitching posts. Here His Highness was abandoned while Skook saw to the packing. At this point, His Highness felt an internal stirring, and he deduced quite correctly that the little house beside the corral was the place to go for relief. He opened the door but could see no toilet paper, and was unaware of the purpose of the religious magazines piled inside (all other magazines were used to light fires in Skook's stove). He went to Skook who was still busy with the horses and asked quietly if toilet paper were available. Skook slowly turned to him.

"So," he replied in a voice that all could hear, "you want to take a ----? Well, if you're through with it, you take that pine branch flappin' in the breeze between your legs and ride right down. That's how we do it in this country!"

The prince gasped, but he was a sensible man for he exploded into laughter. But his ordeal for the day was not over—not yet.

The pack train was soon ready, and prince, outfitter, guides, wranglers, and cooks mounted and headed down the trail. They had not ridden long when the prince motioned to halt. He was not feeling too well, which was more than forgivable considering the travels he had just made. When Skook rode up, the prince asked for a little rest.

"You sure can stand here if you want," retorted Skook, "the rest goes on."

And they did.

It is hard not to like the crusty old man, and the prince did grow fond of him in the weeks on the trail. The hunt was a most successful one. Upon returning to his home, the prince sent Skook a present, which reached him via air from Watson Lake, along with his mail, some groceries, and several bags of oats for his horses. The pilot was curious about the box's contents but held his tongue, till Skook—who knew human nature very well—opened it as the very last parcel to be inspected. Out came a truly princely gift that only an oriental prince could give—a hammered silver bowl with gold inlays, of the finest workmanship. Skook held it under his big, red nose for closer inspection and put it down again without comment. He betrayed his thoughts with no word or sign and went on as usual. The pilot left.

Several months later, the same pilot flew another load of oats and Skook's mail in to the Diamond J. Ranch. He was most curious as to what Skook had done with the bowl, but true to western fashion he asked no questions. He nursed a cup of coffee—while Skook rummaged through the mail—his eyes searching the cabin, moving over the shelves, the cupboards, and the corners, but without seeing the bowl. Then a clatter close to the door caught the pilot's attention, and glancing down he saw one of Skook's cats enjoying a meal—from the golden bowl.

The pilot hid his surprise and sipped his coffee.

"Skook," he asked a little later, "how did you like the gift the prince sent you?"

"You mean the golden bowl?"

"Yeah, the golden bowl."

"Well, I'll tell you. It's no damned good. I made pancakes in it, and they all turned black!"

Skook did not keep that golden bowl. When his brother-in-law died, his sister made an effort to find Skook through the Royal Canadian Mounted Police. When Skook got her letter, he cleaned up the golden bowl and sent it off to her. He had no use for the damn thing, anyway.

When fall comes again along the Kechika the hunting parties will be traveling in and out. The Diamond J. Ranch will be in the throes of its busy season, and Skook's horses will be doing their work to earn a living. At this writing, Skook is 86 years old. Arthritis has crippled him severely, but he stays on, helped by one or two hired hands from Lower Post. Last January his cabin burned down, with all the records Skook had kept, his diaries, and photographs of former days. It was a blow to the old man, but he soon recovered.

"He's OK again," Stan, the Beaver's pilot, commented. "He's been shouting on the radio as usual."

Skook's old age has not been reached without shadows. He represents an earlier time in Canada's North when much was asked of the individual, when the law was far but justice near, and fair play the order of the day. One did not lock cabins in those days. When one left, one saw to it that dry wood was stacked beside the stove, that some kindling was cut and put on the wood, that a little food, sugar, and coffee were placed in a mouse-proof tin, just in case a visitor came by in one's absence. One might never know, it could save a man's life. One entered cabins, used them, and left them just as one found them—clean and tidy. I recall how painful it was to stand in front of the first locked cabin in the Yukon wilderness, a cabin at a lake but far, far away from a road. Why was it done? Had the callousness toward others so typical of our cities reached into the far corners of this land already? What was this person doing here, anyway, if he could not respect the unwritten rules of decency practiced in this land? Yet I was familiar with the ways of our urban south; Skook was not. How much more must it have pained him to stand in front of his first robbed cache? The old man was incredulous. He had not recovered from the shock when I stayed with him, and he came back to it again and again. To rob a cache is one of the lowest, dirtiest, most despicable things that one can do. Someone had boated up the river and demolished the cache, destroying some items and carting off others. That kind of malicious thievery was unheard of in former times, and the petty theft and senseless destruction of food and implements that one might need on one's return, upset Skook severely.

However, much worse news was on the horizon. Old Skook was upset that the Kechika and Liard rivers have been under investigation for potential dam sites by British Columbia Hydro. The possibility now exists that the Liard River will be dammed to create another monstrosity akin to the one on the Peace River, Williston Lake, that lies behind the W. A. C. Bennett Dam. This dam has created a two-armed lake 635 square miles in size, by flooding the Finlay and Parsnip rivers. To me these are megalomaniac constructs of a petit-bourgeois mentality, which ultimately will be considered not as achievements but as criminal acts. Even today this dam is not the panacea it was drummed up to be, with the difficulty it has caused along the Peace River, the Athabasca Delta, and the Mackenzie River, plus the expensive power it provides, not to mention the loss of the fertile flood plains, their productive forests, ranches, and rich wildlife. The dam catches the silt-laden waters of glacial streams and creates a catchment basin which promises a short life expectancy for the reservoir—huge as it is. The same fate is to befall the Liard and Kechika rivers, some of the muddiest rivers during flood, and the last major river basins in the North with good productive forest growth. These are also outstanding wildlife regions, and areas with good agricultural potential. Be that as it may, Skook's heart aches for the magnificent land that distant planners are condemning to the flood. He has attempted to gain the help of others in order that a national park may be created in the area—thus far with little success. He is old. His days are numbered. He will probably die while the mighty valley of the Rocky Mountain trench, which holds the big, braided Kechika, is still much as he first saw it. He was a young man, then, and he returned to it to build his cabin, plant his garden, and winter his horses there. The land was good to him. Walk through this valley with its tall aspen forests and big white spruce trees, its dense willow flats on the river bars, its low-lying meadows of sedges, or the bunch-grass meadows on drier land. Note the rich wildlife that dwells here: the moose that stream to this valley in winter; the wolf packs that roam the land; the black bears and grizzlies that fatten on buffalo berries in late summer along the streams; the bands of big Mountain caribou; and the mule deer and large Stone's sheep that graze the rich slopes that are now under threat of flooding. Walk through it, see it, hear it, smell it, contemplate what happens when the waters rise and the land dies. Then realize that for hundreds of miles this valley will be under water, that for hundreds of miles the life that lived here ever since the big glacier left ten millennia ago, the life which gave sustenance to the people of this land, will be dead. Rivers are the lifeline of a land. The richness in plants and animals of an area depends on them. Kill the river, and you kill wildlife that depends on the river in a wide area around. And what does one gain in exchange for damming the river? More neon lights? More street lighting? Can you understand what stirs in the old man's breast and in my heart when we look at the land of the Kechika?

You call my response here to the damming of a river emotional? Well, you're damned right. It is! It is very emotional—almost as emotional as your response would be if something valuable and dear to you were under sentence of death. I will not object to the human use of this land that potentially can give a stake in life and sustenance to many a man and his family for millennia to come. I have no quarrel with the sensible uses of the surface of this land, of the harvest of timber and crops and wildlife, of the days of joy, and soul-and-body-forming experiences that await the people born and raised here. I will not object to the rational extraction of its mineral wealth provided the land is rehabilitated. But I do object to its being flooded. I do deplore the callous, irrational destruction of its soil, its life, its wealth of renewable resources, and the submerging of its nonrenewable resources. I protest, also, because wilderness is not a common thing anymore, because the frontier is gone forever, and that which we had regarded with contempt, which we conquered and altered, is now an appreciating treasure. I protest because power and a few jobs do not pay for the damage, not by a long shot. Yes, there are emotions involved.

I left Skook's ranch in mid-December. Stan's Beaver circled once over the cabin and landed on the airstrip. Skook drove me out to the aircraft with a team of horses, and took Harry Moosenose along to help unload the sacks of oats from the Beaver. The weeks here had been eventful and had passed quickly. When Skook found out on my first arrival that I was a German, he registered a plus point. That I was a zoologist he registered with a minus point, maybe two. This placed me in the category of "god-damned wolf lovers," and wolves Skook hated. Wolves had killed horses and maimed some others, hence wolves were not favored by the old man. Sheep he loved. He put salt out for them not far from the cabin and delighted in the daily appearance of the animals. He prohibited all his helpers from hunting while they worked for him and in his earlier days would probably have been very nasty with any man who harmed any creature on his ranch—except wolves of course. As we rumbled along, he sat hunched forward on the cart he had built, holding the reins with hard, knotty hands. His cap, old coat, and pants were ripped and dirty, and his feet were stuck in moose-hide moccasins, and these in turn into rubber boots. One saw little of the man himself, except the big, red nose, bushy eyebrows, and white, stubbly whiskers and, occasionally, his deep-seated blue eyes. There was little welcome for anyone when we reached Stan's machine. The oat sacks were unloaded, the mail passed, my baggage stowed away. There was a sudden loud shout, the horses lurched forward, and the cart rolled off accompanied by a clatter of hoofs and a cloud of powdered snow and Kechika dust. Skook did not want to say goodbye. He did not stand for soggy sentimentality.

10

The Hunting Game

𝒟 More than four hours had passed since I had first seen the mountain goat on the cliff below. It was a male, a big billy. Not far away, across a scree slope that poured forth from a big cleft in the rock wall, was another goat, also a male, as the curvature of his short horns told me. I had noted the goats in passing and moved on, for I still had to check the valley of Sanctuary Creek for rams. There were none. The remainder of the day, I decided, I would put to good use and get one of those goats. We needed food. I returned by way of a high trail since this would lead me past the goats. Now I was in the cliffs where the big billy had been. Would he still be there? Probably. There was no likely reason for him to leave. As I rounded a corner in the cliff, I spied the second billy. He was resting in the opposite bluff, his back toward me, looking out across the valley to Cliff Mountain. That confirmed my hunch that the big goat was still below me, somewhere down there in the brown, lichen-covered rocks but hidden by the cliff's curve.

The second goat was quite far away, about 300 yards, a small white speck to the unaided eye and too far for a certain shot with the iron sights of my short rifle. The big goat below me would be closer, much closer, if I could only see it. There was no point remaining behind the rock, so I grasped the rifle tightly and stepped forward along the ledge. The sound of rolling stones coming from beneath made me turn my head and steady myself on the ledge. More stones rolled. I raised the weapon and waited.

Eternal seconds passed. The wind tugged at my parka, and played my hair over my eyes. An eagle soared past below me and vanished behind brown rock. In bluish haze the valley stood below, the creek blinked its reflection of the late autumn sun and lost itself in the greenish-blue spruce forest that extended far along the mountain flanks, becoming ever bluer in the distance. Another trickle of pebbles. Still no sight of a living thing. Time ticked on. The seed heads of a bunch of blue grass nodded in the breeze against the steel of my rifle barrel. Suddenly a big white object shot out below the cliff and onto the scree slope. It was the goat, the big one, and it was running fast. My rifle flipped to my shoulder, the gleaming brass bead of the front sight moved past the running object, stuck to its nose a moment, then blurred as the shot crashed. The goat slid to a halt, rose on its hind legs, and flipped over backwards. On it went, rolling down the scree slope, trailed by a small cloud of yellow dust. Now it slid out of sight behind a projection of the cliff on which I stood. The rifle came down. The familiar click of the bolt told me that I had repeated, and a new cartridge lay in the chamber ready to burst should the need arise. But the big goat was dead. Its body once again emerged into view, still rolling on, now at greater speed. I began the descent. The goat rolled on. Further on, I glanced over the cliff shoulder. The goat was still rolling, tumbling more than a thousand feet until a willow bush, protruding from the rubble, finally caught and held it.

It was some time before I reached the goat. While the climb down the rock was not difficult, it was time-consuming, although the going was good on the loose scree downhill. The long descent had not damaged the billy, except to scratch his unusually short and curved horns. He was a large-bodied six-year-old, and with some difficulty I moved him into position to gut, skin, and dress him. My prize was fat after a leisurely summer, and there was no trace of the unpleasant odor exuded by big mountain-goat males during the rut. After all, it was late September, and the rut still six weeks away.

I pushed my hand through his thick, white coat, observed the long, stiff hairs on his rump that exaggerate the height of the animal, and noted the position of the bullet hole high up on the shoulders. I pulled my knife from its sheath; the steel gritted through sand as I made the first cut. Goats sand bathe, and the grains fill the hair, even next to the skin. He rolled in fat, I noticed with much satisfaction, for I had shot this goat for meat. I cut around the diaphragm and drew out the rumen, liver, and intestine. Then I reached far forward and freed the heart and lungs. Liver, heart, and kidneys were impaled on a willow stick for the trip home. Next, I removed the colon and bladder and cleaned the carcass of blood by pulling the billy uphill, letting the dark red mass spill out between the legs. There was much more work to be done: the goat had to be skinned, its innards examined for parasites, its carcass checked for old injuries, and then it had to be quartered and weighed. In total, the goat weighed 265 pounds—a big billy indeed.

Evening was beginning to fall by the time I loaded the hind-quarters—all I could carry on this trip—onto the pack-board and secured them with a diamond hitch. Then I proceeded with my "security" storage measures. I cut off the goat's shoulders and stuffed them into its rib basket, over all of which I placed the hide. There was no fear of the meat spoiling, since it had cooled out sufficiently; moreover, the night would be cold, and I would be back early next day to pick up the remainder. If all went well, neither wolverine, wolf, nor bear would find the remains, and the hide would protect the meat from ravens and magpies. I jiggled my load on the pack-board, making sure the diamond hitch held it tight against the canvas. It did. The time had come to shoulder the pack, pick up the gun and the goat's edible innards, and descend the mountain to the trail that led back to the cabin and home.

The weight was heavy on my shoulders, but it was a cheerful weight. The excitement of the hunt had faded: from the tense moments when one knows that game is near, to the chilling flush when one's eye spies the desired form, to the icy moment when the sight traces its mark, when the rifle barks, and the quarry falls. Then the heart begins to pound and the breath comes quicker, and then a brief feeling of antipathy as one moves up to the kill, hesitantly examines it, touches, strokes it, and maybe sits down for a moment or two to get over it. With the drawing of the knife there is a return of joy to the chest. The eye scans the carcass to evaluate the meat and searches for the parts that must be saved for the table, while the mind projects and anticipates the quiet satisfactions of aging the meat, of cutting it, of the first small delicacies one will prepare at home.

It's a welcome weight on one's shoulders when one hikes home with game in the bag and a set of antlers or horns protruding from the pack. During a rest break, the hand touches the gleaming points (or the horn tips), caresses the antler beams (or the burr), and plays with the soft hair on the head. Hunting is a passion better men than I have tried to describe, have philosophized about, eulogized and justified, romanticized, sung about, and attempted to explain. Some have called it sport. I disagree. Some have called it cruel and unjust—an uncultured act, done for the sake of killing. I disagree. It is no more "sport" than is gardening; it is no more done for the sake of killing than gardening is done for the sake of killing vegetables. If it is sporting, with whom is one competing? The animals? I should blush at such a comparison, given the weapons we possess and the skills in hunting we are capable of. If it were done for the sake of butchery, it would be a poor second to a job in a slaughterhouse. Were someone to call it an intercourse with nature, I should shake my head at the choice of words, but I shall know what that person gets out of hunting. When stalking, one's guts must tell one that one is doing something right, that one is reliving the very drama that caused man's ancestors to rise from the apes to become men. For whether we love hunting or hate it, eulogize its blinding passion or condemn it, hunting was the force that shaped our bodies, moulded our souls, and honed our minds. From this conclusion there appears to be no escape.

Who are we? Everyone is entitled to ask that question; every generation has to answer it anew. It is an old question, and one that will never cease to be asked; not as long as there are human beings to ask it. Who is this creature that swelters in extremes? The ultimate destroyer, second only to nature? The ultimate builder and inventor, again second only to nature? The being so infinitely wise and clever in some strategies; the being so insane in shortsighted greed, convenience, and dogmas? The creature who cheerfully kills its own kind to the sound of applause, and with joy and efficiency? The creature who cheerfully and eagerly dies for others of its own kind? Who are we?

One ponders that question. It flashes on to the scene in New York's teeming canyons of architectured concrete; in a storm-tossed boat on foaming waters; on a dripping, cold mountainside in gray fog; at a three-ring circus alive with acrobats, elephants, and clowns; at the sight of a blazing sunset; beside the flicker, smoke, and warmth of a campfire; and it can be a burning question in the winter loneliness of a mountain valley when the peaks are white, and the sky is black, and the green laces of the northern lights quiver overhead. Hear the sound of the snowshoes as they crunch along the crystalline white, feel the cold bite at the face and ice forming on the eyelashes, taste the silence, the eerie long silence that is almost a sound. Men had been here before: men without steel knives, or steel axes, or rifles, or matches, without the finely made parkas insulated with down, without woolen pants and socks and felt boots. How had they lived? How had they been able to colonize—with their poor and primitive gear—a land so harsh and alien to warm, throbbing life that I, favored with excellent equipment and with ample food flown in from outside, cannot but tremble in fear over the prospects of survival? In company of chilling adversity or sparkling wonder the old question moves into focus.

In recent years, the question of who we are has been tackled with increasing frequency. So much has thrown us into turmoil—technological advances, the decay of ancient dogmas about man, increased leisure time, increased spread of education, increased communication readily available—that we are rightly uncertain of ourselves. In addition, a number of unexpected findings unearthed by scientists, and the rapid growth of unnerving knowledge of the rules governing the life of wild animals, have given the experts pause and plenty to contemplate. The result has been a flood of books on man. They have been great books—great, not because of the truths they contain, but because they stimulate and fan the search for truth about ourselves.

Central to the latest synthesis of our new understanding is that man arose as a hunter. It is unfortunate, however, that the first theorists who arrived at this conclusion, forced on us by fossil evidence, were neither hunters nor ecologists. They did not treat man's ecological profession during his evolution; they failed to apply much zoological and ecological knowledge; and, hence, they failed to deduce the many consequences pertinent to an understanding of man. Second, the authors themselves were not hunters, familiar with the demands and consequences of making a living by hunting in inhospitable climates. Rather than refute arguments, I shall, instead, attempt to sketch a picture of man's emergence in a somewhat different framework from that accepted today.

Somewhere in the beginning of the little ice ages—the Villafranchian, which preceded the major ice ages by at least three million years—we can find the remains of our kind. Zoologically he differs little from us; he is much smaller, his teeth are relatively large and more complex than ours; his brain is smaller, relatively and absolutely, and poorly developed in the frontal and temporal lobes, which are the regions associated with the attributes that characterize man, his language, and his constraint over instinctive and reflex behavior; his feet are less elegantly built than ours, an indication that his gait was not quite like ours and that walking as we know it had not yet emerged; his arms still carry the signs of adaptation to tree life and indeed in trees this little man-creature would have to seek safety at night, granted his puny size and strength and the great diversity of predators of the Villafranchian South African plains. Like so many of the true ice-age creatures, modern man had a rather puny pre-ice-age ancestor, or conversely modern man is a giant like so many ice-age mammals.

We need not enter into controversy over how to name this little man-creature; *Homo africanus* will do. He had for all of his existence—as far as it can be traced paleontologically—a larger hominid as a companion, albeit one which probably occupied more mesic savannah habitats. This rather larger and more primitive—that is, more apelike—hominid we shall call the robust form or *Paranthropus*. We had, then, a robust and a gracile hominid: the latter is directly in our ancestral line; the former may have given rise early in its evolution to the gracile form, but it became a species distinctly its own, and a successful one at that, which remained on this earth for at least some four million years. It was by all available evidence a vegetarian, but one which used hands to select the most digestible plant parts which means not only to pluck fruit, seeds, flowers, and tender shoots, but also to carefully pull free the meristematic parts of grasses (the growing, sweet, and tender parts) or pull free roots, bulbs, and tubers hidden in soft soil. The gracile form by contrast concentrated on eating small packages of highly digestible food, be they of plant or animal origin, much as gatherers do in southern Africa to this day. The gracile form may have used some crude tools to free tubers from deep but loose soil, but granted its small body and long legs it probably filled its daily food requirement by roaming over a large area rather than exploiting small areas of land intensively as the robust form was wont to do. The hands of the gracile form would have been capable of a strong grip but not of a precision grip, and anyway none would be required to live the essentially gathering, omnivorous way of life of the gracile form.

The finding of the gracile and robust hominids was sensational enough, but it became even more so when Professor Raymond A. Dart, of Johannesburg, South Africa, later popularized by Robert Ardrey, author of *African Genesis*, insisted that the gracile form was a carnivore from its inception and even worse—a cannibal. There was evidence to support this contention in the form of distorted and cracked or damaged skulls of hominids, baboons, and other creatures, as well as a murder weapon in the form of antelope humeri. The paleontologic evidence has been controversial and far less secure than Dart assumed or Ardrey popularized. Careful assessments and reassessments have made it evident that the distortions of the soft limestone and the slow movements of hard rock through the soft limestone over geologic ages could account for the damage reported by Dart. Worse still, there is absolutely no ecological reason why the gracile form should be a hunter, granted the adequacy of gathering to supply all essential food as demonstrated by present-day gatherers. Nor is it an easy, snap-the-finger routine to change from a herbivore to a carnivore, despite the fact that chimpanzees, which are essentially plant eaters, on rare occasions practice carnivorism and even cannibalism. Moreover, the gracile form, only 3½ to 4 feet in height, would be able to generate a blow with less than ⅛ of the power of a man close to 6 feet tall. It was far too small to be anything but an opportunistic killer of small, defenseless prey such as antelope fawns or fledgling birds; it was too small to be a big-game hunter and could support itself without hunting anyway. The claim that early man was a hunter is probably a myth.

At the beginning of the major glaciations, somewhat more than a million years ago, the gracile hominid form changes into a larger form which we call *Homo erectus.* This hominid is nearly our size, has somewhat smaller teeth than *Homo africanus,* a larger brain, and a body which is essentially ours. At the transition from *H. africanus* to *H. erectus*—it is a long transition— fashioned stone tools become common. These are simple, pointed pebbles, but they are crafted tools just the same. These pointed pebble tools change to the simple, crude Abbevillian hand axes which are part of the early Acheulian tradition that survived in Africa up to 60,000 years ago. With the advance of pebble tools the gracile hominid expands northward into central and north Africa and, with the advent of *H. erectus,* into Europe and Asia as well.

Homo erectus is considered to be a capable hunter by most students of man's early history, but unfortunately such a view again ignores ecological realities. Nor is the fossil evidence indisputably in favor of such a view. It does show that *H. erectus* almost certainly ate red meat and that he almost certainly was a cannibal, an excellent indicator of carnivorous tendencies, since we know by now that probably all large carnivores are also cannibals. There is also little doubt that the late *H. erectus,* in contrast to the early populations of this species, was a hunter, since

shortly before the advent of *Homo sapiens* we find spears fashioned with stone tools from wood. Yet the view that early populations were big-game hunters is almost certainly false.

To begin with, must one invoke big-game hunting for early
H. erectus? The answer is no. Gathering would have sufficed to
fill the food requirement in the tropical or subtropical savannah. *H. erectus* appears to have expanded into dry steppe from
the savannah. Thus he would have been exposed to a period in
which green vegetation and concomitant fauna would not be
available, namely the dry season. At such time green vegetation
is available along watercourses and at the edges of receding
lakes, and food is available in these areas by gathering. However, the amount of such habitat is relatively small, and the
pressure would be on to exploit alternative food sources. The
hand axe gives us a first clue. It is by and large not associated
with butchering sites and has thus little significance to hunting.
It is obviously a tool designed to penetrate something hard
which fingernails cannot penetrate. This hard crust could be
hard-baked soil, rotten tree trunks, or bark. Such hard surfaces
would conceal various bulbs—particularly plentiful in the dry
steppe where plants store food in their underground parts in
order to emerge when the rains fall—as well as edible pith,
phloem, and various insect larvae. Hence, the difference in diet
between *H. africanus* and *H. erectus* would be caused by the latter's emphasis on hidden plant and animal foods in addition to
those accessible to the unaided hand above the earth surface.
The hand axe made it thus possible to exploit the dry steppe by
living off its hidden plant foods as the staple diet.

The subtropical savannah and steppe is also characterized by
an incredible biomass of animal life, in particular represented
by large herbivores. Granted this, there would be frequent kills
by large carnivores and thus the opportunity for scavenging.
Such may be crucial during the dry season when there is reduced availability of plant food. Since kills are frequent, there
exists the potential for male bands of hominids to approach
kills and by mimicking the sounds of the predators—by parasitizing those cognitive systems which to the predator signal

danger and cause him to withdraw—to reach the kill and obtain some food.

Why male bands? Because under the existing conditions, granted our knowledge of primate social systems, it is most likely that females and juveniles would be split into small groups guarded by adult males and foraging in the pockets of abundant plant food, while subordinate males would be in bands relegated to poorer habitats. It is they who would be most frequently confronted by hunger and would specialize toward scavenging and toward the beginnings of systematic hunting, in contrast to the opportunistic hunting probably practiced by *Homo africanus.*

At the pain of being repetitive let me once more sketch out the ecological argument against the view that early men were big-game hunters.

Warm climates were characterized by an immense diversity of plant and animal species as well as by a great and continuous biological productivity. Put crudely, there was something either growing, ripening, or crawling that was good to eat throughout the year. As we are aware from present primitive societies that live by gathering, it is possible not only to collect, but also to sustain a rather good living off a great variety of seeds, berries, tree fruits, nuts, tubers, melons, succulent stems, leaves, and flowers, and insects, grubs, and honey, as well as the occasional turtle, lizard, snake, frog, fish, fledgling bird, young mammal, snail or mouse, bird or reptile nest filled with eggs. The early hominids had no more need of hunting to maintain an adequate and balanced diet than do members of today's societies that rely primarily on the collecting of diverse natural foods. Even without hunting, the early hominids would have had ample opportunity to eat meat. They lived in areas that supported a diverse and rich fauna of large mammals. Scavenging would have added significantly to their diet, just as it does in some hunting-gathering societies today. At the least it would have added the marrow of unbroken long bones, and the brain and flesh of skulls; at best it would have added intact carcasses. Fresh kills can be spotted by the descent of vultures to kills.

Homo erectus, in groups, armed with the most primitive of clubs would have had little difficulty chasing away hunting dogs, dholes, hyenas or even leopards. *H. erectus* was a big fellow, almost as large as we are. The odd carnivore bold enough to attack would probably have died of skull-bursting club blows and become prey in turn. This cannot be claimed for the small-bodied *Homo africanus*.

It would have required a bare minimum of tools to survive and live well as a gatherer and scavenger. Sticks for digging roots can be broken from trees or bushes and discarded after use; similarly, they can be employed for knocking down fruit or smacking a snake over the head. Fish can be caught by hand or collected from natural traps one occasionally encounters along streams. There is little need for a fire to make foods digestible—although in primitive times fire would have been an excellent protection against predators, particularly if used to block caves. It is not inconceivable that scavenged bones and skulls were taken to the safety of a cave where they could be smashed open with rocks and scraped clean of meat with rock chips and flakes. A generalized diet as postulated here would require precisely the kind of heavy jaws and large teeth found in the *H. africanus* and *H. erectus*. Such a chewing apparatus would be needed to grind raw tubers, tough fruits, and fibrous stalks to a fine consistency in order to extract a maximum of energy from it during digestion. A meat eater with highly advanced tools who also consumed cooked tubers, nuts, and so on, would not require such massive jaws and teeth (excepting the late Neanderthal man, for reasons to be mentioned later). Furthermore, the great neck muscles of *H. erectus* and the *Australopithecinae* would be highly functional in the absence of effective cutting tools, allowing tough plant fibres and sinews to be ripped off when gripped between teeth and hands.

The existing evidence from anatomy, tools, bone assemblages, and ecology is compatible with the view that hominids from the early Pleistocene—who then enjoyed warm climates—were not hunters of big game, but were generalized food gatherers and, at best, opportunistic killers of animals. To practice such a life they would need no refined abilities to visualize strategies, to cooperate with one another, or to learn great stores of strategic and technical information; nor would they be required to practice refined value judgments or to exercise discipline, all of which hunters are forced to do if they are to survive by hunting. We need not attribute compassion and altruism to these early hominids; rather, in a food-gathering culture it would be "every creature for himself," and particularly in areas of marginal productivity. Here, an egocentric, callous, individualistic, quarrelsome disposition is adaptive—just as we see it in such human gatherers as the Jk from Uganda and the Sudan. Each individual in a troop would forage for itself. There would be no aid to the sick. The old would limp along as best as they could, their fate, inevitably, to be left behind by the troop, finally to die of scavenging fangs. There would be no language, since vocal exchange presupposes the need for close cooperation, and such would have existed, at best, when the troop confronted danger. The troop would be noisy though, and, during scavenging, loud, harsh sounds would be raised, similar to the roars of animal predators, to frighten away competitors. Perhaps the ability to imitate sounds—a skill unique to humans among mammals—had its roots here. These early men would have possessed at most, a bare rudiment of culture or tradition, hardly advanced over that possessed by gorillas or mountain sheep. The picture that emerges of *Homo erectus* is not pleasing to our egos, for we would hardly call this callous, dull, egocentric, cold, opportunistic, and aggressive creature "human." Yet this is the inevitable picture that arises if we invoke Occam's razor, and refrain from too much wishful thinking.

And yet the scavenging activities and the requirement to cooperate, the search for helpless game that could be overpowered and eaten and which thus occasioned a change from opportunistic to systematic hunting, and the guarding by the male of the females and of the dwindling plant-food resources, all laid the foundation for the human condition. The changes caused a revolution in the primate way of life that must have been typical for *Homo africanus*.

In the highly productive tropical and subtropical savannah

and steppe the female can be totally independent of the male in her reproductive effort, except for mating. She can raise her offspring entirely on her own, and no case can be made on ecological grounds that early hominids did any food sharing. We can conceive of their bands as spreading out at daybreak over the dry savannah from their protective cliffs where they spent the night and beginning a search for diverse small bits of food. There would probably be very large gatherings of such man-creatures, since it is in very large gatherings that we find the conditions favoring selection of females that are similar in size to males. That is, in large groups exploiting open plains there is selection against sexual dimorphism, and selection for large, malelike females that can successfully compete with males. The fossil evidence indicates little differences in the skeleton of the two sexes of *Homo africanus*. The troops would hence be mixed, with larger males occupying the center and smaller males moving about on the periphery.

Such a social system will function in the dry savannah only as long as food is relatively abundant. When food becomes scarce it is first necessary to disperse, to abandon cliffs as refuges from predators at night in favor of other antipredator adaptations, and to begin exploiting alternate food supplies. Once the groups are broken up, it becomes adaptive for a large male to guard limited areas of good habitat during the season of scarcity and allow their exploitation only by the female or females he inseminated, as well as by his children. Conversely it becomes adaptive for the female to align herself with a large, physically capable male who can chase off troops of peripheral males and thus reduce competition for her and her offspring. At the same time it is advantageous for the male to restrict the number of females that he protects, since a large number of females on a limited piece of habitat can quickly exhaust its resources to the detriment of all. This requirement would select for male-female bonding, since evolutionary laws dictate that male and female must each work for their personal reproductive effort—that is, *only* for their *personal* reproductive effort. It would also select for sexual dimorphism in *Homo erectus*—which apparently is found, since males are indeed larger than the females.

The above social system would work only as long as the food supply protected by the male could be readily accessible to the female; when the break between vegetative seasons increases in duration, and hidden plant foods become increasingly difficult to procure, then the female must curtail her reproductive effort. If she is suckling a young, her milk supply must decrease, to the detriment of the young unless food is forthcoming. It is at this stage that it is adaptive for the male to supply food to the lactating or gestating female, since in so doing he supports *his* own reproductive effort. Food sharing, however, is not practiced by primates, only by carnivores among mammals. Food sharing could only arise by a truly revolutionary change in the social behavior of primates, for social behavior is most conservative and hence difficult to change via natural selection since it requires simultaneous changes in the sender and in the receiver of social signals. Food sharing would have to be based on some precursor in the normal behavior of primates. This precursor is indeed found. We see it in the chimpanzee, where during the females' estrous period, males do indeed permit females to eat favorite food uncontested, and they may even share some food with females, provided they are satiated. An expansion of sexual receptivity would hence lead to increased bending of custom and the beginning of some forage sharing.

As the break between vegetative seasons in the savannah increases, so it becomes less and less adaptive for the male to bond with and guard several females, and increasingly adaptive for the male to remain with one female only, to ensure an adequate supply of forage to his reproductive effort. Also it becomes increasingly more adaptive for the male to eat foods other than those eaten by the female and so to reduce competition and ensure a maximum of forage and nutrition for his children. If he were to abandon his female, then other males could come in and compete with her and his children for available plant foods, much to the detriment of his reproductive effort. So the male must remain as a guardian. He cannot band together with other males in order to scavenge, but he can develop systematic hunting which cannot be practiced in the presence of a large troop anyway. I shall explain systematic hunting a little later. At the present it is important to note that the moment systematic hunting provides a significant amount of food during the dry season, and systematic hunting by the male begins to support his reproductive effort by making meat available to the female and tiding her over while she is pregnant or lactating, another set of new rules appears in man's social behavior. These rules are at least as revolutionary—if not more so—than those which led to food sharing by the male.

We noted earlier that dominance displays in mammals emphasize size, height, mass, weapons, and fighting ability. They permit females to select the most dominant male, as is dictated by the rules of evolution. In the early gracile hominids it is indeed adaptive for the female to select a dominant male to father her children. When the female becomes dependent in her reproductive effort on defense by the male of essential plant-food resources, there is even stronger selection in this direction. However, once food sharing and systematic hunting are important in supporting the reproductive effort by the female, selection on the basis of dominance only is not sufficient for the female. A large, powerful male may be a good protector but at the same time an inadequate systematic hunter, and a greedy individual on top of it. Yet the female must select a male that is not only a capable protector, but also a good hunter who can supply food in excess of his own requirements during the dry season and be willing to share it. Dominance displays that emphasize only physical might are now a poor guide to a successful mate. If the male is to be chosen by the female as a potential mate, he must add to his dominance displays new behaviors, behaviors reflecting his skill as a provider; moreover he must enter into a longer courtship to "convince" the female. Since hunting demands great flexibility and rather specific attributes of body and mind, as I shall discuss below, dominance displays now begin to incorporate skill displays. Here begins the shift from innate dominance displays to cultural dominance displays so typical of the human animal. The young males begin to compete for females on the basis of skills useful in systematic hunting, as well as on the basis of physical strength and fighting skills. The males must also show traits such as food sharing during courtship and assume a protective role against other males early in the game, as well as ignore females other than the ones they court. It is to the female's disadvantage to bond with a male who is easily attracted to other females, since such a male is not likely to support her reproductive effort during the dry seasons, and he may abandon his older children as well.

Males are of course also subject to the rules of evolution when selecting mates. To maximize his reproduction a male must choose the best possible mother for his children, as well as a female who is not promiscuous, since then he would support the reproductive effort of another male and not his own. He must not support during the dry season a female who is a poor mother, for in so doing the male selects against his own genotype. He must choose on the basis of external signs and behaviors. It becomes highly adaptive for females to display signs of adequate potential motherhood. These are secondary sexual characteristics subject to hormonal control. Since in the dry savannah or steppe it is the nuclear family, not the female, which is the effective reproductive unit, courtship, dominance displays, secondary sexual characteristics and child-raising behaviors take on new forms which deviate totally from the primate pattern that was probably still found in *Homo africanus*. It is important to note that as the *Homo erectus* forms became increasingly more capable of exploiting dry steppes the male had increasingly to procure more food through systematic hunting during the dry season and to share such food for an increasingly longer time with his older children until they were capable enough to satisfy their personal food demands during the dry season. Food sharing by the male is not to be considered a sign of altruism but strictly a means of supporting his reproductive effort.

One may wonder why the gracile, small-bodied *Homo africanus* grew into the large-bodied *Homo erectus*. Among large mammals, a species dispersing into new, uncolonized lands increases in body size, a development which is due to the better nutrition in the unsettled areas during the population's dispersal, as well as to the selection for vigorous, large adults. Thus, we expect that the dispersing *Homo africanus* increased in body size and was largest at the periphery of his range. In growing larger, however, even an opportunistic hunter can increase the range and size of his prey species and become increasingly effective as a scavenger. Hence, the protein intake in the diet also increases. The rewards are, potentially, still-larger body size, better health, increased ability to exploit marginal habitats, improved reproduction, and a reinforcement of tendencies to hunt opportunistically.

If geographic dispersal extends far enough, a rather different creature must stand at the end point of the journey compared with the one who started out. Had *Homo* been a pure herbivore there would be a great diversity of species today. Granted even opportunistic hunting tendencies, however, a reversal would set in and the large-bodied form would reinvade areas occupied by the smaller and more primitive parent populations. Such a reinvasion would lead to a displacement of the smaller by the larger form.

The large-bodied robust hominid who was a specialized plant eater lived for a long time concurrently with *Homo erectus,* for we find his remains in Africa until well into the middle of the Pleistocene. This supports the earlier contention that early *Homo erectus* did not possess hunting weapons effective enough to kill prey as large as *Paranthropus.* This he could have done had he possessed and been able to use spears. These are weapons found no earlier than the latter half of the major glaciations when *Homo erectus* changes to *Homo sapiens*—and *Paranthropus* disappeared from the face of the earth. This may have been coincidental, but I doubt it. The foregoing suggests that our present knowledge of early and mid-Pleistocene hominids is compatible with the view that they were far less dependent on hunting—or the use of tools—than is presently advanced by anthropologists. Moreover, no case can be made for the selective advantage of altruism, compassion, or increased intelligence, as long as *Homo* remained a gatherer, an opportunistic hunter, and a scavenger in warm climates. Man's humanity was not cradled in the tropics but in a different environment—in the cold forests and steppes, in the face of huge glaciers, and in the periglacial zones. With the adaptations as described for *Homo erectus,* man could not have survived in the cold zones. He could not have sustained himself through six to eight months of winter by food gathering, nor go undressed, nor indeed exist without a skillful technology of starting and maintaining fires. Not even bears, much stronger and faster than man, can continue their omnivorous diet in winter but must hibernate to survive. Barring hibernation, there is no means to sustain an omnivore, except to turn him into a specialized, efficient carnivore—a hunter of slow, dangerous game, for the niche of the fleet-footed carnivore who kills the smaller ungulates is already occupied by the wolf. The large herbivore niche is filled by a variety of cervids, bovids, horses, rhinos, and elephants—there is no place for a slow, herbivorous ape.

What did it mean to live in the cold climates? The productivity of the land was generally very low and very spotty. The species' composition was smaller than in the tropics. Plant food was available only during the short summer and early fall—that is, on a seasonal basis. Within that period availability of a specific food, be it berries, nuts, seeds, sprouting stalks, or whatever, was confined to two or three weeks per year—at most. The fauna was adapted to take advantage of the seasonally available, dispersed food sources, and then it migrated. Hence nesting birds or migratory fish or mammals were in short supply unless the hunter followed the prey. There was a short, intense plague of biting insects in summer that tormented animals beyond belief and could even kill them—an ancient Finnish execution method was to tie an offender, naked, to a stake and leave him to the biting flies.

Once the snow descends, it covers most edible plant parts. Those above ground, such as berries or fruit, freeze, then thaw, and quickly disintegrate. Tubers and corms—even if found through the snow blanket—are virtually impossible to remove from the frozen soil, even with pick and shovel. Most small mammals—accessible for hunting in summer—hibernate in winter and are unattainable to man; so also are many birds since these leave for warmer climes in fall. The fauna is generally greatly impoverished once the snows arrive; one finds mainly overwintering, large mammals plus a few small mammals, usually below the snow blanket, and a few birds. Great areas of land are almost completely devoid of huntable game. Moreover, the presence of clothing on one's body, plus the presence of crunchy snow, makes silent stalking—the most elementary of hunting methods—quite impossible.

If a kill is made, the meat soon freezes, and one requires a sharp axe or saw to hack chunks out of the carcass; human teeth are totally inappropriate for the job. As an alternative, one may thaw the meat, if one has a fire and knows how to keep, transport, or kindle it. One must protect oneself from the cold, in particular from blizzards. One must have means to cover one's extremities such as toes, fingers, ears, and even the nose, in very cold weather. One must be able to sleep comfortably at 40°, 50°, or 60° F below zero. One requires much more food than is necessary in warm climates. One must be able to move on and over deep, loose snow. In short, one must be able to accomplish many things in cold climates that would be inconsequential in warm ones. Primitive hominids, faced with cold climates, had four choices: to hibernate in winter; to trek across continents to the south—a task mastered only by birds; to become efficient predators of overwintering large mammals; or to become extinct.

It is likely that, in the early to mid-Pleistocene, extinction was exactly what happened to the populations of *Homo erectus* living at the species' northern fringe in Europe and Asia. These hominids moved in at the time of the warm interglacials, during which period they could practice their way of life gathering food and hunting opportunistically and systematically. When the weather grew colder it is not likely that they packed up and left—a view expressed too frequently by both laymen and scholars. More likely they suffered increasing reproductive failures and infant mortality due to a decrease in food resources, seasonal starvation, and increased energy expenditures in obtaining food. The milk production of mothers declined; infants grew more slowly and were more susceptible to diseases; their injuries healed more slowly; and they were weakened by periodic absence of food and the hard work required to get it—all of which would cause higher mortality of the young. The return of cool climates would have proceeded much more rapidly than would have any system of natural selection to increase the reproductive fitness of these hominid populations, and *H. erectus* would have perished due to insufficient reproduction.

Yet somewhere on that northern rim of hominid distribution in the areas destined for glaciation, a new species of humans began to emerge. *Homo erectus* was fated to become increasingly capable of acquiring food in the dry steppe during the non-vegetative seasons; he was forced to become an increasingly more efficient systematic hunter, increasingly more monogamous, and increasingly more dependent, within the periphery of his distribution, on animals as a source of food. It is in his latter existence that he becomes a big-game hunter, and that spears are invented. It is also here that for the first time cooperative hunting must have become established as a rare but regular occurrence. This change could only take place when systematic hunting became impossible, and such would become impossible if snow and even mild hoarfrost became a common occurrence in areas inhabited by *H. erectus*. Even when *Homo sapiens* does appear, he is still for a long time a creature of warm interglacials, an indication that little cooperative hunting needed to be practiced, or that he was not yet fully man, fully human, and capable of cooperative hunting.

When *Homo sapiens* appears he is by no means abundant. He did disperse across Africa, as is evidenced by his handiwork, and the Acheulian hand-axe culture. He is larger in body size than *Homo erectus* and probably displaced him. He makes spears from wood hardened in fires, as shown by those found in European interglacial gravels, and by the concave flint scrapers which probably served as tools for spear making. His artifacts became associated with remarkably large animals: elephants, rhinos, and bisons. His hand axes improved in time. He was a creature that could probably have survived wet winters, rather than cold ones of relatively short duration. His absence from

Europe during the Riss glaciation, and the very crudeness of his tools, suggests that he had not yet invented clothing, nor the process of tanning furs, nor the tools capable of making clothing. His shelters were likely those that could be made from branches breakable with bare hands. One can build rather good shelters with one's bare hands, which, in combination with an open fire, are also remarkably comfortable.

The value of caves as shelters would depend on the availability of wood. Once the wood that could be gathered by hand in the vicinity of the shelter was depleted, the shelter was likely to lose its attraction. Since these early men lacked effective tools for cutting dead trees, they probably had to move from one area to another quite often during the cool season, simply to have wood accessible for burning. In the absence of effective wood-cutting tools which would allow the economic use of wood, the ability to exploit herds of big game probably depended upon the availability of firewood to survive cold, wet nights. In addition, the lack of clothing to protect the extremities would have reduced early *Homo sapiens*' capability to exploit cold climates. He would have been, given the foregoing reasoning, an occupant of the ecotone between forest and grasslands in temperate climates, exploiting big-game animals in the plains during the cold season, and reverting to the more productive gathering of food during the warm spring, summer, and fall seasons. This is probably how *Homo* became adapted to the forest-steppe ecotone and was later able to invade and exploit forested areas. In warm regions we would have been able to exploit areas marked by seasonal shortages of plant food by hunting large mammals. His human attributes would still have been quite modest: he would have been a rather egocentric, callous being of relatively low intellect, but of improved manual skills over those of *Homo erectus,* and a much better hunter. Pre-Neanderthal man probably represented the stage of the individualistic, systematic hunter, highly adept at stalking, with rudimentary abilities to employ strategies, and some tendencies for cooperation with others of his kind.

During the long Riss glaciation man did not dwell in the cold zones. He appears again as the generalized Neanderthal man in the following interglacial. Then with the advent of the last major series of glaciations, the Würm glaciation, he becomes for the first time an inhabitant of the cold, but exceedingly rich, periglacial steppe on the dry, southern side of the Eurasian ice sheets. Neanderthal man is the first human experiment in periglacial living, and he exists more by biological adaptations than with cultural ones, as is typical of the wave of people, the Cro-Magnon, our direct ancestors that replaced him. Neanderthal man had incredibly crude tools. His face, teeth, skull, neck musculature, and shoulder girdle were shaped by his method of ripping flesh into mouth-sized pieces; we must remember that the only food source for at least eight months of the year was the flesh of large mammals. Granted his crude cutting tools, he must have gripped meat with his powerful incisors and worried off one bite after the other. This requires powerful jaws, a large facial musculature, a massive neck, and powerful arms. The "brutish" appearance of the classic Neanderthal man must have been the result of his poor tools; and since his tools were too crude to form gloves or boots, his thick appendages were probably also an adaptation to the cold climate. His sites are not common and are usually in association with cliffs or river terraces, an indication that he obtained food by driving game over cliff edges in winter. He was not a very successful form compared to the Cro-Magnon which replaced him, for his remains are not abundant; his life expectancy as revealed from the fossil evidence was quite short, and he probably went to natural extinction when the first major Würm glaciation withdrew, causing in its retreat the collapse of the rich, periglacial ecosystem and an advance of forests which covered the loess steppe once populated by mammoth, bison, horses, and rhinos. We find a similar collapse after the last Würm glaciation and signs of desperate struggle of humans to adapt to the postglacial environments. This happened during the Mesolithic when population levels dropped drastically in Europe, large areas became free of humans, the individuals decreased in body size while their skeletons showed a high rate of diseases, deformities, and evidence of traumatic deaths. Compared to the large-bodied, large-brained Cro-Magnon of the Aurignacian, Gravettian, and Magdalenian cultures that flourished during the Würm glaciation, the postglacial populations are of poor quality and greatly impoverished in culture and in the workmanship of their tools. If these technologically advanced people had such difficulty surviving, it is not too astonishing that the culturally primitive Neanderthal man vanished after the first Würm glaciation when deglaciation caused the rich periglacial steppe to collapse.

At this point it is necessary to take a close look at some mental attributes and elementary facts concerning opportunistic, systematic, and cooperative hunting. The following case can be made: the ability to conceive four-dimensionally as well as to understand the complexity and quality of value judgments, the ability to store diverse learned information, and the ability to produce effective tools are very closely related and interdependent. These capabilities arose from similar ones readily detectable in animals, albeit in less-developed form. Their development to human levels of performance can be linked to the survival and increase in reproductive fitness through hunting which took effect, significantly, no earlier than the mid-Pleistocene when man adapted to live first in temperate and then in cold, periglacial climates. This implies that the complexity, diversity, and craftsmanship of tools are a fair reflection of the intellect of the men who made them for the following reasons: in order to choose a tool—let alone make one—one must be able to produce a mental picture of it. Such a mental picture may be the result of previous experience, trial and error learning, or what have you, but one must have it in order to choose the most appropriate object available. As Wolfgang Koehler, well-known early psychologist, showed long ago, chimpanzees can form a quite adequate concept of what is required and can fashion primitive tools. Choosing a tool depends on the ability to visualize it and to compare the mental image with the object at hand—whether it has the right shape, the right length, the right weight, the right resistance, and so on. One must be able to recognize if the conceived tool has been found, and select it from similar, but less preferable, forms. One must exercise a rudimentary value judgment, deciding what is better than the next. Animals can also do that much. Note the oyster catcher preferring the larger egg over the smaller eggs in his nest, or preferring the six eggs beside his nest to the three in his own nest. Regardless of how we camouflage the oyster catcher's choice in scientific jargon, the bird still exercises a choice, depending on the recognition that larger is better, or more is better.

The same argument for choosing a tool applies also to shaping one. One must have a rather good notion of what a finished tool will look like before beginning to build or shape the raw material. Thus, tool building depends on one's ability to imagine and to apply past experience. Clearly, the better the imagination and the more experience one has, the better and more effective the tool will be, and the more diverse one's equipment can be.

Somewhere in man's early history came the point in time when he kept a tool he found after using it, in anticipation of future use, rather than throwing it away and making a new one every time the need arose. That is, the individual practiced foresight and exercised a value judgment that was refined through anticipation of his future needs. His reward was greater efficiency—by having a good tool just when needed, by saving time and energy, and by conserving raw materials in tool crafting. In short, the ability to *make* and *keep* tools depends on a great ability to visualize spatially, to visualize future events, and to store much experience—be it with materials, craftsmanship, or strategies, including a refined value judgment. Clearly, man, to be an effective tool user, had to become a possessive animal unambiguously and strongly expressing "what is mine" and "what is thine."

However, refined tool making and use could hardly arise without refined ability to plot strategies (to imagine alternatives of events and objects in space and time), and this ability, in turn, could only evolve if there were sufficient economic return in such exercise. An opportunistic hunter needs little strategy to hunt successfully. He takes what comes along. He can, of course, improve his hunting efficiency by evolving or learning a method of approaching silently and taking his prey by surprise.

He can increase his chances of meeting a desired quarry by revisiting places where he had surprised a previous victim. While these are methods practiced by other carnivores, there is one in which I believe man surpasses anything alive—that is our adeptness in approaching an animal or man silently.

Have you ever wondered why your feet are so tender? Why they are soled just so? The feet are extremely sensitive to common nuisances of the ground such as thorns, pebbles, rocky ground, and the like. Of course, one can become fairly adept at moving on bare feet, but every so often one is reminded painfully of their limitations. Why did we not evolve soles as solid as those of a bear, or wolf, or a hairy pad with heavy claws as rabbits did? Why not thick calluses instead of pliable cushions where we step and force down our rather great weight? Don't compare the tender feet of other primates, because they are so light of body or because they live in such soft-floored forests that tender feet do not matter. Of what use are tender feet? Plenty, to a hunter. Had you trained for it and practiced, you would be able to sneak up on a deer in the forest close enough to pet it. I am not aware of any other carnivore that can do as well. Strip off your clothes—a major cause of noise—and with some experience you can sneak quietly like a shadow up to your quarry and surprise it at arm's length.

Such silent stalking, plus a quick rush, would bring early hominids on top of many small and medium-sized game animals. There was need to dispatch them quickly. Almost every type of game bites, and it is not wise to grasp with the hands. However, with a short club the victim can be quickly dispatched. We can regard our tender soles as an old adaptation, an echo from environments past, that has come to us from those time spans when warm, productive landscapes were our evolutionary home, when we made our living by gathering and a little hunting. Like our appendixes, so tender feet can be regarded as adaptations which were useful in the distant past; and both are still with us since they are not a great hindrance, even though they are of little use. In a similar manner, we are likely to carry some behavioral adaptations that were useful to our early ancestors—of the *Homo erectus* type or prior—but which were of no use in later formative environments such as the periglacial zones, although they still crop up occasionally. Not all of our antisocial acts are necessarily pathological or un-natural—they may be remnants of old adaptations, as useless to life in the periglacial zones as are tender soles, which are worthless on snow and ice. When it is cold and we must wear clothing, silent, systematic stalking is, for all practical purposes, next to impossible. The clothing makes noises. Snow crunches under our feet. While it is possible, under such conditions, to stalk within bow-and-arrow range of animals, it is impossible to get within clubbing distance. The type of hunting successful in warm climates is out of the question in the cold north; one must develop new techniques. Thus, the change from making a living in warm climates to making a living in cold climates was fraught with great difficulties, and it is not surprising that man did not become a periglacial creature—a permanent member of the tundra fauna—till very late, indeed, in the Pleistocene. He was evolving and slowly developing into a cooperating, sys-tematic hunter, and much more slowly than most recent au-thorities assumed.

Yet man achieved it. Why did he go into business as a cun-ning, cooperating, disciplined hunter rather than as one who runs down the game as wolves or hyenas do? There appear to be several reasons. Given the gathering way of life of *Homo erectus* and his opportunistic hunting, there would be selection for silent, slow stalking—not fast running—and for a certain amount of craftiness. There would be selection for endurance in order to sustain roaming and to increase the chances of find-ing the bits and pieces of highly digestible food required by man. Just as we greatly enjoy exercising adaptations that sus-tain us and reproduce our kind, so we still like hiking and prac-tice it. Given the way of life of *Homo erectus* there would be no selection for running down game; nor the ability to starve for long time periods and still be able to muster resources to hunt; nor for the ability to bolt food in a great hurry when it is avail-able or to digest a lot of food in short order. Yet such abilities were essential for a roaming, culling predator of big game that hunted in groups, predators such as wolves, hyenas, and hunt-ing dogs.

We shall try a little game now. A flow diagram will indicate the adaptive syndromes of humans that lived in the periglacial environment and made a living by hunting. Adaptive syndrome? Let me explain this one by illustrating it on the now familiar mountain goats. As discussed earlier, goats have short, needle-sharp horns. Since they fight in reverse parallel, most punctures should be found on the rumps of fighting goats. However, here goats have a thick, tough, skin shield that serves as protection against the sharp horns. Therefore, in the goat, sharp horns led to the evolution of rump shields, as drawn in Figure 1.

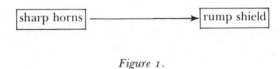

Figure 1.

Since blunt horns had no effect against the shield, but very sharp horns could still penetrate the shield, very sharp horns were quite advantageous. The effect of a rump shield was the evolution of sharper horns, as noted in Figure 2.

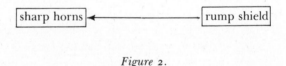

Figure 2.

Therefore, there was a mutual, reciprocal effect: sharp horns selecting for thicker, tougher, rump shields, and rump shields selecting for sharper horns, as noted in Figure 3.

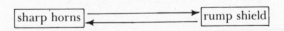

Figure 3.

A consequence of sharp horns is that baby goats must not play-fight, once their horns start growing, since they could easily injure or kill each other. In particular, the rambunctious yearlings—the "teenagers" in goat society—must be discouraged in their playful bouts with the younger kids. I saw one kid severely wounded, probably in a play fight, and a friend told me of finding a kid dead of horn punctures. Consequently, a mother mountain goat keeps a watchful eye on her kid and chases yearlings and two-year-olds away the moment aggressive interaction begins. Hence, sharp horns led to very protective and very aggressive goat mothers. It had to be. A mother goat not so endowed would lose her children to accidental wounding; thus the sequence moves on in Figure 4.

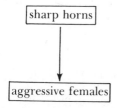

Figure 4.

In addition, it was most adaptive for the youngster if he could call mother should he get into trouble. After all, mother may be out of sight behind a rock when big brother, the bully, shows up. Therefore, a loud and effective distress call became a most essential part of a little goat's equipment. That is, of course, exactly what we find. Little mountain goats have a unique, absolutely ear-splitting yell that urges mountain-goat mothers to come running in great haste and in very visible excitement. Therefore, as depicted in Figure 5:

Figure 5.

Now comes the real dilemma. How does boy meet girl? She is aggressive as hell, big, and exceedingly dangerously armed; this is, in short, quite a traumatic combination. He is also big and also very dangerously armed. Let us assume that they meet, and she takes no guff, and he takes no guff. She strikes; he strikes; and, in short order, there are two badly wounded, dying goats. Hence, if she is aggressive, and he acts dominant they cannot get on with the job and breed. But breed they do.

As indicated in an earlier chapter, the solution that mountain goats have adopted is absolutely deflating to the male ego. He, the big, husky, dangerous boy, goes down on his belly and crawls to the female. Playing subordinate, he makes himself very small. He buzzes and squeaks tenderly like a baby goat—and it works. At first, she confronts him with lowered horns, and chases him away. But on his belly he is irresistible to her, and slowly, slowly, she accepts him, allowing him to drop his belly-to-the-ground performance, allowing him to be dominant, even be rough, during courtship when she is in heat, and when it is all over, she chases him off. Thus, as Figure 6 depicts, we have the following consequences of sharp horns and aggressive females on courtship.

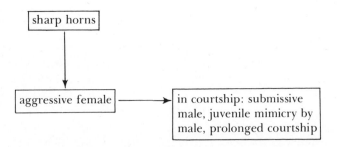

Figure 6.

Now, it so happens that mountain goats occupy some of the coldest, poorest, and most inhospitable habitats found anywhere. Yet, within this wilderness, the female must find sufficient forage above and beyond her daily need to nurture inside her body a baby that is big and strong enough to survive birth during the cold spring. Thereafter she must produce milk for her offspring, and that requires a lot of feed. The last thing in the world she needs is a male hanging around her home range in winter eating up the scarce food. He would probably try courting on the side, as well, generating useless excitement and in the process raising the cost of living by wasting all those precious calories. For her, the best way to live is to rid her home range of as many males as possible, and she certainly has a go at it. I witnessed several males being chased off by females, who allowed only relatively young males to remain with them in winter. The sequence is expressed in Figure 7.

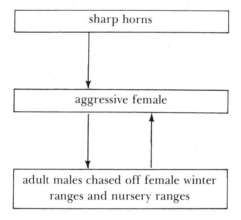

Figure 7.

Now, clearly, the more aggressive the female the more likely will be her success in chasing off males, and the greater the likelihood of her raising viable offspring. Hence, the act of chasing males off feeding grounds reinforces female aggressiveness in the species. Thus, there is an arrow as shown in Figure 7 leading back to the box, "aggressive female."

Granted that the female and her kids are well served by

removing males from their winter range, it is also adaptive or favorable to the female to insure that the male goes with as little back talk as possible, and that he leaves at once without the female needing to press home the attacks she threatens. This she usually accomplishes by looking very dangerous to the male. As it happens, male mountain goats are unlikely to start fighting anyway and readily withdraw from each other. The female takes advantage of this by retaining the image of a dangerous male. This step is described in Figure 8.

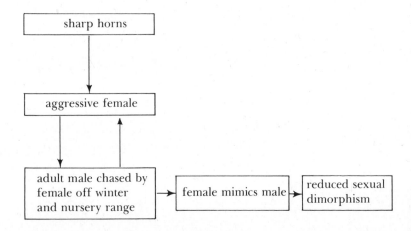

Figure 8.

One last thing: since sharp horns cause wounds, and goats—despite dermal armor on the rear end—get wounded in rare, minor skirmishes, they are well served by mechanisms that quickly stop bleeding and soon heal the wounds. This facility is vital to males in the event they get into a serious fight, where the consequence is always dangerous wounds. Hence, the better their facility to reduce the flow of blood and promote healing the better off they are. While this has not yet been demonstrated, there is some evidence for the phenomenon, since goats severely punctured in fighting bleed very little. Also, once a goat is wounded, it takes an awful lot of punishment to kill it.

This, hunters familiar with goats, are well aware of: one badly placed shot and it is hard to kill the goat. Figure 9 depicts this relationship.

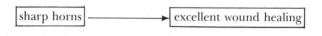

Figure 9

Now (as the schematic in Figure 10 portrays) we can put together a major part of the adaptive syndrome of goats as dictated by the passion for sharp horns.

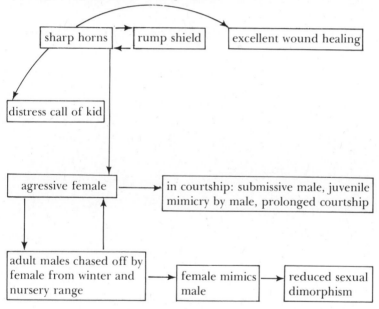

Figure 10

One could, of course, add further boxes and arrows to the schematic. Sharp horns also lead ultimately to reduced overt aggression and an increase in display behavior of males, as dis-

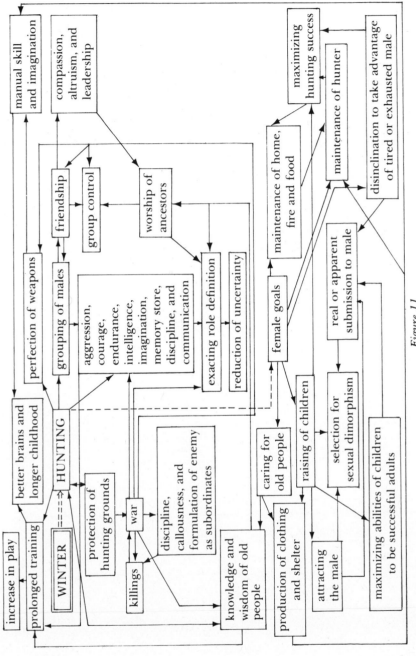

Figure 11

cussed earlier. Clearly, a female must be sensitive to the distress call of the kid, so obviously there must be a box with sensitizing mechanism drawn in, and an arrow leading from "distress call of kid" to that box. One could go on and on for some time before exhausting the possibilities of refining the above logical system. This also illustrates the "messiness" in biological sciences: there are so many related causes. Nothing is clean and elegant except in its simplest form. Nevertheless, even the simple diagram in Figure 10 explains much of the readily observable biology and behavior of the goat, and predicts that some day a physiologist will discover an excellent wound-healing mechanism in goats, whatever that mechanism may be. In a similar vein, we can contruct an adaptive syndrome for the human who lived in periglacial climates and made a living as a hunter (see Figure 11).

There it is. A complex mess, isn't it? Well, whoever said we were simple? If you were expecting a detailed explanation, you erred. I shall discourse only on a few aspects and leave the remainder for the enjoyment or frustration of those who enjoy puzzles. Whatever else I write on humanity is based on this adaptive syndrome and will be evident enough; to explain it fully would take volumes. However, before discoursing, let's look at a few attributes of man not usually discussed.

11

Man Mysteries

∅ Man is a peculiar creature. Why, for instance, should he be the only mammal that mimics sound—which is the biological prerequisite for verbal communication as well as for music? What caused us to acquire this ability? While some birds can mimic sounds—parrots, ravens, and myna birds—not a single mammal is able to do so (the pitiful attempts of chimpanzees on this score only serve to prove the point). The example of the birds illustrates aptly that in order to communicate verbally one needs more than the ability to mimic sounds, but mimicry of sounds is the fundamental need. How did we acquire it? I do not know.

Then there is music and dancing. Why do we enjoy hearing music, and seeing as well as participating in dancing? It does not help to know that some of our poor relations—the gorilla and chimpanzee—depending on species, have drumming of chest and ground, and wild whooping and jumping around accompanied by the waving of broken branches as dominance displays. It does not help much to know that most dancing, and certainly the most acrobatic, is performed by men. It does not help to realize that music, like conversation, follows the rules of predictability. That is, we enjoy listening to known tunes, enjoy singing "old" songs, and of course dancing is no enjoyment unless we know the step. We enjoy doing things we know, and exercise known skills, sometimes ad absurdum. I know that singing can make one brave, can rouse the spirit, or whatever it is, to emotional heights. The first time I marched on parade behind the wailing of bagpipes, I realized what made Scotsmen fight. I, too, was roused to kill. In fact, songs can make one braver than can weapons, as I recall from one incident.

Some years ago an assistant accompanied me on a moose study. He arrived on the job armed with an old army rifle, a gift from his aunt, and announced his determination to kill a bear that spring. We observed moose in shifts during the long spring and summer days from the top of a hill that rose from a steep mountainside. From here we had an excellent view over the valley and could look down almost directly from our dizzy height into a number of big meadows, burns, and shores of several small lakes. One day, shortly before I was to be relieved for the day, I noticed two big bull moose lift their heads from the sedges they were munching and look toward the base of the hill I was on. Almost simultaneously, a cow moose in another meadow also lifted her head and looked at the hill. It was not long before a fourth moose, a mile away or so in another meadow, also stared at the hill. How peculiar! Why the interest? I could not see the base of the mountain I was on since it was obscured in forest. So I strained my ears to pick up some sound. And indeed there was a sound. Whenever the wind settled a little, I could hear something that sounded like, well, it was peculiar, but it did sound as if someone were singing. The noses of the four moose had shifted a little, and by their alignment I gathered that whatever had aroused their curiosity was moving along the hill. Then I heard it clearly. Indeed, someone was singing down there. The tune faded in stronger now. The singer was obviously getting closer; in fact he must be zigzagging up the trail. Then there was no doubt left, it must be my assistant coming to take over the next shift. But why was he singing so loudly? That was unusual behavior for the Canadian bush, to say the least.

About 300 yards below, the singing stopped and soon my assistant arrived, rifle at the ready, and greeted me. I pointed out the moose, and related a few of the observations made that morning, and then mentioned that he had a rather good voice. He turned red from ear to ear. Well, that was strange! "Why did you sing?" I asked. "To keep the bears away," he stammered. Be that as it may, it does not take music to rouse one's emotions for combat. The Indian war whoop was no song, nor was the roar òf the Russian soldier storming from his trenches, rifle at the ready; nor did the German tribesmen confronting Roman legions make music with their swords on the shields, or by yelling into their shields. I have seen wolves become extremely emotional when howling, which is particularly evident in zoos when one can see how they close their eyes during the long, mournful song. On a number of occasions, I have seen wolves howling in the wilds, and have conversed with them by howling—but I still do not know what I told them and what they replied in return. We do not know why wolves howl, or coyotes howl, or hyenas howl. No one has yet come up with a plausible explanation as to what these social carnivores gain from howling, or what they stand to lose by being silent. However, the answer will be forthcoming, it is only a matter of time. Then we shall also know why music became our speciality, although it will not tell us why we mimic sound. For the present we must take it for granted.

Less puzzling is our love for ritual and the structure of most of our daily conversations. They both relate to predictability in the social and intellectual environment. As noted earlier, animals strive toward predictability and are well equipped to familiarize themselves with their habitat (make it familiar, predictable) and to create and maintain a predictable social environment (by means of combat, threat, display, submission). We have not escaped the need for predictability in our daily lives. Have you ever noted what two train conductors, truck drivers, or medical doctors talk about when they meet? They will talk about their work. They will go on and on—the truck drivers about the virtues of certain engines, tires, oils, batteries, truck models; about road conditions several miles back; about pretty waitresses in roadside restaurants where truckers stop; about load restrictions, accidents, employers, wages, other truck drivers, driving feats, and so on. The train conductors will reminisce on how many tickets they clipped; how busy it was the day before yesterday; how they expelled passengers with improper tickets; how they closed an eye for some elderly passenger improperly ticketed; how some fellow they both knew handled similar situations poorly; how good a conductor was some old hand that died recently; how poor were some of the young conductors on the job, and so forth. Nor do we need to note what doctors talk about. Like everyone, they tend to harmonize in conversation on and about things they know. Whatever is news, is really variation on the old. It tends to be a comparison of parallel experiences, a confirmation of competence, and a belonging to a given field. Conversation balks if this is not possible.

We can safely conclude that conversation rises to the highest level of common experience. When one has little in common, conversation can still go on about girls, the weather, cars, politics—but especially about the weather. Conversely, do you remember the emotional response you experienced when, in casual conversation with a stranger, you discovered that you had something very important in common? What a delightful experience it is to discover in a strange land a person who comes from one's home town, or attended the same school, or is dedicated to the same hobby, or that you and he have a common friend. Why is such experience delightful?

Our animal nature gravitates toward exposing ourselves to the predictable, and exercising it. If it were not so, would we bother listening to old tunes, familiar sermons, beloved symphonies, and concerts? Would we reiterate familiar subjects? Would we enjoy dancing? Hobbies? And yet, we also love new stimulation. We enjoy *slight* deviations from the known, but only if we have the option to withdraw again into security should the need arise. That little bit of new experience we quite correctly call exciting. If there was a lot of new experience, and little if anything familiar to run back to, be it physically or intellectually, the experience would be traumatic. To my surprise and delight I discovered that Professor John Kenneth Galbraith in his book *The Affluent Society* had discussed this principle in his treatment of "conventional wisdom." His chapter on this subject is a fine study of our animal behavior at the cultural level and provides a wonderful basis for predicting how changes in accepted theories, traditions, and practices come about. Intellectually, we explore new conceptual ground like a mouse explores a new cage, by carefully moving out a little and darting back to the familiar corner.

Harmonizing in conversation is, of course, only one form of establishing and maintaining a common bond. Drinking or celebrating together helps in the same direction. Better still is to do things together, and experience a common fate. Best of all is to hold in common secret knowledge or rituals. This sharing not only forms a strong bond—but also excludes others. We long for the predictable social relations of an in-group. Since our psychic capacity to remember faces and fates is limited, we can form only a small circle of friends. We form an *in*-group and begin to contrast it with the *out*-group, inevitably by vilifying the *out*-group. This is not at all surprising in view of our superiority displays. This of course reduces contact with the *out*-group and increases contact with the *in*-group. It really saves on intellectual labor and emotional upset if the *in*- and *out*-groups are clearly labeled. In very large gatherings, some labeling and rank designations are inevitable, be it in the army or at a convention. We also signal our allegiance in dress, hair style, our belongings, the place we live in, and the pubs we visit. When establishing the *in*-group, we know at once how to behave, whom to help, whom to like, whom to invite, whose argument to listen to, and so on. Even in our intellectual dealings we are likely to be guided strongly by our emotions when dealing with members of the *in*- and *out*-groups. I cannot conceive how it could be different. That in business it is most important to *belong*, to ally oneself with powerful families and individuals if one wants to get ahead, to marry the boss's daughter, to dress acceptably, not to have idiosyncracies, never to be a loner—these are all ideas that have been well and humorously dwelt upon by Professor Northcote Parkinson.

Anthropologists have noted that evidence for religious beliefs appeared rather late in the prehistory of man. From the foregoing adaptive syndrome of man adapting to the periglacial environment, this is not surprising. One can make a plausible case that religion, in the form of worship of supernatural beings, did not become important till leadership became important, when command had to be backed by authority. Closely coordinated group hunting was not necessary till man adapted to the cold or periglacial environment, as argued earlier; then religion became an extension of leadership.

At this point I shall not discuss leadership in animals but must point out a rather significant observation one can make repeatedly. In mountain sheep or mule deer, young males appear to be fascinated and attracted to older males. In the sheep this ultimately reveals itself in leadership, or followership, for the young males follow the largest horned ram in their group. Similarly, we note a certain attraction to men held by young boys. We are aware that they adopt heroes or idols who may or may not be their own fathers. They are known to justify certain acts by claiming that their father, older brother, or their idol had done the same thing. This gives authority to their own action. And so, in hunting we equip ourselves largely on the basis of the authority of other better, or better-known, hunters. We accept the authority of the experienced.

Let us now conceive of a hunting group of men. The leader's strategy is followed because he is well respected, but he increases his authority by claiming that he learned such from a still greater hunter, one who is now an old man. When that great hunter dies, our leader can invoke the memory of the dead to enhance his authority. From this it is but a small step to worship the deceased; to imagine happy hunting grounds; to conceive of superhunters to whom one's thoughts are to be addressed; to make offerings, ceremonies, and sacrifices to the great leaders. Authority can now be claimed by reference to mythical powers, which all can understand. Since the ability to conceive four-dimensionally, as well as the need for authoritarian leadership, did not arise till man colonized the cold regions, it can be safely predicted that little evidence for religious cults will be found prior to the Würm glaciation. The skulls of humans which had been cracked open to extract the brain are signs of cannibalistic activity, not ritual. We now know that baboon skulls are cracked open by chimpanzees for the extraction of brain, much in the same manner as were those ancient human skulls. With Neanderthal man, a cold-adapted human form, we find the first recognizable traces of religion in the form of burials with artifacts, and of bone assemblages indicating the existence of a bear cult.

Another line of evidence proving that modern man evolved in the periglacial regions comes from an unexpected side. It is known to anthropologists that many cultures emphasize the male sex organs. We find indications in symbolic forms on old Greek statuettes, which, according to Dr. Wolfgang Wickler, were used as border markers; we find similar statuettes on Bali where they are used in the hope of warding off spirits. In ancient cave paintings, the male's organs are usually shown overdimensionally. In Melanesian, in some Indian, and in Australian tribes, the male's organs are emphasized by decorations that make them most conspicuous, and in Australian aborigines by subincisions. The erected penis as a symbol of power and manliness is found in pantheons of gods. In the Khoisan races of humans the penis is maintained in a semierect posture by biological rather than cultural means, by means of a ligament which runs the length of the penis and attaches to the pubic bones. In these races of humans we find the only convincing biological means of penis display, although we do know that, in other races, on the average, males sit differently from females, namely in a fashion that would display the sex organs of the male were it not for the clothing, while male infants have erections when crying in rage. The facts are such that one cannot escape the conclusion that penis displays have been important in our past, that they are performed with the aid of cultural means—since the biological means have been largely lost—but that such displays are quite rudimentary in modern man.

What significance has penis display? In man it has some connotation of manliness, power, and aggression. We can see the significance of penis display much better in primates. Here it is clearly associated with dominance. This has been noted and discussed earlier. A comparison of the primate and human conditions clearly leaves one with the conclusion that penis displays have a biological foundation which can be studied in lower primates, that humans have largely lost this biological foundation for penis display but still practice it in some cultures with the aid of cultural means. This of course raises a question. If we are still sensitive and somehow impressed by penis displays, as their presence clearly demonstrates, why then have we lost the biological means of display?

We can answer this question with a little experiment in thinking. If we assume that in the periglacial environment a male did produce a showy erection when angered, what would happen at 50° below zero? In fact, we need not even postulate such temperatures. If the penis were covered to prevent it from freezing, what kind of garments would it rub against? Rough, hairy, filthy, roughly tanned leather or rawhide? Even if it did not freeze, the penis would still rub against those garments and be injured with each violent motion of the body. In short, a male with his penis displayed would not likely remain long with his penis intact in the periglacial climates. The trait would be quickly selected against. When *Homo sapiens* reinvaded the warm zones following his periglacial evolution, the need for a penis display on the naked body was still present but not the biological means to deliver it. Hence the cultural aids to penis display. One must not fail to mention here that symbolic forms of penis display crop up every so often in the male fashions of Western society, as Professor Otto Koenig amply demonstrated.

Earlier on, I indicated that we had not escaped the rules that governed the evolution of ice age mammals. These ice age mammals tended to be giants of their respective families, and this certainly does apply to us. Of the 166 species of living primates, man is the third largest. When we compare the evolution of the Hominidae with other families of large mammals, we find man followed a rather common pattern. In the early ice ages, there was a radiation of species which resulted in the appearance of the first giants. In the case of our family it is *Gigantopithecus,* a species at whose size we can only wonder. The teeth of the beast were enormous and would presuppose an 8-

192 Mountain Sheep and Man

to-12-foot stature if it stood on its hind legs. The Villafranchian produced many giants: lions were the size of oxen and cheetahs were about twice as large as the present species, as were the African hunting dogs. There were giant deer with incredible antlers, giant oxen, giant sheep, giant goats. These giants disappeared prior to the major ice ages.

We also find larger body sizes with increasing ecological specialization in large mammals. This rule is valid both for tropical areas as well as for areas with cold climates. Since the movement of a genus from tropical to periglacial climates would be linked with ecological specialization, there is also a concomitant increase in body size. In the lineage of *Homo* we see an increase in body size from *Homo africanus,* a savannah-dwelling omnivore from the early Villafranchian, to *Homo erectus,* a toolforming steppe and temperate-climate omnivore, to *Homo sapiens,* a cold-climate carnivore, who ultimately adapts culturally to all major ecosystems of the world.

Recently it has become evident that in ice age mammals evolution and geographic dispersal have a close relationship. This is well illustrated in several lineages of hooved mammals but best of all in the mountain sheep. In general, as sheep dispersed in the wake of glaciers across continents, they became larger in body, grew bigger and bigger horns, became increasingly specialized in fighting techniques, and in the males reduced and ultimately lost a number of secondary sexual characteristics typical of primitive sheep, i.e., the flowing neck manes and bibs. That is, they became increasingly "younger" in looks. When I applied this concept to the behavior of sheep, I surprised myself, since even among the closely related thinhorn and bighorn sheep of North America, the more highly evolved bighorns are more "juvenile" in their behavior than are the thinhorns. What concerns us here is that where sheep colonized last, they are most advanced and most juvenilelike or neotenic. What is surprising is that exactly the same can be said about humans. Where they colonized last, in America, they are more neotenic than where they colonized first, namely in western Eurasia in the Würm interstadial. (This interstadial is a break in the cold climate within the last big glaciation, the Würm glaciation, characterized by a retreat of ice fields.) Let us compare the way in which typical inhabitants of the area first colonized by modern man differ from those in America. I well recognize that such a comparison is fraught with danger, but let us do it nevertheless. What we expect in modern man of aboriginal origin in America is a retardation of characteristics typical of older age in aboriginal man from Europe, and a freezing of physical development or maturation at a slightly earlier stage. Thus aboriginal man from Europe is characterized by heavy growth of facial and body hair after sexual maturation, the development of frontal baldness in a high percentage of cases, the appearance of gray hair in middle age, while females after sexual maturation develop differently and assume the all-familiar form. Aboriginal man in America has a distinctly smaller sexual dimorphism and displays considerable underdevelopment of those features typical of adults in aboriginal Europeans: there is little facial and body hair, frontal baldness is exceptional, while graying of hair is delayed until a greater age. Somehow, aboriginal Americans have sipped longer at the fountains of youth than have their more primitive European counterparts—primitive, zoologically speaking, that is.

Shortly after the appearance of Aurignacian man in Eurasia, the decline and extinction of much of the megafauna began, that is, of the large mammals and birds. Creatures which had lived and thrived with early man during the ice ages go to extinction, and their extinction coincides roughly with the appearance of modern man. We can trace such waves in Africa, Madagascar, Australia, America, and Eurasia, as Professor P. S. Martin and Professor H. E. Wright, Jr., of the universities of Arizona and Minnesota respectively, presented in a book they edited. Oh, I know the evidence is not always conclusive (but often enough), and one can find alternative explanations for one continent or region that are as good as the overkill hypothesis, but the pattern is there just the same. It ought to be, if my hypothesis on human biology and evolution elaborated here is valid. We should find, once man became a highly efficient hunter of large mammals and began colonizing other continents, that the large, relatively rare, highly specialized large mammals would be hunted to extinction. We should have no such expectation of this happening prior to the last glaciation at a time when man was not yet a cooperative hunter.

The .conquest of warm-climate regions by periglacial man inevitably had to lead to a fundamental change in life style. In the periglacial hunting economy, it was the male who was the major provider and in winter the only provider. In such a situation, although one's hunting territories must be protected, warfare is a risky thing. The males are indispensable as providers, and one heedless about fighting jeopardizes the lives of his wife and children should he become even temporarily disabled. In the warm climates the situation is quite different. Due to the continuous and greater biological productivity of warm climates, females can not only provide much of the food through gathering or primitive agriculture, but can also provide a surplus. This frees the males from the need to provide food and increases their role as protectors of the tribal area. Males freed from providing can engage in risky wars, hence we would expect an increase in hostility in tribes from fertile, productive regions. This should lead to great male ceremonies and much emphasis on combat potential, hence severe initiation ceremonies, and war-preparatory games. In essence, though, the role of provider shifts in productive areas from male to female, while the territorial protection becomes the major if not sole responsibility of the male. It has happened before. We find a parallel development in lions, as shown in a study by Dr. George Schaller, a noted field zoologist. In lion society the female provides most of the meat to feed the tribe, while the territorial males, often several brothers together, protect the hunting grounds from intruders of both sexes, thus not only safeguarding the food supply, but also protecting female and offspring from cannibalism.

12

Of Dinosaurs and the Anti-Society

✍ It may be noticed that pronouncements of gloom and doom often contain some references to dinosaurs. The implication is that we shall all bite the dust and disappear from earth like those big, unfortunate reptiles. Next, another piece of wisdom about dinosaurs is pulled from the hat and, while a finger is wagged at us, we are told that if we do not change our ways and adapt to new realities, if we remain as unbendable in nature, as outmoded, as ill adapted as those dinosaurs, well, we will all be dead.

There is a dreadful secret about this dinosaur simile, so dreadful that I am almost afraid to reveal it. Dare we speak of the *poor dinosaurs?* Or say they were unlucky? They only lived more than *250 million years* on earth, while we cannot even boast a half million as a species. If we were to do as well as dinosaurs, or if we are today what the eosuchians were to dinosaurs in the Permian period, then we would have to plan to survive 249.5 million years from today. If that sounds like a little too long a time span, do you think we can survive just half as long as dinosaurs did? If 120 million years or so is still too long, can we make it for so trivial a time as 5 million? Biologically speaking, that is a very modest goal. If we were to survive

just another mere half million, we would have been outdone by
mountain sheep by at least two million years. Our stay on earth
would have been terribly short in the span of earth's history.
An extraterrestrial archaeologist banging our bones, our beer
bottles, and our power-line insulators out of Pleistocene rock
some 50, 100, or 300 million years hence will not even know if
flint axes preceded ceramic toilet bowls or vice versa. He would
know little beyond the fact that some peculiar creature had
roamed the earth then. He would examine a few of our teeth,
our skull fragments, and our long bones and on the overall evidence conclude that we were a short-lived, unsuccessful form
of earth life. He would not need to worry about us, or even
allot us a separate chapter in his book on Earth Life. Dinosaurs? Ah, that's a different story. Yes, they were rather successful but of course nothing outstanding. Clams lived twice
as long as dinosaurs.

Such extraterrestrial conclusions do not sit too well with me,
even though one would have to agree with them. Are we destined to be outdone by sheep, dogs, dinosaurs, and clams!
Shall those dumb creatures really put us to shame? Are we not
something special? Something better? Aren't we? Maybe we
would be something better if—when feeling terribly important
and proud of ourselves—we were just to remember that the dinosaurs we debunk were highly successful while we, by comparison, are at best a rash experiment of nature. From the
viewpoint of a zoologist acquainted with the history of life on
earth, to survive half a million years is most unspectacular, although from the viewpoint of a historian it is a time span far
beyond comprehension. Clever as we may be, wise as we may
wish to be, the thought of surviving just another trifling half-
million years is virtually unthinkable, and certainly no topic for
popular discussion.

How and why did we survive in the past? Maybe we should
take a closer look at it. Then we can fruitfully contrast our
present condition with our past, notice how far we have de-
viated from our original and "natural" way of life, and ponder
what the deviations will lead to. We will be able to recognize
from this contrast some of our strengths and failings for what

they are—as old adaptations or means of survival in a distant and strange, but "natural," physical and social milieu. We will find reasons for familiar cravings that once were satisfied, not at the expense of society, but to its benefit. We are, after all, creatures shaped by past environments, and we have lived in the present artificial one only a very short time. We should not be surprised if our present way of life strains and dissatisfies in a nebulous, unfathomable manner, or if it hurts without our knowing just where the pain originates.

Moreover, in explaining our attributes as a unique species, we must not forget the likelihood that we still carry behavioral "appendixes" with us, expressed strongly in some, weakly in most, that were once functional behaviors and cravings in earlier formative environments. To this concept we will return later, for it may explain some social "problems" that are too often found on psychiatric couches and in jails.

Although man, over a long stretch of time, changed from an omnivorous creature to an opportunistic hunter, and ultimately to a systematic, social hunter, the last and decisive step occurred when man colonized the cold regions of the earth. Here, in the cold climates, in the vast areas close to mighty glaciers, lies the cradle of human evolution. Here, man became man, and was forced to do so through the necessity of providing food during the long, cold winters. From the cold regions, man again and again spread to warm continents, and in the process decimated the large mammals with his newly developed skills and attributes. He also probably decimated, in the process, the earlier human inhabitants he found in his way. What were the requirements placed on man in the cold zones? What were the demands of a hunting way of life?

The demands were severe. Opportunistic hunting by individuals armed, at best, with spears is quite impossible, given clothing and the presence of snow, both of which make silent stalking very difficult. Men, of necessity, formed into cooperating groups for hunting. They concentrated on large prey, particularly on social ungulates such as horses, bison, and reindeer—mammoths that were found mainly on the open steppes and tundra. Such species can be herded and are easier to locate and more rewarding to hunt than such relatively solitary species as moose or roe deer. Hunting with primitive weapons required considerable knowledge on the part of the hunters, such as how to find, stalk, herd, lure, deceive, and kill the prey; it required great physical strength, skill, and stamina to travel long distances, to haul heavy loads of meat, to avoid charges by wounded, enraged bison, mammoths, cave bears, and such, and the skill to place the light spear accurately and forcefully into the vitals of a prey on first try. It also required great courage. Picture a man armed with a short, flint-tipped throwing spear four paces from a mammoth. It took no small amount of courage to get that close and go through with the task of attacking the animal. The foolish would hardly live to tell his tale; the coward would hardly venture within spear-throwing distance, nor would he respond to the urgent need, should it arise, of distracting the quarry's attention from his endangered hunting companion. Such an act requires self-discipline and the ability to calculate one's moves, as well as the need to keep a very level head while only inches from possible death. These requirements had to be met, not once in a lifetime, but on every hunt, and every week, month, year of a man's life span as a hunter.

It is evident that for a group to be successful at hunting it had to have individuals loyal and selflessly dedicated to each other. We find such dedication among soldiers on the front lines of battlefields, a dedication that requires compassion for others of great—indeed of very great—order. We need not postulate that the recognition of mutual advantage kept the hunting group of men together. We can safely postulate that it was friendship, deep friendship, that did it—the consequence of natural selection for compassionate, loyal, altruistic men faced with the need to kill dangerous big game for food.

The hunting group of men had ideal conditions to forge strong, deeply felt friendships. They would have been born within the same band, since periglacial hunters lived in small groups. Some would have shared common childhood memories of adventures and pranks they pulled, would often have confronted dangerous game together, would have made long trips through the winter landscape and shared common joys and hardships, would have lost common friends and been united in grief over the loss of loved ones. They could have harmonized on common experiences to an extent quite impossible to us, and thus psychically reinforced and supported one another. They would have moved through life's stages together—from childhood, to boyhood, to manhood, to old age—with the bonds of friendship and loyalty linking them more closely with each year that passed. They had to exhibit, for the sake of mutual survival, the very best of human attributes, such as love, compassion, tolerance, loyalty, dedication, and ruthless selflessness.

A coward would not have survived or reproduced. He who ran when danger threatened would be scorned and ridiculed. What girl would marry a cowardly hunter? What girl would share her life with a man who could not pass the initiation tests of single-handedly killing a big game animal, so common a task for men to be admitted to manhood in hunting tribes?

Altruism would be further enhanced by their relationship to each other, being brothers, fathers, sons, uncles, cousins, nephews, and grandfathers. Thus, self-sacrifice would be sacrifice for one's genotype and would hence be selected for. The success in a life which dictated that men must hunt large, dangerous game depended on aggressive, brave, clever, loyal, compassionate, *and* altruistic men—and natural selection succeeded in evolving them only too well. We know that men will go out and die on order, that they will run into hails of bullets and shells, rather than let others down, rather than disobey an order, rather than question the rationale of those that gave the order. Of course, under "natural" conditions in the hunting bands, virtually no order would be foolish and suicidal, since the man who gave the order and the one who carried it out were not only the closest of friends, but also relatives. It is quite foolish to postulate that hunting has made us into cruel, soulless beasts. On the contrary, we would never have hunted without possessing love and compassion for others.

Discipline also had its rewards. The hunters would often have been wounded in their dangerous tasks. Hunting accidents were likely common. Yet wounds must not impair the hunting efficiency of the healthy men, lest the group be inconvenienced unduly and the lives of women, children, and the elderly be put in jeopardy. Is it so strange, then, that in many initiation rites the test of manhood depends on withstanding wounds and pain? Is it any great wonder that we admire him who can take the "slings and arrows of outrageous fortune" without flinching? Is it so strange that we admire him who dies bravely, be it through execution, torture, or disease?

One may raise the question whether, in the periglacial hunting societies, warfare was not an important selecting force. True, the hunting grounds would have to be protected from intruders. Yet such a need could be satisfied only with dire consequences to both the aggressors and defendants. Warfare would kill grown men, an eventuality which would be an intolerable luxury to a people who depended on hunting for their livelihood for a minimum of eight months of the year. Nor would warfare be very rewarding. What would one gain? Artifacts the warrior could have produced himself? Women, which meant more mouths to feed? No, under conditions where men must provide and were indispensable for the survival of their families, war was a nonsensical luxury. It was less a luxury where food could be produced quickly and abundantly, whether through highly efficient hunting tools or by the labor of women in the productive warm climates; in either circumstance men were forced into idleness for much of the time. Then dominance displays became very important; rituals could be developed, possessions produced and accumulated, and great epics told, while the possessions of others provided incentive for raids. Then polygyny became possible, and desirable, since it was a status symbol for a great hunter and warrior to multiply his kind, and not only to do great deeds in battle, but also to provide for several families. Moreover, an increase in the tribe's size was highly desirable since it was safest to live in a large and prosperous tribe: it gave the tribe security from attack by lesser tribes, and also permitted it to raid with little cost in men relative to its size.

Under periglacial conditions, polygyny was quite unthinkable in a hunting society. It would have required a super effort on the part of the man to provide for two families. Moreover, the sex ratio would be tipped in favor of men, since (in a hunting society) they were not exposed to mortality by warfare or in childbirth. It is likely that there were fewer women than men, and lucky the hunter who had a woman to make and mend his clothes, to keep the fire going—without which no human life was possible in winter—and to thaw the meat and cook it in his absence. Under conditions of cold, snow, and long winters the woman was the center of the family. The need for women's services as well as the need for harmony among the men would not have permitted polygyny. We can indeed postulate with reason that monogamy would have been the original "natural" condition in the cold environments that shaped modern man.

The role of the woman, as the keeper of her family and a person of great importance, cannot be overemphasized. Her labor not only provided for the elementary comforts of her husband and children, but also freed her husband to become an efficient provider, thereby insuring life and prosperity to the family. Hers was an enduring task, requiring an orderly, industrious person. Hides had to be scraped, tanned, cut, sewn into clothing, and decorated. Fur clothing did not last long and had to be replaced. She had to be very knowledgeable on which skins or parts of skins served which purpose best. She had to transform complaints about clothing into improvements. She had to gather fuel for the fire and maintain it. She had to cook and look after several children, and she was probably pregnant or caring for a baby much of the time. Without a guardian of the fire, meat would freeze into ice in winter and could not be cut with primitive tools. Fire had to be present steadily in the cave and had to be looked after carefully and checked several times a night. Hers must have been a life of persistent, orderly toil, in which there was a premium on exact, level-headed thinking.

Since male and female roles were strictly separated but complementary in nature, quite different demands were made on each. The male became an aggressive, potentially very dangerous individual. A female who was aggressive to the male would likely severely disrupt family life and, if successful in slighting the male, her behavior would probably undermine his self-confidence sufficiently for him to become ineffective in his dangerous daily tasks. A female in competition with the male would, under the conditions postulated, become widowed quite soon and face life as a beggar and burden to the band. Without going into detail, it can be argued that a woman capable of producing maximum harmony in the family, appeasing and psychically reinforcing her husband, would maximize the chances of raising children to maturity. Such harmony would permit the male to live long enough to teach his sons, and ultimately his grandchildren, to become efficient hunters, and serve as a model for his daughters to form their image of a successful husband. Not the individual but the extended family is here the unit of reproduction.

We saw earlier that we are slaves to the Great Game which dictates that the successful female is the one who raises the maximum number of children to adulthood. As suggested above, this entailed maximizing the male's efficiency as a provider. We also noted in an earlier chapter that aggression tends to be accompanied by sexuality in primates and other mammals; we also noted that in periglacial societies aggression would be selected for in the males. This would also result in an increased sexuality in men. Here appears to lie one root of our unusually flourishing sexual behavior and our rather generous organs—when compared, that is, with those of other primates. Furthermore, since a female's secondary sexual characteristics and her typical "feminine" behavior depend upon hormonal levels produced by specific endocrine glands, well-developed secondary sexual characteristics would signal potential compatibility to males. If, indeed, shapely females and brave, aggressive males raised the largest number of offspring to maturity, then, very quickly, natural selection would create a mechanism whereby girls fall for brave, skillful boys, and boys for shapely, charming girls. Such an attraction would increase sexual dimorphism in shape, voice, behavior, and other characteristics. The preferences of Aurignacian and Magdalenian hunters at the dawn of modern man's emergence, as depicted in their

"Venus" carvings, are remarkably similar to those of today's readers of *Playboy*.

While the conditions of the hunt demanded a high degree of cooperation and friendship among the men, such was not necessarily the case for women. They, burdened by children, were left to themselves in the camps. Each hunter returned with his share of the quarry and placed it at his family's disposal. In hunting tribes, sharing of kills was common, but the size of families differed. Hence, the female had to protect the meat her husband brought home from excessive free-loading by others. If she failed to do so, her children, her husband, and she herself were likely to suffer shortages. Therefore, it was advantageous to the family for the woman to exert some control over how much of her family's food could be removed by outside clan members. In short, there would be an element of strain introduced into the woman's position as guardian of the food supply. In times of dire need each had to maximize the amount available for her family. As it is in Eskimo cultures, a man would not likely interfere with anyone helping himself to the meat supply, since this would be admitting that he was a poor hunter incapable of supplying all within the clan who might need his help.

Furthermore, the Great Game dictated that the woman determined early the most successful potential mates for their children. In order to secure good husbands or wives for their children, a considerable amount of downgrading of others in social competition was inescapable. In short, while men had to cooperate in their tasks, the woman had to protect not only food in intergroup competition, but also had to compete on behalf of their offspring. Women married to less prestigious and efficient hunters, in particular, would have to live a rather strained life, often attempting to secure food from other families while protecting their children from social stigma. It takes little imagination to theorize that, whereas men led a hard life, it would have been socially very much more idyllic than that of the women. Notwithstanding the foregoing, for most of the time women would not lead a socially strained life, but only in times of want.

Unless one has been out in winter in the wilderness and provided for oneself, it may be difficult to conceive how much knowledge is required simply to stay alive. Even when supplied with modern equipment, such as our superb sharp axes, knives, matches, and rifles, managing to stay alive is by no means an easy task. How much harder must it have been when there was no equipment with which to quickly fell dead trees, splinter dry wood out of the trunk, and get a fire going at will. Early man had to compensate for poor technology with great knowledge of materials and microclimates, an exacting knowledge of the landscapes inhabited, and the locality and seasonal availability of resources. It was necessary to observe and correctly interpret weather patterns, lest one be surprised by inclement conditions unprepared; to know all possible food sources and means of conserving them; to be able to imitate in sight and sound various game animals and be aware of the idiosyncrasies of each species; to know basic first aid and what to do or not to do under various weather and hunting conditions; and to learn how to make effective implements from the natural materials at hand. For it takes time, much time, to master well the knowledge and skills required to become a consistently successful hunter and to support a family. This makes it evident why prolonged parental care was so important. The more one had to master, the longer the learning period must be. The longer the receptivity of the mind to accumulate, integrate, and exercise knowledge on demand, the longer the juvenile period must be.

In a sense, brains had to substitute for technology. The poorer the technology, the better the brains had to be—the greater the ingenuity a person had to muster to fulfill his daily tasks. It follows that evolution toward a better brain must come to a halt in man when an increase in technological capability makes further development unnecessary. The better the communication and the better the technology, the greater are the possibilities for intellectual decadence, since the intellectual efforts of a few can support the reproductive efforts of less capable minds. Once the increase in an individual's intellectual skills is not rewarded with an increase in reproduction, relative to the reproduction of less capable minds, evolution toward increased intellectual powers which characterized man during his emergence must come to a halt. Thereafter, the average quality of brains must of necessity decrease as technology and communication improve, and the ones who benefit are those who would have been incapable of survival under the conditions which formed our mental powers. To a zoologist our parasitic relationship toward technology has an ominous ring for the future: the host—technology in our case—takes on the task of providing, and gradually takes on more and more functions, leaving the parasite to concentrate all its energy on reproduction. The parasite degenerates into a mass of relict organs, except for big ovaries and testes that reproduce, reproduce, and reproduce.

Be that as it may, our brain size reached its peak in the late Pleistocene; it has apparently declined to about ⁴/₅ of its former size since then. The big brain was reached through prolonged growth of the body, giving us our unusually long juvenile period. This had a secondary benefit: we know from experiments with animals that if we artifically stretch their juvenile period, we also stretch out their period of senescence, that is, we increase their life span. In general, the longer it takes an organism to achieve adult size, the longer it lives as an adult, and the more slowly its body degenerates with old age. Conversely, the faster an animal attains full body size, the faster its body degenerates after reaching its peak of adult vigor. Hence, a by-product of increasing man's juvenile period is to increase automatically his life expectancy. For man this added another benefit: long after its reproductive period was over, a human could enhance the welfare of its offspring by counseling them, by guiding them, and by educating his grandchildren, thus transmitting precisely the information and skills which had allowed him to survive to old age. The more slowly man's body grew, the more intelligent it became, and the longer it lived, the greater its store of knowledge, the longer that knowledge could be passed on in old age. Hence an individual could contribute to his reproductive effort long after he or she ceased reproducing.

In the periglacial society the position of old people must have been one of great importance, and they must have been held in great esteem. They held a store of experience unrecorded anywhere except in their minds. They could give wise counsel based on previous experience, could entertain with tales and stories from times gone by, could counsel and guide children when their parents were occupied, and could teach the youngsters many skills elementary to their future success. A brilliant old man or woman could, for a long time, give superior advice to his descendants and assure their success in trying times. These old people would be loved and honored; they would be central to the life of the band; and they must have been sincerely missed and mourned when they died. Lucky was the tribe that had enough old people.

The society pictured above is the one in which man has lived for the greater part of his existence. He has been shaped by it and is best adapted to it. He has lived not a millennium in it, but for thousands of years, changing in minor detail only, even in the great civilizations that have arisen in the past 6,000 years. We were born into a group of people, and lived with the same group of people, and died with the same group of people. By "nature" we formed few social relationships, but these were strong and lasting ones—until death did us part. We relied on old people for wisdom and guidance. We entertained ourselves by learning to become players, singers, and storytellers. We were built to "like" physical exercise, since, in so doing, as hunters we explored the land, and maximized contact with the game we sought for food. What other animals beside group-hunting carnivores go on long, "pointless" hikes? We and the wolves share this in common. Robbed of sustained physical activity in our daily lives, we search out gyms for a "workout." We love excitement and search out the action, since in our formative days this insured our participation in the business of hunting game and protecting others when danger arose. To this day we pay for the chance to participate, be it only as spectators. We have moved a long way from our natural way of life and have replaced the *natural* action with artificial activity to satisfy ancient, inbred urges. Let us look at modern suburbia.

In the morning father is shipped off to work. He is separated from his family for the rest of the day. His boys have generally little chance to see him at work, nor is his job usually so simple that it can be readily explained to children. Father returns tired and sometimes quite late from work, leaving even less time for activities with his children. The stage is set and the die is cast for a rift to develop between father and son. On the job, father is usually surrounded by men he may or may not know. If he is lucky, he will know a few men well. The great cultural and technological diversity of our society has made it difficult to find persons one can harmonize with on one's work and hobbies, except where people clump together in cities. The relatively frequent shifts of jobs have made it certain that social bonds are constantly broken and formed—a trying, hard process filled with uncertainties and little brotherly love toward one's next acquaintances. By the time father knows the employees at his place of work well, he moves on, or someone else moves, be it through promotion or unemployment or the offer of a more attractive position elsewhere. The slowly formed precious contacts are destroyed, and new ones have to be made. In such an atmosphere of uncertainty, one notices withdrawal on the part of some persons, excessive dominance displays on the part of others, and a search for security and predictability through various coalitions of mutual interests, through hard legal contracts, and through entry into professional unions. The old friendship bond that once guaranteed personal safety, that once triggered the concern of others if one were in need, and that held men together in our old evolutionary environment is largely gone, or is weak and short-lived. However, we still strive to form it, despite obstacles.

As noted earlier, due to the great diversity of experiences, father has a hard time harmonizing with others except on mundane subjects that represent the common experience—weather, politics, females. Although he is surrounded by many, he is still lonely, always on guard, filled with uncertainties, although he may camouflage this well. He is experiencing the very opposite his body is designed to experience.

While father is isolated from his family, mother is also isolated but in a different way. She has several energetic children to attend to, and from these there is no respite. Her sisters are married and live in another town and cannot help her. Her mother, who could have helped her, is also far away. She knows some of the neighbors, but not really well since she came into the community only recently. She has her hands full in keeping the house and family together and has almost no one to fall back on for comfort, for very personal advice, or for a respite from her brood. Both mother and father are lonely, frustrated, and plagued by uncertainties and probably do not even know it. They find themselves caught in a way of life that is so demanding and moving so fast that it does not permit them to reflect on what alternatives there might be.

In suburbia, the need and desire to contact neighbors are severely reduced compared to habits in many less affluent societies. The television, the stereo, the radio, and the newspaper see to that. We need not depend on entertainment by our neighbors; we need not contact them for the latest news; we need not listen to their talents as musicians, storytellers, or actors—we do not need them. We have electronic "neighbors" to entertain us at the flick of a switch or the turn of a dial. Moreover, those "media personalities" save us the trauma of meeting them personally and getting to know them; they allow "faceless communication." Canned entertainment like canned food is easy to serve, undemanding, and so convenient. The neighbor remains a stranger.

The "media personalities" also influence our standards of judgment. They sing and perform their acts so well that we as individuals cannot possibly hope to attain such skills. When music is easily available, if we personally cannot hope to match it in quality, there is no point in trying to sing or learn to play an instrument. We would much rather listen to the stereo or the radio; it saves us the bother of applauding and of being nice to a performer at the end of the show. Just as our media have deprived us of the will and courage to diversify our interests in entertainment and become entertainers ourselves, so the media have also impoverished us and isolated us from our neighbors. The argument that our lives are enriched by the diversity of entertainment and information available to us by means of electronic media is not entirely valid. We do experience a flood of stimuli and impressions, which, for the sake of sanity, we largely block out anyway. But enrichment is equivalent not to dumping unprecedented quantities of impressions on us but to the experience of getting to know and understand some subject well. The electronic media further enhance our isolation from the people around us, the real people, and provide artificial substitutes.

In the meantime grandpa and grandma live alone somewhere, isolated from their children, perhaps in an old folks' home. Their children have deserted them. They are superfluous. They are not needed for their wisdom, since today that is fed to us via radio, television, newspapers, books, magazines, and such. The wisdom and knowledge of the old folks are quite inappropriate to modern conditions, so there is little they can tell us. Their tales are less entertaining than those on the television set, and their presence is sometimes an embarrassment to us. They are not "with it."

In the meantime, the old folks linger on. They survived retirement though some of their acquaintances did not. They live now on a meager pension that somehow has the aura of being generously given, rather than self-earned which it is. Their bodies are failing a little with each year, and the dusk of life is descending. They have time for grandchildren, and should, by the rules of our past, be associated with them, telling them what they know, comforting pains, settling quarrels, teaching them little skills, and showing them the best places to go fishing, berry picking, and so on. When the young folks do come for a visit, they are familiar strangers. Something is not quite right, and both parties know it and try to ignore the fact. The experiences and worries of both generations are different, due to the rapid technological changes by which we have been torn along, and the gulf between old and young is very real. When the grandparents' bodies fail, they are put up in hospitals—strange, frightening environments. They are as isolated from their loved ones as ever, and that at a time when they most need a little care and attention from their children.

Maybe the children do realize what awaits them, despite the youth cult promoted by our news media, and despite advertisements for hair coloring and expensive wigs to obscure gray hair. They, too, will be deserted by their children in turn; they, too, will face retirement with devastating finality and a feeling of uselessness; they too will face the old folks' home, the terrible isolation, and the long, lonely death on a white hospital bed.

In essence we have isolated the nuclear family and, by presenting substitutes, we have reduced opportunities for meaningful contacts with others. We have created circumstances that increase the isolation of the members of the nuclear family, thus estranging them and inducing uncertainties. Given this situation, it can be safely predicted that isolated individuals will do all they can to find certainty and emotional predictability, whether it be in channeling their energy into work, into religion, into dogmas, or into hobbies, thereby intensifying the common "rat race."

How and why did we get into this situation in modern times? The reason appears to be that we have developed "antinature" values, which, if followed, create an "antinature" society. Please allow me to explain: we strive to reduce, in all our doings, the need for physical work. Our gadgetry essentially is labor saving, or antiwork. We have worked against work for a long time, first by capturing the labor of domesticated animals to reduce our personal labor and to increase our efficiency. We then captured the forces of wind, steam, and electric power to do work on our behalf, including the reduction of labor in daily activities. This has reached absurd dimensions—witness the electric toothbrush and the electric carving knife. Yet, as indicated earlier, we were built by evolution to do plenty of physical work as roving hunters. Screened from the demands of physical work in our daily lives we seek to substitute by going for periodic "work-outs" in gyms, playing games of golf or tennis, or going for a hike. We essentially satisfy inherent laziness by our work-reducing technology. Yet, laziness is a biological adaptation that made a lot of sense in a hunting society. The demand for physical work was great, and laziness insured that we did not overwork ourselves, wasting precious food energy for nothing. Laziness insured that when demands were made upon us, we were ready to respond. Similarly, it is advantageous under conditions of hard physical work to seek means to reduce labor or obtain greater gain for the energy expended. The more efficient hunter could support a healthier and larger family. There was, in a hunting society, a premium on labor-saving devices. We are still following that trend.

In a similar vein, we are antisickness and antideath; we do everything possible to conserve health and life. This is in response to an ancient demand, older than the formal moral codes that impose it, for a tribe's strength was maintained and its collective wisdom was conserved by extending the life of old people. Today, we are, by and large, following these old demands to save and extend human life—regardless of consequence.

We are antidiscomfort in many ways, not only in the design of utensils, homes, and furniture, but also in our social life. To have a sick person around is often difficult and frightening, so we are relieved when sending to the hospital is prescribed. So also with a dying person. We are grateful to get him out of the house, and we believe it is better for the children not to see the dying. And in a nuclear family there simply are not enough hands to keep the household intact and to look after the needs of a dying person. But is it better for the dying? It is only too true that most dying persons long to be with their loved ones, and long not to die alone. Paid attendants in strange, sterile surroundings are poor substitutes for a family and a home.

Our desire for "creature comforts" is largely responsible for creating the antisociety referred to above. And yet our longing for creature comforts served us well during our emergence in millennia past and has safeguarded us from excessive energy waste. Today, given technology and affluence, we are able to satisfy these creature comforts to an unprecedented extent.

At this point I must pause for a brief review. In the preceding chapters I have elaborated on man's early environments as well as the consequences to man in adapting to these environments. The purpose of that exercise was to shape a tool with which to judge how and when our present mode of life deviates from our old, "natural" way of life. Applying the tool in this chapter, although only partially, I find that the deviations noted are the very kind which promote isolation of individuals, increase emotional strain through psychic insecurity, and consequently stimulate activities by which individuals regain predictability in the social milieu. The extended family has been disbanded in favor of the nuclear family—by isolating generations and relatives spacially. The social bonds between close relatives have been weakened by isolation through a decrease of common experience, whether from different jobs, hobbies, or place and region of residence. Isolation has reduced the amount of common experience within which relatives can harmonize and has increased "strangeness." Cultural and technological diversity has reduced the common experience between persons on the same job, thus isolating individuals. High job mobility has caused frequent shifts of allegiance; it has broken social bonds and forced the strainful re-establishment of new social bonds, and has been counterproductive to the development of strong friendship bonds. Members of the nuclear family were also isolated from each other by economic and social dictates, a situation which resulted in fewer common experiences, thus reducing opportunities for meaningful communication and promoting generation gaps. The satisfaction of creature comforts, through cultural and technological developments, promoted not only the acquisition of toil-reducing implements but, by the use of "faceless communication" via various news and information media and the telephone, at the same time reduced the need for face-to-face contact with new and different individuals as well as between neighbors, and this isolated individuals still further. In other words, in place of "real" experience, through human personal contact, the entertainment media substituted "fake" experience. Since interactions with neighbors have been reduced, it is notable that "horizontal" communication typical of a closely knit community has been replaced by "vertical" communication, which of course left nuclear families in a suburb isolated from one another. "Vertical" communication refers here to information flow from institutions, such as government agencies, via the electronic media to the family; it is an ideal structure to promote propaganda by whomever has access to the media.

The storage and ready accessibility of pertinent information, combined with the growth of technology and specialization of jobs, have made older generations useless as stores of knowledge and wisdom—and this has led to further isolation. In addition, reductions in real experiences of suffering, joy, sickness and death—and their replacement by televised suffering, joy, sickness and death—have created a way of life in which little compassion for persons outside the very small *in*-group circle of individuals can be expected. In short, we can expect persons to grow callous and shallow as their social bonds weaken and the quality of personal contact lessens. As a consequence of reduced real social bonds, and concomitant insecurity, it can be expected that individuals will channel activities into restoring security, be it through memberships in small groups with common beliefs and experiences, or unions with clear goals, or contracts safeguarding jobs—as well as through dominance displays in peer groups and the associated promotion of the "rat race." Personal insecurity has also promoted the search for unambiguous dogmas, black and white solutions, and—unfortunately—simplistic explanations. These considerations do suggest that the formation of small groups of persons of common background, age, and ambitions is a very "natural" happening. For reasons indicated earlier, it would be expected that such groups should be bound strongly by friendship and loyalty and should be rather hostile to similar groups and/or to society as a whole. While the formation of street gangs, motorcycle gangs, and other antisocial groupings may be quite damaging to the life and property of nongang members, their existence cannot be considered evidence of "social pathology." That the groups exist, cannot be equated with disease, but rather with the psychic health of the gang members.

Where does this lead us? A contemplation of our present society as seen through the eyes of an ecologist leaves little doubt that we may well be the last civilization. This is no pleasant prospect, but it does pose a very real challenge—it also leads me to the point where courage may just leave me. If nothing but physical survival of the human species were the goal, continuation of life could easily be achieved by destroying human culture and technology as we have seen it evolve in the past six millennia. We would then revert to an aboriginal way of life, with its proven survival value. However, physical survival alone simply cannot be a goal. Rather, the problem is to find ways and means to continue our life on earth with the fruits of our magnificent cultural attributes. Better men than I have pondered this and searched for solutions. From a biologist's viewpoint the solution entails linking the reproductive efforts of individuals to superior physical and intellectual performance—to escape the gradual randomizing of genetically controlled growth processes shaping the micro- and macrostructures of our organs and bodies. It would also entail as a way of life the dictatorship of knowledge over our behavior. Please remember that we lived under a dictatorship of knowledge in our evolutionary environment as hunters, while today we live under a mixture of blind dictators—economic, social, technological. The alternative, embracing an egalitarian philosophy, would inevitably lead to greater diversion of technology to prop up failing human minds and bodies, to an increased regimentation of the individual's life, and ultimately to dictatorship by technocrats and machines. It would also entail a very great danger of accidental extinction. It takes little insight to recognize which dictatorship would most degrade the human. It also takes little insight to recognize which path we must travel if we want to survive on earth only one one-hundredth as long as did dinosaurs.

13

Paradise Lost?

⌀ We were progressing on our hands and knees. I had planned to approach the sheep from above in order to obtain some photos. After all, this strategy had worked with Stone's sheep, and it should work with bighorns. Karli, my brother-in-law, was sweating from the strenuous exercise, and so was I. A moment earlier we had reached a little rock platform, and I had peered across only to discover the ewes and two big rams peering back at us. The sheep were about 150 yards away. I slowly sank back behind the rock and paused, wondering what to do. We had been discovered. Maybe the sheep would run; maybe they would stay. I decided to creep on. We had barely begun to advance when a rumble erupted above us. Before I could lift my head, the rumble had changed to a drumbeat of hooves, swirling dust, and clanking stones, and seconds later we were engulfed in a band of bighorn sheep. We crouched on our hands and knees looking up; they stood, taller than we, looking down. We appeared—pardon the expression—sheepish, to say the least, not knowing whether we were dreaming or hallucinating. As the dust began to settle, another roll of hoof beats sounded, and two big rams burst through the females into sight before us. There we were, face to face with the legendary creature of the wild and towering Canadian Rockies—the bighorn ram. But this "legend" was flesh and

The author's bighorn friends. They would see him and come, looking at him with expectation.

blood and was breathing into our faces, since our noses were only a foot apart.

When I raised my hand the "legend" licked it, while another "legend" pulled my parka with its mouth. We stood in their midst as they gazed at us and pressed closer. I tried to think of a parallel to this occurrence, or for some clue to an appropriate action, but there simply was no precedent. Nothing I had learned previously equipped me for this surprise. Mountain sheep were not supposed to act like this. I had stumbled onto another "accident."

Much of my research has been a progression of accidents. To someone blessed with the asset of an orderly mind, it would be intolerable to have his plans dissolve in a string of calamities. But then, for research in the field in Canada's western mountains where unpredictable weather patterns, sparse animal populations, and highly seasonal events are customary, an orderly mind and polished research plans are, at best, a doubtful asset. One must learn to take advantage of the unexpected and let plans go down the drain without shedding too many tears. The best course is to make every calamity an asset.

The puzzle of the tame sheep had a perfectly rational explanation—as we discovered later. For fourteen years prior to my arrival at Banff National Park, a park warden, Ernie Stenton, had tamed and tagged a group of sheep at Lake Minnewanka. In early summer, shortly after lambing, the animals crave salt, and they had learned that this treat could be had close to Warden Stenton's station. Soon they were licking salt out of his hand and—while they were licking—he clipped small metal tags onto their ears. Stenton was mainly interested in learning if his sheep went beyond the park boundary where they might fall victim to hunters. Over the years a few rams were shot, but there were so few that Stenton concluded, correctly, that his sheep were confined mainly to the park. Some hikers or exploration parties brought back word of tagged sheep approaching them, but a systematic search for the animals had not been undertaken up to the time of my arrival, and I had no warning that the Palliser sheep were the very ones tagged by Stenton.

In earlier years, Stenton stood in rivalry with another warden, Green, who pre-empted the right to tag sheep above the Vermillion Lakes where the Trans-Canada Highway now runs. Since Green used green ear tags and Stenton used red ones, it soon became evident that they were tagging different groups of sheep. A third group at Aylmer Pass was kept under close watch by another old gentleman, Norman Tithrington, who for seventeen years occupied the Aylmer lookout tower each summer. When Tithrington was not watching sheep (for which he provided a salt block at the foot of the tower) he was spotting for boats putting out illegal set lines on the lake below, or for parties making an illegal campfire in a hidden bay during the preseason, or for couples making legal love on the beaches. Nothing escaped his eyes and telescope. Tithrington reported his observations vividly to his friend Ernie over the wireless—to the mirth of other operators on the same frequency and to the dismay of Department of Transport supervisors of radio.

Tithrington had fallen in love with the sheep and kept daily counts on them. He also observed cougars each summer and is the only individual I know who saw a cougar stalk and kill a young bighorn ram. The Aylmer sheep were a group quite separate from the Palliser group, even though they lived on different sides of the same mountain, and they were not quite as tame as those tagged by Stenton. They tolerated humans well, though. Tithrington had tried his hand at tagging, but a ewe had clipped him across the hand with her horns, and the old fellow declined any closer contact thereafter. Thus, when I arrived in Banff National Park after my Stone's sheep study, a group of enthusiastic amateurs had long known something professional zoologists were not quite conscious of: namely, that wild, unhunted animals can get along with man in a fashion reminiscent of the Biblical paradise.

In retrospect it is hard to understand why such insight had not come to me earlier, although I was not alone in my mental blindness. I had spent hours close to Stone's sheep, dressed in white coveralls and pretending to be a mountain goat; I had tamed whisky jacks and a weasel at my cabin; I had seen tourists with tamed mountain sheep along the Trans-Canada Highway in Banff. Yet we did not get the message the animals were shouting at us. It was this group of bighorn sheep—far away from tourists and out of contact with the wardens, galloping up to us and surrounding us—that made me see the obvious for the first time. In the years following I got to know them well and with their help I tamed others—in the process gaining a deeper insight into the habits of this beautiful animal.

Have you ever sat on a mountainside and observed a ram graze below you, watched the ram finish feeding, then look up and come to you, paw a bed that sends the dust and pebbles striking your legs, and then lie down beside you? There you sit, the cunning hunter and the cunning prey, while the wind plays gently with your hair, and his heavy eyes blink, ready for a little nap. The clouds move past overhead and their shadows play in the valley, the grasses rustle in the breeze, and the eagle soars past along the slope below both of you. The creature resting beside you is as free and wild as the mountains that nourish it. It can choose to leave you, but it does not. For the moment, it prefers your company.

I well remember the day when Number 48 returned after a long winter of absence. Number 48 was a five-year-old ram and a particularly trusting type. He disappeared prior to the rut, and I wondered what had happened to him. In the previous spring he had limped a little, and I speculated that perhaps his leg ailment had returned and finished him. So I often wondered if I would see him again in spring.

One evening in May I saw him. There was no doubt: it *was* 48, and at a distance he appeared to be quite well. Since dusk had fallen, I postponed climbing to him till the following morning. Early the next day I began the ascent, although I could not see him anywhere. "He must be *somewhere*, though," I thought, and I searched all morning in vain. Then I climbed across the range to its precipitous opposite side and continued my search. Suddenly I spied a lone sheep far away across many gorges and snowfields, but so far away I could identify the figure only as a ram in my field glasses. The sheep was feeding. I waited until it raised its head, then I began waving my arms to attract its attention. The sheep paused, only momentarily, and then it came—dashing at a full run across scree slopes and gorges, across cliffs and snowfields. The dust flew, the stones rolled, and the snow splattered as it ran. Ever larger grew its image until, frolicking and bouncing, the young ram descended the slope and slid to a halt in front of me amid a cloud of dust and rolling stones. His breathing was heavy, his nostrils flared, and those big eyes glistened. It was, indeed, little 48.

I gave him what he wanted most, a bit of salt. But, even after I had signaled that no more was forthcoming, he made no move to leave me. Together we climbed through the cliffs to the southern side of the range, where I eventually left him with a group of other sheep. His leg had healed well—and yet it was the last spring I saw little 48. He vanished during summer with the other sheep and never appeared again. I could not know whether a coyote had killed him, or a hunter at the distant boundary, or a poacher inside the park.

These sheep that trusted man gave me opportunity to study at close range much that I had previously seen at long distance, and they allowed me to gain insights that only work with free-

The author in 1970 with some bighorn ewes and yearling rams, Banff National Park

living, yet tame, animals allows. Some of my concerns were rather mundane, such as checking if chronological age, as determined from dates of tagging, did coincide with the age rings on the horns. It did. I could demonstrate to my satisfaction that the sheep were exceedingly loyal to their seasonal home ranges and reappeared at the same seasons each year in the very same places. I could show that females tagged in the Palliser female group stayed in the Palliser female group, while rams moved between the female groups. Thus, the female sheep in a group were largely related by maternal descent.

The scientific discoveries pale, however, beside the recollection of the individuals I came to know for a few years of their short lives. Some were shy individuals who waited a long time before they decided to come to me. Such a one was ram 616, who took about a year to make up his mind. He was one of the few sheep whose body was found after death. His floating body was picked up in Lake Minnewanka where it must have been deposited by the swift waters of the Cascade River which 616 crossed in spring on his return to the Palliser Range. Apparently he was drowned while attempting to cross the swollen, rapid river.

Others, in particular the females, became exceedingly tame, and stuck their noses into everything—my pockets, my rucksack, my camera lenses, and even my cameras if I had to change film. Soon I learned to change film while sitting in a tree since, up there, the eager crowd could not reach me. One young ram pulled a camera from my rucksack and dropped it down the mountainside. I recovered the camera's remains 300 yards below. The sheep allowed me to pluck ticks from their withers, and they went out of their way to stay with me. This gave me my first opportunity to observe how sheep search. I had anticipated that, if I ran off, they would seek for me where I had been last. This, however, they did not do. Instead, they searched on the basis of a priori expectations, or hypothesis. They always sought first where I *should* have been, had I continued in a *straight line*. Failing to find me, they searched against the wind. If this also failed, they reverted sometimes to tracking me.

It was soon after my initial surprise over their search methods that their significance became clear. Of course, it would be highly adaptive to track something mentally; usually this object would be a wolf or coyote. On such occasions it is pertinent indeed for a sheep to anticipate the movement of the predator. If the predator *fails* to appear where expected and cannot be found, it is obviously time to flee. The predator may be stalking by this time. As long as he is in sight, all is well, and young rams in particular may follow wolves on the uphill side for some distance. As long as sheep are on the uphill side of wolves, many will stand and observe the predator, even if it is only a dozen paces away.

My next surprise came when I discovered that, if I climbed a tree out of sight of sheep, they would fail to discover me even though I sat close enough above ground to touch them. It appeared that once I was in a tree, I became somehow unrecognizable. However, if I climbed a tree in their sight they clustered around the base for a while, looked at me, and then returned to grazing. I wonder to this day if a mountain lion maintains an advantage over sheep simply by sitting in a tree.

After a couple of years the females performed another maneuver which surprised me. My usual manner of breaking contact with the sheep was to turn suddenly from the group and run downhill into the timber. The animals generally stood watching me, and, by the time they had decided to follow, I was usually at the timber's edge and soon out of their sight. Then one day a female sprinted after me, overtook me, and then pressed her body against mine, pushing me off course, away from the timber. This is identical to the behavior used by lambs to stop their mothers in order to suckle. Here an adult, even old, female was using this method apparently in an attempt to hold me back—a rational act, since I did carry salt, which the animals craved.

The craving for salt, particularly in spring, is quite understandable. During winter the skeleton of wild sheep probably grows thin, light, and porous, just as did those of domestic sheep or reindeer where this subject was investigated. During winter, the mineral content of the forage is apparently quite insufficient, and the animal attacks its own skeleton to satisfy its metabolic needs, as well as to grow the skeleton of the lamb inside the uterus. Shortly after the lamb's birth, the female must provide many minerals in the milk, and again she attacks her skeleton. Only after lactation do females rebuild their skeletons in readiness for the next winter. Hence, the highest demand for minerals comes in spring and early summer, and sheep then flock to salt licks. So do other big-game animals, in particular mountain goats.

While the craving for salt is great, it is not so great as to cause sheep to commit acts dangerous to themselves. They would not, for instance, cross deep, loose snow in a gorge in order to reach me. They would come at once, however, if I plowed a trail for them. Then they would navigate the deepest snow—just so long as I went first. If an avalanche descended and left hard-packed snow in its path, the sheep used the avalanche paths like a highway for their travels. If the snow grew soft, one could see at close distance how they placed their feet—

namely, in a fashion so that both the hooves and the dewclaws were almost flat on the snow surface. Simultaneously they spread their legs. In very deep, loose snow the animals preferred to jump, which is, of course, a difficult and wasteful way to move.

On the whole the sheep regarded me as a two-legged salt lick, as a curiosity, but not as one of their own. This was fortunate. In sheep society, subordinates have the prerogative to be aggressive, and had I belonged to their pecking order, I would have been butted to a pulp. There is no way that a human body could accept the crushing blows delivered by bighorn rams. Hence, it was fortunate for me that I was excluded from their social hierarchies. Yet, attacks did occur.

The first ram to attack me was one I had known for two years, and it came as a surprise. During a cold day in late November I ascended a steep slope, well covered with fresh tracks of rutting sheep. No animals were in sight, and I expected to find them somewhere on the other side of the mountain. On the top of the slope was a tiny plateau, and when I reached it I was confronted by about 40 sheep, including a half-dozen large, rutting rams. They came to me at once.

The purpose of my climb was to check on the tags of ewes, checking out those that had been on the range as well as searching for new animals. I was quickly surrounded by the animals, and my task, reading small metal tags partially covered by hair on sheep's ears, became very difficult. The big rams, each one of which I knew anyway, pressed around, making it difficult for me to get at the females. The big boys wanted their bit of salt and grew noticeably impatient. My efforts were in vain. I could scarcely remain upright as forty sheep pushed, forcing me downhill. The animals were rather cheeky, which they always are in big bunches. In small groups, or in pairs, sheep are quite careful, even cautious. But give them a mob, and they grow bold. These were rutting sheep, and they were terribly brave. There was nothing to gain by staying further, so I turned and in long jumps hurled myself down the steep slope. Suddenly, about four jumps from the sheep, something solid hit my pack-board. Glancing over my shoulder, I saw one

Sheep following the author through deep snow, so long as he plows the way

of the large rams, Crooked Horn, with his head lowered to the ground. He had rushed me and hit a glancing blow at the parka trailing behind me, thereby hitting my pack-board. I stopped, and at once Crooked Horn was confronting me—face to face. Taking a little piece of salt from my pocket, I let him lick—a grave mistake as I soon realized. I had rewarded him for charging and butting me. The reason I was undamaged, thus far, was due to a sheep's habit of aiming a *downward* blow at a *specific* part of its opponent. The specific part is usually that closest to the sheep—in my case the pack-board.

Again I turned and ran off, and again Crooked Horn charged and hit my flying parka and pack-board. This was not funny! I had still a quarter mile to go to the timber, and with a big, rutting ram blasting me all the way I could expect not to make it. The moment the ram aimed poorly he would probably wrap me around his horns, or he could cut me deeply with one of his broken horn tips. At that point I realized that my piece of salt was just large enough to place it into the ram's mouth sideways, meaning he would be unable to spit it out for a few minutes. It worked. Crooked Horn stood still, completely absorbed in sucking on his "candy." I departed—in haste.

In later years, Crooked Horn showed that he had learned his lesson well. A number of times he rose against me, but I had also learned a trick or two. First, a ram cannot clash uphill effectively. Hence, I stayed uphill from him. Second, I faced him in a firm no-nonsense fashion—even though, inwardly, I was not full of confidence. If I walked toward him he would noticeably lose assurance and hesitate, then turn, glance back at me, and begin feeding. If he rose against me, I stood and looked down on him, and he dropped down on his legs.

How well these rams noted if someone were afraid of them I saw when a friend of mine first visited them. He was clearly ambivalent as the big rams came closer. Within minutes one ram lurched forward and butted him. A year later he confronted Crooked Horn who proceeded to crash into him, knocking him flat on the ground. Clearly these big animals can be dangerous, though minimally so to someone unafraid of them.

Crooked Horn did me a number of favors, however. Twice I acquainted colleagues with my work by taking them on the sheep ranges. Each of these colleagues was a passionate hunter. Keeping this point well in mind, I informed them of the terribly dangerous ram that roamed the mountains who took out his vengeance on people on sight. Each time Crooked Horn did me the favor of appearing, and each time, as soon as he spotted us, he came at a run from about two hundred yards away. A big ram approaching at full blast is a sight that causes anxious moment in the hearts of even brave men. When Crooked Horn was about 150 yards away, I yelled "It's him! It's him!" What splendid results! My pals took to their heels, lickety-split, down the mountain. What a sight it was to see a dedicated hunter running as hard as possible from a fine bighorn ram.

One of the dangers in the mountains in late winter is the possibility of a fall on a steep snowpack on a mountainside. At that season the snow melts a little each day and freezes hard at night, forming an impenetrable snowpack that may have not only an ice crust on top but an ice crust on the bottom as well. I had not realized how dangerous a fall on a steep slope could be till I found a ram just after he had suffered the mishap. The ram had slipped on the hard crust and rolled downhill, as the trail revealed. While I did not witness his fall, I arrived shortly after and could see his trail.

I followed this track with my binoculars and saw the sheep lying in the avalanche gorge below. Believing him to be dead, I took the camera and commenced the hour-long climb to the fallen animal. It had rolled down a good four hundred yards before hitting the avalanche gorge.

When I arrived beside the big ram and began to set up the camera tripod, he suddenly flailed weakly with his front legs. At once I glanced at his head. The ram's eyes were open and alert; his tongue darted weakly in and out of his mouth. Far from death, the poor animal was alive but badly paralyzed. In fact, both his neck and back were broken, as the autopsy shortly revealed. To judge from the tracks, he must have rolled over and over again coming downhill, gathering speed with each foot of descent. It was a wonder and a tribute to the tough bodies of bighorns that he was not killed at once. I plunged a knife into his heart and cut short his suffering. Other rams were less fortunate.

One ram apparently walked on a snowdrift beneath a telephone line that ran to a distant fire lookout. The animal caught its horn in the wire; next spring the wardens removed its lifeless body hanging several feet above ground from the wire.

Old Tithrington saw a young ram walk out on a snow cornice. Suddenly the cornice caved in, and the young ram sank into his white grave. I saw several rams and ewes return with broken legs. How these legs were broken I shall never know. Some healed, to give the sheep a clubfoot and a limp; but other sheep disappeared after their mishaps, never to be seen again. In one case a young, lamb-leading female broke her hind leg. For days she lay in one spot while her lamb tried in vain to get her up so he could suckle. The little fellow stole short suckles from other ewes while they fed their own lambs and was frequently punished for it with severe butts, for a ewe rejects all but her own offspring. Yet the lamb only rose to try again. The female did finally rise and feed, but I soon lost sight of her. Several weeks later I saw her again with her poorly grown bedraggled lamb. She had become little more than skin and bones and limped pitifully, but her leg was well along in healing. I saw her for a few more days, and never again thereafter. Nor do I know what happened to her lamb.

Another female had a clubfoot and was blind in one eye. She was butted around pitifully by other females, but she hung on to life. For the last two years of her difficult life I made periodic contact with her. She had no lambs of her own but was a favorite "aunty" for lambs to cluster around. In spring, when the other females were off lambing, she was followed closely by a group of yearlings wherever she went. I still don't know why this ewe (or other old girls) attracted lambs, causing them to gather around. In spring these old ladies perform a very real service to sheep society by acting as focal points for the motherless youngsters to group around, while the adult females lambed in hiding. One of these old girls even licked lambs—a most unusual behavior; I saw her bounce and frolic through the cliffs followed by a stream of frolicking youngsters, and I saw her turn and call after departing yearlings. Could it be that, barren as they are, these old females somehow begin to "mother" the youngsters that have just broken contact with their dams? The period when old barren females act as a focal point for the yearling sheep is very short, however—a couple of weeks more or less. Then the first females with the newborn young return, and the yearlings begin following them, deserting the old ladies. Oh, how fascinating the new little lambs were to the old ladies and the yearlings alike.

During my daily association with the bighorns it began to dawn on me slowly, ever so slowly, that maybe paradise had not

Week-old Dall's sheep lambs, gamboling

been lost after all but only mislaid. Were not these creatures trying to tell us that man and beast can live together in almost Biblical harmony? My mind wandered back to my first surprises in the Spatzisi at being able to approach Stone's sheep closely. I attributed it then to my white coveralls and the white towel I wrapped about my head in an attempt to imitate a mountain goat. I thought I had successfully faked goat to them—today I shudder at such innocence. The sheep had begun to accept me because they had seen me for many months while I was walking in the valley and on the slopes; they had been habituated to my presence. I could have exchanged my "goat suit" for that of a circus clown with equal effect. It was I and not the "goat" these animals had begun to accept as a part of their landscape and had grown to tolerate.

At the cabin, the whisky jacks (or Canada jays) had long ago become tame and were taking food from my hands. They settled on my outstretched arm wherever I encountered them. This permitted me to experiment a little, to observe their behavior, and to follow their fate closely.

There was "Old Terror," who with Dina held a territory around the cabin and punished any other whisky jack that dared to come close. His favorite trick was to land on the big spruce behind the cabin, then silently sail down, around the cabin, and land among a crowd of shrieking jays that hastened to take wing. Usually all managed to become airborne except one who would be hindered from takeoff since Old Terror held on to his tail and tugged, beating hard with his wings. Once all the "opposition" had fled, Old Terror stood slim and upright on the chopping block, the very image of young Siegfried in jay society.

Old Terror and Dina were different personalities. If I held out a scrap of meat for Old Terror, he landed with a burst of wing beats on my hand, pecked my finger, picked up the meat, instantaneously dropped backward off my hand and took off in a fast hard flight. He was a forceful, exact, stern sort of a fellow. His wife Dina acted differently. She fluttered gently onto my hand, settled, folded her wings, tilted her head to look at me, and uttered a soft "tjuk." I, of course, returned her greeting with "tjuk." Then Dina looked over the offerings in my palm. Taking her time, she gently took a piece, the biggest if there were a choice, or she carefully stuffed her bill till no more would fit. Dina was meticulous about this. That done she looked up, turned around, tilted her head to look at me, said "tjuk," and then fluttered off.

"Little Terror" was the most subordinate whisky jack around and played "baby" all the time. Threatened by Old Terror, he fluttered his wings and shrieked, but loud. If that were to no avail, and occasionally it was not, he would spread himself silently on the snow, extend wings and tail, bury his bill in snow, and show his black neck cap to Old Terror. The dominant would stand over him ready to peck, but he never did, and eventually he left Little Terror alone. What the latter had done, in essence, was to replace his adult face with the black mask. Since juvenile whiskies are black in the face, he had, in essence, mimicked a juvenile. And that Old Terror could not attack. Such faking of juveniles is of course useful to jays. It allows a jay to eat at a carcass of, say, a deer or moose in another jay's territory where he is subordinate. There is virtually nothing accidental in nature.

In April Old Terror and Dina courted and mated. It happened just outside the cabin while I was watching sheep through a spotting scope. I noticed their activities and made several quick sketches and notes, for I had never heard of anyone having seen the courtship of these birds. Then I rose and carefully walked into the cabin to get the camera with a telephoto lens. Cautiously I returned to the door and stuck my nose around the corner to see how the jays were doing in their courtship. They were not. They both sat, stiff, necks way outstretched, peeking at me—in anticipation of the food they thought I would bring out. Obviously, love took second place.

Then, one day in spring, I noticed that Dina was missing. She had not been around for several days, I recalled. Old Terror was still as nasty as ever. Little Terror was there, and so were two newlyweds, Mary and Jack. Little Terror was also in the process of courting, a procedure he interrupted every so often with loud baby screams if Old Terror came in sight. As the days went past I noticed a change in Old Terror. He did not persecute Mary as he had when Dina was still around. He followed Mary and concentrated his savage attacks on Jack. However, he only attracted a turned back from Mary and a string of sharp hard calls from her. Although he beat up Jack mercilessly, Jack and Mary's marriage held. One day Old Terror was gone too, and I never saw him again.

For as long as I stayed at the cabin, Jack and Mary held a territory there. Little Terror left in spring but came back in fall again, alone. There was no evidence that he had raised a brood that year, and neither had Jack and Mary. If there is one point I regret, it is that I kept no notes on the whisky jacks and thus could not double check by observations and conclusions. "Whiskys" (as I called them) were no scientific subject to me—just fun. I have sometimes wondered what would have happened had a stranger stumbled some sunny day onto the clearing where the cabin stood and seen a long-haired, bearded man, standing there with arms outstretched toward the sky shouting, "Whisky, Whisky, come here, Whisky."

Some years have passed since I left my whisky jacks or last saw my bighorn friends. In my work as a scientist I have since encountered other occasions when animals and man have lived harmoniously. I regret that I arrived in the wilderness not knowing that taming was possible, for it has surprised me again and again how quickly one can get along with animals; my little weasel friend I tamed in one day but only in the last months of my stay in the Spatzisi; how I wish it had been earlier. In the St. Elias Range in the Yukon, while working on Dall's sheep, I tamed a red fox within a few days, soon after he had picked up heads of lake trout from beside my cabin. Within a week he followed at my heels up the mountain—a behavior I had to discourage since he spooked the sheep. Thereafter he often joined me when I returned to the cabin after a day on the mountains. Then came the mule deer . . . but I will tell about that some other time.

No, paradise is not lost, just mislaid, and it can be found—occasionally.

14

Farewell

✒ Christmas had come and gone. I had packed my belongings and was now waiting for the aircraft that would pluck me from my land and take me back south. These were the last days in the cabin. I remember the blue skies and crisp cold, the rugged peaks, brilliant light and sharp shadows, and the white of the snow everywhere, while through the icy silence rang the chop of my lonely axe. These were days of glistening powdery snow, of bright moonlit nights, of cackling ptarmigan, and the mournful wails of shy timber wolves. These were long days, stretched by the agony of waiting for the sound of the aircraft, which had failed to appear on the appointed date. The cold Arctic front had grounded the bush plane. The waiting gave me time to contemplate, to recall the events that were now history, and to turn to thoughts that normally one has no time for.

When I had packed my things I went to Ghost Mountain, for I wanted to sit on its ridge for a last time. It was a clear, brilliant day with the temperature rising toward 35° F below zero. For once I had no scientific business to attend to, and my eyes and mind were free to look at what normally I hastened past. The familiar trees, stumps, and willow bushes, the curves of the trail I had cleared of brush so many times, the gurgling of Connors Creek, the sedge meadows, now deep under the snow—all lay there before me as I made my way to the foot of the mountain. Each landmark awakened memories from the past. The climb was easy and pleasant, since I took my time and since I knew the way so very well.

I looked down from Ghost Mountain to the Spatzisi Plateau, its flanks painted a light blue by forests in the distance. At the foot of its ridges lay Hyland Post where lived my friends who had come to say goodbye to the crazy white man a couple of weeks ago. They once worked along the Alaska Highway but had chosen to see as little of the white man's life as possible after that experience. They preferred to live here and make do with a meager but adequate income while retaining their sanity. They were probably the only Indians I met who were not afraid to kick the white man in the arse, just too polite to do it. On their last visit Charlie Abu had told me of his old father whom he had lately visited after an absence of a decade or so. The old man went trapping every winter and refused his old-age pension. He had gotten along on his own well enough, and old age was not going to change him. Charlie had shaken his head at such stubbornness and pride, for the old-age pension was the due of every Canadian and applicable to rich and poor. His father need not be ashamed of accepting it. But the old man would not.

My eyes moved on from the Spatzisi Plateau and the distant Cassiar Ranges. My gaze stopped here and there on familiar shapes and moved on, on over the steep cliffs of Sanctuary Mountain, over the ridges, glaciers, and peaks of Mount Will, over the smooth white of little Gladys Lake with its steaming outlet where soon the whitefish and grayling would be swirling, over the forests of white spruce and alpine fir, over Cliff Mountain, and on to the distant, hazy peaks of the Klappan Ranges barely visible in the blue. Traveling on, my mind recalled the joys and sorrows that formed my link with the land— little glimpses from the past which would become my wealth for the future.

It was in that hollow below, just where the alpine firs form a last big thicket before succumbing to altitude, that Renate and I had first seen mountain goats performing their elaborate threat display. And on that same slope, last spring, I had watched a

Bighorn ram in the Canadian Rockies

group of mountain goats playing. There were thirteen of them. At first they bounced and bucked a little, and then all thirteen of them began cartwheeling down the slope, spinning around horizontally in spirals. An incredible sight, and one I had not witnessed since. Only a little beyond had once lain the big yellow wolf I shot that desperate October day. Over the crest of the ridge I had found the badly wounded male mountain goat and filmed his pitiful ascent—silent evidence of the terrible wounds members of this species may inflict on each other. Over there I saw my first Stone's lamb, a little, spunky, mouse-gray fellow with a ridiculously short, black tail. His birth was a joyful moment, for I had anticipated its advent and had watched his mother for days.

In the valley stood my cabin. How small it was in the distance. I raised the binoculars to take a closer look. Its tin roof was shining in the sun; a thin plume of whitish smoke drifted from its stove pipe; its irregular peeled logs seemed to be smiling. Oh, that irresistible tempting smile. How well I understood the men who wrote poems to their cabins, for, to them and to

me, cabins are not just houses but living spirits with character
and idiosyncrasies.

I recalled how we built it, how we cut and peeled the logs,
how we joked beside the fire at noon while biting chunks off
roasted caribou rib and drinking pots of steaming tea. I recalled the spring cleanups at winter's end a few weeks before
the ice went out on Gladys Lake. How well the cabin was
scrubbed then, till all of winter's grime was gone. I recalled the
first chimney fire, and what a mess I made in quenching it. I
recalled the day in spring when Charlie Abu and old Alec came
for a visit. It was June 9, to be exact. I had just scaled Ghost
Mountain, but then I saw them in the valley; I fired a couple of
shots to let them know that I had seen them and hurried back
to the cabin.

We were sharing a pot of tea when the radio crackled, and
Marge Smith's voice called for me on the air. It was quite an
announcement. My daughter was born.

Old Alec beamed, Charlie stretched his hand out to congrat-
ulate me. "You lucky man," he said. They were so happy, as if
they had become fathers, not I. From beneath the bed I dug
out a 26-ounce bottle of navy rum. Although I had rationed it
carefully, since I had only two such bottles to last the whole
winter, there was but one inch of rum left. I was wishing I had
more, to match the occasion, but it was sufficient to toast my
daughter and Renate, and we did so. Charlie had two big
grown boys but was hoping that his wife might yet bear him a
daughter. I am glad to say his wish was fulfilled that very year.

Again I looked out into the distance beyond the sunlit plateau, where caribou gathered in the fall to rut, to the hazy Cassiar Ranges beyond. What would the future bring? What would
happen with this land? It had a long history, and I wondered
how it would continue. It was humbling to realize that I was
here by the grace of modern technology, that my food, my
clothing, and my equipment were not of this land but of the
civilization beyond. If I had to depend on this wilderness for
my life, I would have developed the pioneer's mentality, who
saw in it the threat to his survival, who regarded it as the
enemy to his security, and who hated wilderness and fought it

tooth and nail. I, too, had felt this hate a number of times. I had to admit that technology had liberated me so that I could come to know, and ultimately fall in love with, this land. Technology had been a liberator, but it also dulled my senses and judgment.

This lack was brought home to me vividly in a blizzard. I had forgotten what Canadian blizzards are like. I had seen blizzards from the comfort of a house. I had seen them from the safety of a car or truck, and I had ceased to remember what blizzards felt like on the Saskatchewan prairie. I had managed to forget the cutting gales and blinding snows that numb the face and hands, that choke one's breath and cut sharply and painfully into exposed flesh. I had forgotten how one fights the gales with each step, leaning a shoulder into the wind and turning the head away, while the ears freeze right inside the parka hood. I had forgotten that men will live but an hour exposed to these storms. I had seen cattle drift up against fences or crowd below the crest of hills where the wind was least. But from the inside of a car or truck, such sights meant little, at least emotionally. The drifting snow conveyed no message except that of an eerie beauty. I grew careless of blizzards. Then, one day, while I was studying deer where mountains and prairie join, the memories returned with a vengeance.

In the morning it was not bad. The wind was hard, the snow did drift, the temperature was well below 0° F, but with my back to the wind and keeping close to the mountains at the forest edge it was bearable. I was out to find a mule deer buck I had left the previous day at the forest edge. He had been wounded in a fight, and I wanted to see how he made out with other bucks. Within two hours I found him in the forest and stayed close to him. Among the dense Douglas firs the wind was negligible. Below, I could see clouds of snow blowing past and small trees bending and jerking in the gales. Above, the branches were waving, and clumps of snow thumped to the ground. The buck was nervous, as are all deer in the forest during a storm, and he finally decided to move to a more peaceful place, an aspen forest on the next ridge, a half mile across the valley. On the prairies, outside the protection of the

thick grove, the winds had long turned to gales. A wall of airborne snow was singing past, obscuring all sight at ground
level, but above it one could see the mountains and the long
plumes of snow being torn off their slopes by the wind.

The buck walked to the forest edge, paused and looked
ahead into the blinding snow, and then took off. He raced into
the blizzard in hard long bounds to get through the worst of it
as quickly as possible. It was an eminently sensible thing to do.
Within a dozen jumps he vanished in the blowing snow, and I
plunged in after him. But I did not have the speed of a deer. I
could not race through the wind funnel—here a quarter of a
mile wide—as fast as the buck. At this point, the winds could
reach speeds exceeding seventy miles an hour during normal
storms, and this was no normal storm. Cars had been blown off
the road in this valley in lesser storms. It took me fifteen minutes to cross to the safety of the ridge and to the relative calm
of the forest on the lee side of the ridge, where I joined the
buck once more. However, I barely made it. When I reached
the ridge I had to sit down and rest; ten minutes more of that
blizzard and the coyotes would have had me for breakfast.

Such an experience makes one value modern times. I am as
apprehensive as ever of the technological megatroph, the giant
devourer of resources we have created that, on one hand, claws
and tears at mother earth, and, on the other, has freed us from
the fears and wants of yesterday. Let it continue to grow un-
checked, like a cancer, and we shall become its victims—as certainly as the sun will rise.

There is a peculiar and grim satisfaction that only some biologists can experience at the thought of man's extinction. From
our studies we know that, should we disappear—be it with a
bang or a whimper—but still leave some life of our class behind, the earth again will be filled with creatures some millions
of years hence. There will be "birds" flying. Not birds as we
know them, but something similar just the same. There will be
"rhinos" lumbering over the plains and "wolves" running in
packs. The history of life on earth teaches that similar forms,
regardless of their genetic origin, replace each other in geologic times.

I have heard satisfaction expressed at this thought. I have heard it proclaimed as a triumph. I see no triumph here, no reason for rejoicing. If there will be "rhinos," "wolves," "rats," and "mice" on earth, but no "man" among them—a world as it was prior to the ice ages—no more fields of grain or orchards, no church bells to ring out the fading day, no castles on the hills, no wine on the slopes, no ships to plow the seas, will it matter? To me, very much. If my species will be gone—a species so unique, so unusual, a species so young, it hurts me as a zoologist to think that it may disappear. If it does so, we will have failed. Reason will have failed. Our failure would prove intelligence to be a useless, good-for-nothing attribute of earthly life. Intelligence will have been our curse, not our blessing, and we would have to say we might have been better off without it. Our failure would mean that you and I have lived in vain, that you and I did not do enough to assure a future for our children and our children's children, that you and I have been outdone by dinosaurs.

Who has not heard statements that intelligent life will re-evolve if destroyed, or that intelligent life is prevalent out yonder in distant space—statements by astronomers and mathematicians? But can evolution at the molecular level be equated with evolution of complex organisms? Can we assume that all life evolves deterministically toward intelligence. Teilhard de Chardin, the famous philosopher and theologian, notwithstanding, there is no more evidence for this assumption than for the one that all life evolves toward dinosaurs. There is no theoretical reason to believe that something remotely similar to man could evolve again, any more than that a nation's history can repeat itself.

Even if a manlike creature were to reappear, would it be possible for it to develop a technological culture? We are diffusing and depleting the earth's concentrated mineral and energy stores, thereby insuring that mineral and energy extraction will depend on increasingly sophisticated technology. With that, we are insuring that, should we fail, no technological civilization would ever rise from our ashes. With that, we insure that no civilization will rise beyond the Stone Age state. It also follows, since our culture depends upon high-energy consumption, and it, in turn, depends upon high levels of technology, that technology's survival is our survival. Yet, with each increase in the size, complexity, and importance of technology, we enslave ourselves a little more and become a little less its master. We gain a little more security and lose a little more freedom.

Moreover, should we destroy science we need not worry that it would arise readily. Science is a rare development. In all the cultures and civilizations known to us, it rose feebly only three times, to be crushed twice and to survive by default a third time. It reared its head in ancient China, and flourished in early Greece. It rose again in the monasteries in the Middle Ages of our own civilization. Science has brought to us the richest and most exciting period in human history—we are living it today. There are more poets, scientists, philosophers, musicians, and such, alive today than the total number that lived before them. We have mastered much knowledge and yet have with us great cultural diversity; in addition we have some unspoiled nature. We are today rich beyond belief compared to earlier times, and we are probably richer today than we shall ever be again. It is a magnificent age in which to be alive.

Yet there are fundamental questions to which we must address ourselves, and the most fundamental of these is whether man shall be his own master or succumb to the seductions of technology and a market society that panders to his animal comforts, and enter the Brave New World by default. If we do not act toward gaining mastery of our destiny, the techno-politico-sociological system we have just constructed will dictate our future, in a predictable, unpleasant manner.

We will never escape the inherent biological rules that govern our actions. But we need not try to escape. After all, we like doing best what is adaptive—eating well and often, procreating, hiking, watching or participating in controlled forms of aggression, snubbing somebody, searching for new, exciting things. These are desires inbred into us from millennia past, from environments long vanished, and we have added a cultural dimension to the expression of these desires which makes them purely human. We have made art and beauty out of them; we have intermixed them in such a fashion that we do not recognize their inherent biological foundation. In Mozart's *Zauberflöte*, it was only after trial by fire and trial by water, after dangerous journeys and trying times, that the prince Tamino wed his princess Pamina, while Papageno, of lower status though he was, still had to work and fear much before Papagena was his. It takes a Mozart—and the skills of actors and vocalists, of director, conductor, orchestra, and stagehands—to put in such emotional form the epic of these trials and tribulations. And what is this epic all about? What is the last rule of the Great Game? To choose a mate most likely to succeed in the great game! Hence, a bird man Papageno must find a bird girl Papagena, and a prince must find his princess, and neither can be satisfied with anything less. Hence our striving to marry the most beautiful, noble, heroic, rich, generous, kind, and mighty, the one endowed with the finest qualities to make secure our life on earth. Earthy, basic, and biological this rule may be, it is highly necessary for us, given the small number of children we bear and the requirements for their long, loving care and education. Our human uniqueness is that we can see poetry and art in this rule. We can and do make an epic of it. We can relive it again and again by setting it to music and to visual expressions that lift the soul to ecstasy. It is our human lot to take the mundane and beautify it, to complicate it, to put new form and diversity into it, to condense it, to prolong it, and to relive its drama in each performance. It is our lot to make the everyday into art by playing a variation on its principle, to make cathedrals from huts, to make costumes from clothing, ballets from love, operas from fights, philosophies and sciences from horse sense, and, by so doing, subconsciously to reinforce the principles within.

We may grant that we love and greatly enjoy exercising our biological adaptations. Yet what is joy? Fulfillment of the expected? Making the strange familiar? Removal of a great difficulty? Mastering and testing a new skill? Recognizing a friend in a strange crowd? Something is common to all of these. Joy and happiness result from matching an expected or familiar Gestalt with Reality. If this be so, then the converse must also be true: that excitation, stress, and trauma result if we cannot match what our body expects with reality; that when we cannot do what habit dictates us to do we are in trouble; that when we cannot do our daily work anymore, be it through retirement or unemployment, we grieve; that when we are confined and unable to exercise we grow sour and irritable; that if a loved one dies there is a great personal loss and grief; that when an unexpected event dominates our lives, we must adapt to new strains. This cause-and-effect pattern should give pause to anyone trying to impose his or her own ideas of how to do things better, or trying to dictate to others what to do without, and what to do next.

In the past I revolted against ceremony, ridiculing it as senseless, stupid, outmoded; but no more. Ceremonies serve a good purpose. The forms are prescribed, and through their performance give pleasure, security, identity, confidence in social relationships and, as such, an "inner strength." Many ceremonies permit persons to act out their feelings in a meaningful way. Ceremonies bind together those who participate; they delineate an in-group, a gathering of like minds. Ceremonies often arouse emotions, and ensure that we shall remember the occasion as well as the persons who participated. Trials by crisis in fraternities did not appear by acccident; they help strangers to become loyal friends. Ceremonies in war and peace, in marriage, birth, and death, unite families, communities, and nations; they help people to live in security and trust. It is not surprising that even ancient philosophers of human nature expounded the need for ritual and order as a prerequisite to civilized life.

What choices have we in modern times? We are not free to change into whatever pleases us, at least not without cost to us. Yet belief in infinitely malleable man is a tenet of faith to the gods of our present society—the market values. Our socioeconomic system is driven by market values, with the aid of science and technology, toward satisfying the creature comforts of individuals. The measure of success is called the "standard of living": it can be equated almost exactly with goods and services required for ego or dominance displays. Our "standard of living" is hence a function of vanity, no doubt an important biological attribute of man, but one that need not be satisfied at the cost of looted landscapes and broken cultures. Worse still, market values demand a human being quite the opposite from the cooperative, altruistic, intelligent, reflective human creature we rightly value; they demand an egocentric, competitive, callous, ruthless, efficient individual. Market values demand sacrifice to the system. They are intolerant gods. And we obey. Yet the costs are already evident. In industrial nations, urban disease, social breakdown, and retirements at an ever-earlier age are increasing, and so are the concomitant social costs. In order to maximize individual development, to permit our genetic constitution to unfold itself to its full extent, we must live in an environment like the one we evolved in, or a good facsimile thereof; any deviations from it will cost us some of our humanity. We develop best in a stable extended family in a predictable conceptual, social, and physical milieu. Given our old evolutionary environment, or an adequate replica, we can expect to reduce the occurrence of abnormal development in children and to reduce the need for crime prevention, police forces, jails, mental wards, crisis centers, sex therapists and other professionals that try to patch up and replace what the family offers. Indeed, a cynic can cost out a family and say how many dollars a good mother is worth to society.

We face another crippling problem: how to convey important findings from the disciplines and the professions and how to have this collective wisdom readily accepted and acted upon. A "natural" antipathy among professionals to accept one another's findings may be due to a biological factor, namely, that an animal does not readily accept the unfamiliar, and only over a period of time will familiarize itself with the strange. We cannot possibly learn from others as long as their knowledge strikes us as strange, funny, irrelevant, and ridiculous. Politicians and bureaucrats cannot be expected to accept readily the findings of scientists and sociologists. To one, the "environmental crisis" may seem unreal; to the other it may be the "economic crisis" that has no significance. Disciplines and professions have, unfortunately, a built-in mechanism to repel the wisdom of other disciplines, so that new knowledge does not diffuse readily; it gets stuck somewhere. Indeed one has to demonstrate its relevance repeatedly before it becomes accepted and even then not by all who should approve it. For instance, a law tried and proven in one country is not acceptable in another, no matter how rational and reasonable. Here we run into a second compounding factor, the ego-crisis. Readily accepting a point from someone else and praising it seems to imply one's own intellectual and moral inferiority. Hence, ideas that are new, or that come from foreigners, strangers, or enemies often are emotionally unacceptable to us. How do we break down this nonsense? There are two ways: first, by education in the old, classical sense, in which an individual disciplines himself to examine ideas and learns to argue both sides, or all sides of a case, and, second, by grouping individuals from diverse disciplines into functional, long-lasting teams so that strong bonds of trust and friendship may develop. In other words, we must fight biological urges with biological science.

There is also the split between the scientists and artists or humanists. Separate they have become, belittling each other, going each his own way, following a narrow vision and becoming increasingly more uneducated with each specialization. Why did humanists ever think that science was alien to them? Why did scientists ever think that humanists had little to contribute? Why did we ever let knowledge and wisdom be split and frayed, each branch a beginning, growing and proliferating as if it were an independent plant? There were times when men were not considered educated unless they had a grounding in natural philosophies, unless they could discuss the latest in science, in art, in poetry, in politics, in music and in opera, because it was within the realm of knowledge and experience. Such men could mix science and poetry, science and philosophy, science and ethics, science and music.

Science is poetry; science is philosophy; science is art. It is lack of a little courage and vision that makes science only science. It is fear, sometimes paralyzing fear, of the strange men and minds in the arts, as well as fear of making science something less than rational, and the fear of losing face before other scientists that causes us to withdraw. This fear is an animal hang-up, not a human hang-up, and it can be cured. It is related to the harm our tender egos could incur, and it should have no place among educated men.

Think of the carbon, nitrogen, phosphate, and water cycles. Is there no poetry, no art, no philosophy in them? Have they no dimensions beyond the scientific ones? Do they not say something about the stuff that forms *me*, which the *I* gave shape to? They say that the *me* has been eternal and will be so, whichever way we may define *eternal*. The *me* gives shape to the *I* and has been in flowers and ocean waves, in wheat fields, rain clouds, storms, and flies, in forests, in volcanoes and icecaps, in seas and continents, in rock and air, in ancestors past, in apes and in dinosaurs. *Me* was here before *I* and will be here after *I*. The *me* has never died and will never die. Today it is part of *I* but will travel on, leaving *I* with each breath. *Me* cycles and recycles; *I* comes and *I* goes. *Me* is my link to eternity; *I* to the present. *I* is my link to mysteries past and mysteries future. This land is in me and of me. The mortal and eternal, the shadow and the substance have but joined forces to form a being that lives by the rules of the Great Game, that asks the question, "Can we live eternally?"

Does the carbon cycle suffer from such a description? Does it lose any of its validity? Is it damaged by running into questions and answering them in its own way? These are questions raised by philosophers of every generation.

Think of genetics and what it teaches. Think where the *I* came from and where the genes will go—how the genes concentrated from diffused lineages to become *I* and how they will diffuse in the future. What stories genes could tell! The *I* holds them, genes that have come together from many continents and landscapes, that came from different tribes and persons, from tall and short, ugly and beautiful, from genius and dumbbell, from kings, paupers, sages, and criminals. They separate with each generation and yet come together mysteriously, spreading downward from our distant ancestors and diffusing till every bone unearthed of man is the bone of a blood relation. Yet the genes do not stop there. They reach back further, ever further; they link us to the web of mammalian life, to corda-itean life, and, finally, to all life on earth. They all contain the first spark of life; they make me brother to the whale, cousin to the soaring eagle, relative of the lowly moss. What stories could genes tell! Yet they are silent, and the mysterious happenings of the past will largely remain mysterious. No science will dis-cover them, any more than a future scientist, who discovered that old f.c. lived on this mountain, can know of what he did and where he died. Yet there is more to the *me* and the *I*. There is the future when *me* will again become flower and ocean wave, storm cloud and soil, when the *I* is gone but its pieces are as active as ever, forming the *me* into hair and bone, flesh and skin, bulges and hollows, creating the children's laughter, the adult smiles, and the dying groans.

How could anyone believe that science destroys "beauty" and desecrates "mystery"? The "mysteries" we scientists have had to clear up have been arbitrary, ignorant explanations, sometimes pretty, but often dumb and stupid, of people who have tried their best to formulate a coherent story. These "mysteries" have hung like clouds over the sky, blocking the sunrise. Is the sunrise less beautiful without clouds? Is a beautiful girl adorned with flowers or dressed in rags beautiful or ugly be-cause of them?

I suddenly felt very cold. The sun had set behind Mount Will, and now the shadows were creeping up Ghost Mountain. The icy cold descended and bit into my face, signaling that I must descend. Dark lay the valley below. The temperature would plunge very low tonight, and winter would be master for some time to come. Yet, the winter solstice was past. The days would lengthen a little each twenty-four hours; every day the sun would shine a little longer. The earth had completed its full cycle, and summer, the warm, lush summer had embarked upon its return.

Epilogue

꧀ "Once upon a time"—fairy tales begin so, and stories of the past, of events no longer with us. Change is inevitable, alas! The innocent days of the early fieldworkers in animal behavior are over. Old Skook is no longer on the Kechika: old age did catch up with him, and he is now institutionalized. The land I wrote about is found no more, for progress has caught up with the Spatzisi. A railway leads fifteen miles past my cabin, as does a road. More roads are planned to "open up" the country, mainly to strip it of its meager forest resources. Hordes of hunters descend annually on Gladys Lake to shoot sheep, goats, and caribou, and the battle is on to make the Spatzisi a wilderness area before it is too late for nature to heal its wounds. The sheep and goat populations I studied there are already atypical and in part exterminated (as I first witnessed on a return trip two years later, and as I have been told by friends and have learned from a few published hunting stories—Judas tales, I call them). "Progress" has been so rapid that, young though I am in years, I am already an "old man," one who knows how life once was.

Oh suffering wildlife, oh mistreated mountains! The callous abuse today in northern and western Canada must be seen to be believed. Strip mining, short-sighted hydroelectric developments, exploration for minerals and coal, uncontrolled prospectors meagerly financed by the federal government and living off the land, unenforced or poor game laws—all are major villains, as are some resource agencies that have become prostitutes of the client, not guardians of the resources. Much environmental damage is quite avoidable, as oil companies exploring in the Arctic have recently shown. Some people have been lulled into a sense of security by the creation of national parks. The boundaries of the parks, however, have been drawn so cynically that, as in the case of Kluane National Park, the border proposal of even the most determined opponent of the park, the Yukon Chamber of Mines, was on the whole more generous than that established by the government. The wildlife found in Kluane and Nahanni national parks depends for its existence to a large extent on unprotected areas outside the parks. All is not bleak, since public hearings and participatory planning are progressing, but the outlook is still dim.

Can much of the destruction of land and wildlife be justified as an inescapable consequence of economic progress? A lazy, cowardly, thoughtless excuse! Economic progress hardly deserves to be considered holy, bound as it is to a material expression of human vanity, that insatiable glutton. The gods of economic progress—market values—are the progeny of value systems derived from aggressive agrarian societies with temporary economic surpluses. We have lived in surplus economies and expanding populations where these values are tolerable; they become intolerable in populations living at the carrying capacity of the land. We could do worse than look at the values of such people, since they may give us an inkling of the values we ultimately may have to accept. Then we may note with surprise the humaneness of such people, but their values—unfortunately—cannot be maintained without world peace. Could science help us out of our dilemmas? Is there no hope in it? We must ask what intrinsic values does science have. Alas, it tends to serve him who pays the bill. In the meantime we bow to new gods that demand the plunder of our landscapes and the destruction of our cultural diversity, in the name of more energy, more consumer goods, more easy ways, more fads. . . . Après moi le deluge!

These gods, market values, as served by science and technology, and working on behalf of human creature comforts, are locked in a frightening conspiracy, and frightening is the number and power of their priests. We need a new agnosticism to oppose them, and a clarification of the values that will help our species to survive and thrive. Toward that end I write of men and sheep.